# MILITANT LIVERPOOL

# MILITANT LIVERPOOL

## A City on the Edge

**Diane Frost and Peter North**

LIVERPOOL UNIVERSITY PRESS

First published 2013 by
Liverpool University Press
4 Cambridge Street
Liverpool
L69 7ZU

British Library Cataloguing-in-Publication data
A British Library CIP record is available

ISBN 978-1-84631-863-4

Typeset in Chaparral by Carnegie Book Production, Lancaster
Printed and bound by CPI Group (UK) Ltd, Croydon CR0 4YY

# CONTENTS

ACRONYMS AND ABBREVIATIONS     VII

ACKNOWLEDGEMENTS     IX

INTRODUCTION     1

1   LIVERPOOL FROM WORLD CITY TO BASKET CASE     7

2   LIVERPOOL RESPONDS TO THE CRISIS     31

3   THE ELECTION OF 1983     53

4   BUDGET CRISIS 1984     67

5   BUDGET CRISIS 1985     95

6   COMMUNITY AND CONFLICT     123

7   CONTROVERSIES     155

8   THE LEGACY     179

BIBLIOGRAPHY     207

ENDNOTES     211

INDEX     213

# ACRONYMS AND ABBREVIATIONS

| | |
|---|---|
| **AEU** | Amalgamated Engineering Union |
| **AMA** | Association of Metropolitan Authorities |
| **BNP** | British National Party |
| **CBTC** | Commercial Business Training Centre |
| **CDP** | Community Development Programme |
| **CLP** | Constituency Labour Party |
| **COHSE** | Confederation of Health Service Employees |
| **CP** | Communist Party |
| **CRE** | Commission for Racial Equality |
| **DA** | District Auditor |
| **DLP** | District Labour Party |
| **GLC** | Greater London Council |
| **GMB** | General Municipal Boilermakers Union |
| **GMC** | General Management Committee (of the Labour Party) |
| **GMWU** | General and Municipal Workers' Union |
| **MAPG** | Merseyside Area Profile Group |
| **MCRC** | Merseyside Community Relations Council |
| **MDC** | Merseyside Development Corporation |
| **NF** | National Front |
| **NALGO** | National and Local Government Officers' Association |

| | |
|---|---|
| **NATFE** | National Association of Teachers in Further and Higher Education |
| **NUM** | National Union of Mineworkers |
| **NUPE** | National Union of Public Employees |
| **NUT** | National Union of Teachers |
| **PB** | Petty (Petite) Bourgeoisie |
| **SDP** | Social Democratic Party |
| **SWP** | Socialist Workers' Party |
| **T&G** | Transport and General Workers' Union |
| **UCATT** | Union of Construction, Allied Trades and Technicians |
| **UDC** | Urban Development Corporation |
| **UNISON** | (combined NALGO, NUPE & COHSE) |
| **USDAW** | Union of Shop, Distributive and Allied Workers |
| **YS** | Young Socialists |
| **YTS** | Youth Training Scheme |

# ACKNOWLEDGEMENTS

W e would like to thank all those we spoke to for their gener-
osity with their time and their views, including those who
attended the research workshop – *Legacy of the Liverpool Labour Council*
(December 2011), as well as those who were interviewed individually
throughout 2012. Your reflections and accounts were enlightening,
insightful and at times moving; and without your voices, this work
would not have been possible. We would like to thank Helena Smart
and her colleagues at Liverpool City Archives for allowing us access to
their collection. We would also like to thank Mark O'Brien for setting
up the workshop and for conducting some of the interviews. We have
a huge debt of gratitude to the John Hamilton Foundation for funding
the workshop and to the Barry Amiel and Norman Melburn Trust for
their financial support in funding the bulk of the transcripts. This
certainly made the writing of the book much easier. Thanks also go to
Daniel Foy and Damian Lyons for giving up their time and providing
assistance in undertaking the comprehensive and detailed workshop
notes. Also, thanks to Martin Ralph for undertaking the workshop
transcription. Finally, we would like to thank Anthony Cond at LUP
for commissioning the book and supporting the project, as well as
providing a contribution towards the transcriptions. Any mistakes
and omissions are of course the responsibility of the authors.

## LIST OF WORKSHOP PARTICIPANTS 1 DECEMBER 2011, UNIVERSITY OF LIVERPOOL

Heather Adams
James Dillon
James Hackett
Paul Lafferty
Dave Lloyd
Ian Lowes
Tony Mulhearn
John Nelson
Harry Smith

## LIST OF INTERVIEWEES – 2012

John Airs
Gideon Ben-Tovim
Mark Campbell
Ray Costello
Louise Ellman MP
John Flamson
Maurice Gubbins
Derek Hatton
Mike Henesey
Mike Hogan
Malcolm Kennedy
Peter Kilfoyle
Paul Lafferty
Paul Luckock
Steve Munby
Michael Parkinson
Tony Rimmer
Jimmy Rutledge
Alex Scott Samuel
Sam Semoff
Jerry Spencer
Tunde Zack-Williams

# 'THE MILITANT YEARS: MAD, BAD AND NEVER COMING BACK'?

I n 1985 Margaret Thatcher was mid-way through her second period in office and had both defeated the 'enemy without', the Argentines in the South Atlantic, and the 'enemy within', the National Union of Mineworkers at home. Trade unions had been tamed, public spending cut massively and public services privatised. Mrs Thatcher proclaimed that 'there is no such thing as society' (McSmith 2011) and referred instead to individuals and markets. Long term processes of deindustrialisation and the move towards a service economy had led to the destruction of manufacturing and the onset of mass unemployment, especially in the UK's northern cities. Labour had been reduced by its biggest election defeat in history in 1983. The Tories seemed indestructible. At the Labour Party Conference in October 1985, the then Labour Party leader Neil Kinnock made what was widely regarded as the speech of his life, a major element of Labour's return to respectability. It was a speech that went down in history. Kinnock said:

I'll tell you what happens with impossible promises. You start with a far-fetched series of resolutions, and these are then pickled into a rigid dogma, a code, and you go through the years sticking to that, misplaced, outdated, irrelevant to the real needs, and you end in the grotesque chaos of a Labour council, a *Labour council*, hiring taxis to scuttle round the city handing out redundancy notices to its own workers. I tell you – and you'll listen – you can't play politics with people's jobs and people's homes and people's services. (*New Statesman* 4 February 2010)

The object of Kinnock's vitriol was Liverpool's Labour Council which had led a high profile campaign of opposition to the Thatcher Government. While local authorities today have implemented the coalition governments cuts, in the 1980s Liverpool Council, along with many other socialist Labour councils (led by future senior Labour figures like Ken Livingstone, Margaret Hodge and David Blunkett), had resisted the cuts. They argued that more government funding was needed to preserve the jobs and services that residents depended on. They refused to set a budget that would lead to cuts: 'better to break the law than break the poor', they argued.

Liverpool Labour Council was different. While the other socialist councils eventually came to an accommodation with the Government, Liverpool Council stood firm. This led to its denigration by Kinnock and other opponents as a council controlled by a clique of Trotskyite entryists from the Revolutionary Socialist League, also known as the Militant Tendency. In Kinnock's and many other people's eyes, the Labour Party in Liverpool had been hijacked by a gang of ruthless revolutionaries, playing politics with people's lives in a doomed attempt to overthrow the Tory Government. The council, Kinnock argued, had been elected on an unrealistic manifesto which sought confrontation with central government to win more resources for the city. Now the chickens were coming home to roost and in a battle between a city and the centre, the centre would always win. Worse still, the wrong message was being sent to the wider electorate which needed reassurance that Labour was a competent party of government in waiting. Worrying messages were coming out of Liverpool with allegations that a gang of hard men had taken over the city, using a private security force of formerly unemployed thugs to terrorise anyone brave enough to stand up to the hard left. Alan Bleasdale's drama GBH satirised the sharp dressed snake oil salesman at the heart of the problem. The incubus needed to be ruthlessly cast out, and Kinnock was the man to do that. He could take on his own supporters, and make the hard decisions. In time, the 47 errant councillors, who had sought needless confrontation with the government, were fined and disbarred from office, while the Militants were cast out of office.

Fast forward to 2012, and the *Sunday Times* reports on 'How Liverpool got its Mojo Back'. Liverpool's renewed status as a thriving visitor destination was topped off by its year as Capital of Culture in 2008 and the opening of the Liverpool One shopping centre and the waterfront arena and conference centre. Posters around town boast that Liverpool is now the fastest growing city region in the UK outside London. Popular culture presents a brash, confident (if rather, for some tastes) vulgar reinvented city to the world through reality TV programmes such as the conspicuous consumption of 'Desperate Scousewives' and 'My Big Fat Gypsy Wedding', featuring the Liverpool dressmaker to the travelling community. The long awaited inquiry into the Hillsborough disaster of 1998 finally reported that the police and media had conspired to denigrate Scousers as drunken thugs who stole from the dead, to cover up their own failings. A nation saw that a city and its residents had been systematically maligned as at best, over emotional and romantic, at worst, workshy scroungers that claim 'it's never our fault' and who have become residents of a 'self-pity city'.

So the city has reinvented itself. What was 30 years ago a toxic and derelict dockside, with a dirty, unkempt and half derelict city centre is now full of designer shops, clubs and bars. Liners have returned. Planes bring scores of overseas visitors to the city for city breaks. Yet, outside the city centre, the entrenched poverty, deprivation, criminality and drug abuse is still rife. North Liverpool, in particular, has its problems. But, the City Council under its new mayor Joe Anderson, is working with, not confronting, central government to address these problems. Anderson looks to work with, not attack, private business. And the rejuvenation of the city suggests that co-operation, not confrontation, is what a city needs. The Militant years for some, encapsulate all that was wrong with Liverpool. Why rake that up now that all the hard work of changing how Liverpool is perceived nationally has finally paid off? Do we want to see Hatton, Mulhearn, Byrne and their cronies on the front pages again? Let's forget about the 1980s, many say.

The reinvention of Liverpool was a culmination of a number of long-term contributory factors including the regeneration initiatives following the 1980s Liverpool 8 riots, as well as the public and private investment that occurred during and after the 'Militant' years. This book, published on the 30th anniversary of the election of the Labour (not Militant) Council in May 1983 argues that it is now time to revisit those years and properly put them in context. A major objective of this work is to ask what contribution the Labour Council made to how Liverpool navigated the great economic changes that we have seen since the 1980s. With hindsight, how do Militant and Broad Left Labour councillors and their supporters and opponents see their role in Liverpool's story 30 years on? Such perspectives are significant because they are at times misrepresented and at others an ignored part of the story. The 'Militant' years are an important part of the wider narrative on the regeneration of Liverpool.

We would argue that the Liverpool of the late 1970s and early 1980s suffered from a catastrophic breakdown as factory after factory closed. Cities and towns can survive and continue to exist long after the reason for their existence has evaporated, but they do so as poor, disinvested, ghost places where the role of public policy becomes no more than managing that decline. In some American cities like Detroit, we have seen the return of agriculture and woodland to former urban spaces. Cabinet papers recently released under the thirty year rule revealed how the then Tory Government argued that Liverpool should be left to its destiny (managed decline). It was the Toxteth riots of 1981 that enabled Michael Heseltine to argue that 'it took a riot' to get the government to recognise the problems of cities like Liverpool. Even today, maverick right wing voices argue that northern cities have no future, and their residents should be encouraged to migrate south, perhaps to replace Eastern European immigrants in the fruit fields of Kent.

We argue that the actions of the council in the years 1983–1985 mark the time that the city began to turn the tide. Far from putting off or delaying the regeneration of the city, the council's actions represented a shout of anger and pain against years of poor leadership and private sector disinvestment, the economic and social policies of national government, and the global changes in the economy that were at the time only dimly understood. The Labour Council, we argue, did not put off private sector led recovery: the private sector was already deserting the city. The council argued that Liverpudlians needed houses, community centres, decent education, parks and other green spaces – but government cuts were making this impossible to deliver. The council did not just accept this, it fought back. This stance was echoed 30 years later at a recent drinks reception for green investors in the city where a suited investment manager explained, 'what did you expect us to do back then, give up and die?' This was no battled hardened Trotskyite class warrior. When a city in crisis cries 'enough', the recovery begins.

This book utilises a number of oral testimonies to revisit those years of conflict and confrontation and explores a number of themes. Specific issues around racial equality, particularly the Sampson Bond appointment, are discussed at some length since the unforeseen convulsions that emanated from it revealed a chink in Militant's and the wider Labour Council's armour. With hindsight, some have conceded that huge mistakes were made here, whilst others stand by their actions. Through the use of oral testimonies, a range of perspectives is presented from those who defend the actions of the Labour Council, as well as those who offer a number of critical voices. Our account will not be to everyone's tastes: for some we have been too soft on the council and are being naïve. Others will feel that we are building on and amplifying previous attacks. Our account needs to be examined alongside other partial analyses of the events. For an account from a Militant perspective, see Taaffe and Mulhearn's *The City that Dared to Fight* or Derek Hatton's *Inside Left*. For accounts of opponents of Militant, see Peter Kilfoyle's *Left Behind* or Michael Crick's *Militant*.

It is not the remit of this work to join the many voices that condemned, both at the time and subsequently, the City Council's overall stance, nor do we seek to construct a retrospective hagiographic account. What is provided here is an account that lets the protagonists, both supporters and opponents, speak with their own voices. We do not try to label decisions right or wrong, sensible or misplaced. We document how those involved perceived what they were doing, why, and what their experiences mean now the city again faces a Conservative-led government carrying out a programme of spending cuts that disproportionately hit what is still a poor city. We hope that readers from all persuasions will enjoy what we recount, and look back on those troubled days perhaps with more perspective and understanding of other positions that was perhaps not possible in the heat of the battle. Finally, we hope visitors to the city, including our students, many of whom were born long after these events, will understand what they mean to those who lived through them.

The book unfolds as follows. Firstly, we introduce the reader to the Liverpool of the 1970s and early 1980s. How did the recession of those days impact on the city, and what was the political response that led to the election of the Labour Council in 1983? The next section looks at the theme of conflict as the battles over the city's finances and the deals made in 1984 and 1985 are revisited, before recounting what the councillors felt their achievements were. The book then moves to an analysis of how the backlash against the councillors' actions grew, which led to them being surcharged and disbarred from office, and Militants being expelled from Labour. The book then goes on to look at the conflict over positive action policies and in particular Sam Bond – a Militant activist from London who was given the job of Principal Race Relations Adviser in 1984 that provoked a storm of protest and dissent. In the final section we discuss retrospectively what this all means. Were the Militant years 'mad, bad and never coming back', irredeemably awful, summarising all that was wrong with Liverpool? Or did the election of a radical Labour Council of the early 1980s represent the first faltering steps in Liverpool's fight back against many years of decline and more recent unrest, which later years would build on as the city re-invented itself? Was the city right to stand up and fight back, or did it forfeit important allies and influence? Is the current administration right in choosing a more co-operative route?

# CHAPTER ONE

# LIVERPOOL FROM WORLD CITY TO BASKET CASE

L iverpool's recent economic travails need to be understood in a wider context of changing global trade patterns, some of which generated wealth, whilst others laid waste to its manufacturing base. From the eighteenth and nineteenth centuries to the early 1970s Liverpool was a prosperous and vibrant world city where the elite had a tradition of engagement in global trade stretching back to the slave trade. Their wealth went towards funding some of Liverpool's remarkable buildings, including its library. However, that wealth was lost on the majority of its citizens as the city remained socially exclusive not only in rough times such as the 1930s depression, but also during prosperous times. The legacy of the Second World War was a bombed city centre and a housing crisis that took 35 years of rebuilding to address. Bombing had destroyed 6,500 houses and damaged 125,000 more. There were 20,000 unfit dwellings in the city centre, 33,000 people still on housing waiting lists in 1947. By 1954 the problems had got worse, with 88,000 dwellings deemed unfit. Liverpool's working class grew on a diet of casualised work based around the docks that was poorly paid and notoriously volatile. Many of Liverpool's workers occupied slum dwellings that contributed to their poor health. The poor then did not share the city's wealth (Taaffe and Mulhearn 1988: 33).

In 1944 the Merseyside Plan to keep the new war industries in new estates saw a move from military to civilian production. Only around 35 per cent of Liverpool's workforce was involved in industry in 1945, compared with 52 per cent nationally. In the same year the Distribution of Industry Act moved industry away from the South East because of its vulnerability to air strikes. By the mid-1950s, the port of Liverpool showed signs of economic recovery as trade lost during the 1920s and 1930s was recovered:

> The regions of the world were still sea-laned to Liverpool. Within hailing distance of the Liver building were small ships to Paris and Rouen, and a mere ten minute walk took in ships of varying sizes loading for Limerick, Barcelona, New Orleans, Demerara, Lagos and Manaos – it was impossible to exaggerate how much the city of Liverpool was a seaport. (Murden 2006: 402)

More regularised dock work momentarily changed the casualised nature of this work and the docks became the single most important employer. Wages rose in the new prosperous Liverpool:

> A Liverpool docker's life no longer came under the heading of casual labour … 17,000 men worked here and their average wage was over seven pounds a week with overtime. (Murden 2006: 402–3)

By the mid-1960s, unemployment was what now seems a negligible 5 per cent and a manufacturing base was established on the edge of the city seen in an array of industries[1] of which the motor industry (including Ford, British Motor Corporation and Standard Triumph) was prominent. This created 26,000 jobs and an annual contribution of £25 million to the local economy (Couch 2003: 18). The city's strong, confident identity was perhaps encapsulated by *Merseybeat* in which for 51 weeks between April 1963 and May 1964, there would be a recording by a Liverpool artist at No. 1 in the pop charts. Liverpool was 'cheeky and young, un-posh, un-stuffy, democratic to its boot heels' (Du Noyer 2002: 78). Beat artist Allen Ginsburg famously came to Matthew Street, identified by Jung as the 'pool of life'. He argued that 'at the present moment [Liverpool is] the centre of consciousness of the human universe' (Du Noyer 2002: 93) although Liverpool poet Brian Patten, whose floor Ginsberg slept on, said 'I think Allen believed the centre of human consciousness to be wherever he was at the time' (Hickling 2007). John Airs moved to Liverpool in the 1960s from more dour Edinburgh, and remembers:

> I was just bowled over by it because in Edinburgh on a bus you are all sat quietly and no one looked at anyone else, in Liverpool, if you got on a bus at night, it was like a party. They had bus conductors in those days, and they were the MCs. I couldn't believe how different it was. I loved that. (John Airs interview, 2012)

In retrospect, however, it soon became clearer that Liverpool in the 1960s was experiencing an Indian summer, and the halcyon days of buoyant trade were short lived. By the mid-1960s, lack of investment in port facilities saw the passenger liner trade leaving Liverpool for Southampton and between 1966 and 1979 Liverpool's share of UK short-sea trade with Europe fell from 6.1 per cent to 2.4 per cent. Global Trade almost halved from 24.5 per cent to 13.8 per cent (Couch 2003: 12). By 2001 Liverpool had lost half its manufacturing industry and 44 per cent of its population: from 790,838 in 1951 to 439,476 in 2001 (Couch 2003: 3, 22).

Liverpool's inner city was characterised by decline as out of town shopping outlets competed with a city centre that still boasted seven department stores (Hendersons, G.H. Lees, Lewis's, Owen Owen, Blackler's, TJ Hughes and the Co-op) in 1971. In the meantime housing had been a perennial problem in Liverpool and after the war all parties were committed to a programme of municipal housing based on the 1944 Merseyside Plan of massive slum clearance and the redevelopment of slum areas, including the construction of high rise dwellings throughout the 1950s and '60s. Redevelopment went hand in hand with the dispersal of the population to overspill 'model estates' like Speke, Kirkby, Halewood, Croxteth, Huyton and Cantril Farm (Murden 2006: 395–96). From 1972 the Merseyside Structure Plan (Couch 2003: 94–110) led by a small Merseyside County Council team attempted to gain some sort of purchase on the city's problems, but quickly ran out of steam, prompting Couch to argue 'if the County Council could not come up with a strategic plan for the county, what is it for?' (Couch 2003: 97). The main plan was not published until

1979 as a guide for what might be possible in the 1980s. Still, in 1977 half of Liverpool's unemployed were aged 16–24, with many waiting 2–3 years for their first job (Murden 2006: 440). Many gave up on an unequal fight and moved elsewhere to seek work. A city that at its peak had a population of 855,000 in 1931 had halved in size by the end of the 1970s (Murden 2006: 428).

The poor social conditions that were characteristic of many parts of Liverpool in the 1970s and '80s inspired many to want to do better. Labour party member John Airs recalls:

> It clearly was, even then, pretty impoverished, I remember … I was teaching at Calderstones as it is now [Quarry Bank], that was very mixed, a lot of middle class kids from around here, but also a lot of underprivileged youngsters, and they found it quite hard. [...] it could be a tough rough city. I'd [lived in] flats all over the city at different times, and some of them were very damp, downtrodden. I was campaigning with the Child Poverty Action Group. I was interested in free schools and all that. (John Airs interview, 2012)

Derek Hatton was Deputy Leader of the Council in the 1980s. He recalls the changes that resulted from the decline of dock employment:

> As a kid my dad was a fireman and if he was at one of the dock fire stations, Canada Dock or Coburg Dock, I often used to go down and see. I used to walk along the front; there was ship after ship after ship, warehouse after warehouse after warehouse, thousands of dockers. It is hard sometimes to describe the feeling down there and I can smell now the hemp and the cotton, I can smell those smells now.
>
> All of a sudden in the '70s and '80s, the docks were being removed and things were changing. I don't think people fully understand when they look back in history the impact that had on the city and on people's lives. You could argue there was an inevitability that it had to change. Whether there was [or] was not an inevitability, that did not help those people at the time. It did not make any sense to those people whose jobs were changing. It was not just the people on the docks; it was people in all the service industries that were related to

the docks, all the insurance companies and everything that went with it. (Derek Hatton interview, 2012)

Mark Campbell was a local government worker in the 1980s, later becoming part of the team who promoted the council's politics to Liverpool residents. He recalls problems, but also a happy childhood, despite having little money:

I've lived here nearly 51 years now and I've never been unhappy here. That business of grey and grime and 'we haven't got two pennies to rub together', I don't think that's ever affected me. I had a good upbringing, not necessarily privileged, but we lived in a nice suburb of the city.

We're a lot more materialistic now than we were then ... I've got an 18 year old son and he would probably think I was poverty stricken when I was his age because there is a pressure on young people now that ... It probably did exist, but I remember being delighted when I got my Penny Round shirt, because that was a status symbol, or my two-tone Prince of Wales check trousers ... and playing football, as I did, getting a good pair of boots. But certainly, I had a happy upbringing and it was only later on that I realised, when I went into the big bad world, that I realised that, factories were getting closed down and threatened with closure and the rest of it, industry was changing, so... I got politicised. (Mark Campbell interview, 2012)

## Attempts at regeneration

There were varioius regeneration efforts throughout the 1970s, such as the Home Office-run Urban Programme that funded day nurseries, playgrounds and community centres. A Community Development Programme (CDP) in Vauxhall (Scotland Road) funded a study of local employment conditions which found that between 1967 and 1972, 20,000 jobs had been lost. It provided a liaison office for benefits as well as community education and resources. The CDP also became involved with rent strikes during this period.[2] In common with other CDPs, the Vauxhall CDP developed a critical analysis that argued urban problems derive from broader structural factors: working class Liverpudlians should not become a scapegoat for the poverty of the city. In the CDP's publication, *Gilding the Ghetto* (CDP 1977), Alcock (1994: 135) argued:

> To put it bluntly, the workers and academics of the CDPs found that working with local people did not remove local poverty because the causes of that poverty lay elsewhere in economic trends and social politics; and their outspoken and public repetition of this message led to the closure of the programme by the government.

This is not to argue against the valuable social environmental work that was done, including road restructuring. But it is to understand that small palliative measures in an area devastated by global economic forces as well as by local decisions (like the building of the Wallasey tunnel that destroyed the communities of Scotland Road) are insufficient. More and more socialists in the Liverpool Labour Party began to develop an understanding that many housing conditions in the city were unacceptable, but also that tinkering with problems through trivial (if well intentioned) amounts of *ad hoc* or targeted funding was not enough. The city had major structural problems and large amounts of money would be needed from Government to fix them. From 1978 the Liverpool Inner City Partnership developed a plan for 1979–82, agreeing £48 million of public expenditure, a 30 per cent increase in funding for the city.

However, with the Tory win in the 1979 election, public spending cuts were introduced, and the Inner City Partnership's plan was never implemented (Couch 2003: 84). The Tories, it seemed, had turned their backs on Liverpool, and the government's actions reinforced a feeling locally that 'Liverpool has no place in the Conservatives' scheme of things, [as they] simply do not care about its people or its problems' (Parkinson 1985: 17). This formed the basis for later claims that the Tories have 'stolen Liverpool's money'. It would seem then that the various initiatives to regenerate and pull Liverpool out of its social and economic stagnation were not enough.

> Since the 1960s, the city has been the recipient, or victim, of every urban experiment invented, including Tony Crosland's educational priority areas, Jim Callaghan's traditional urban programme, Roy Jenkin's community development projects, the Home Office's

Brunswick neighbourhood project, Peter Walker's inner area studies, Peter Shore's inner city partnerships, Geoffrey Howe's enterprise zones and Michael Heseltine's urban development corporation. Two decades' experience of those policies had not substantially improved the city's problems. (Parkinson 1985: 16)

Such initiatives fell short for a number of reasons including lack of resources for the scale of the problems and a lack of coherence of central government involvement. The enormity of Liverpool's problems was reflected in the city's ongoing housing issues between the years 1979–83 when no social housing was built, repair backlogs had built up under a Liberal-controlled council, rents were the highest in the country and waiting lists the longest. Paul Luckock came to Liverpool from Belfast in 1981 and reflects on the poor state of housing during that period:

I lived in a flat on Upper Parliament Street and fairly immediately the thing that struck me ... [was] the housing and the conditions people were living [was] even worse than parts of Belfast. ... I was gobsmacked, it was very, very grim. I think particularly shocking was the state of a lot of the tenement blocks in the city but also a lot of the housing that had been built well after the Second World War was even then by the '80s in pretty dire conditions. ... A lot of those blocks of flats that had been put up were in a dire state.

He also remembers the working class pride invested and apparent in people's homes:

I remember in the tenement blocks particularly you'd have this abject squalor along the landings. The refuse chutes didn't work, the sewerage systems didn't work, in the courtyards below there were piles of raw sewage and all, but even in and amongst that you would come across people who'd maybe lived there since the beginning. ... When you went into their houses ... [they] were [like] little beautiful palaces, they were absolutely pristine and their little bit of the landing was pristine and they were almost living under siege because even at that time in the early '80s some of the properties were not let, they were just empty, and [of] course it deteriorated over time.

For some, deprivation and poverty resulted in a number of mental health problems:

> My work was with children and young people and their families and many of the problems that I was engaging with were really problems in large part people coping with the poverty they were living in, so they had significant emotional wellbeing, mental health problems. The problems [of] living day to day and that exhibited itself in drugs and alcohol problems and all of that. So I found that really quite shocking and I suppose very quickly in a sense I joined the local Labour Party. (Paul Luckock interview, 2012)

The 1979 'winter of discontent' saw a series of local government Labour disputes across the UK, many centred on Liverpool. Famously striking Toxteth grave workers were pilloried in the press and the militancy of unions like the GMWU who represented them was used by the Conservatives to make political capital against the Labour Government then in office. 'You couldn't even bury the dead', it was said (Kilfoyle 2000: 70).

## Enter Thatcher, stage right

With the election of Thatcher in May 1979, the situation for Liverpool changed markedly for the worst with changes in the rate support grant and the playing down of the role of Inner Area Partnerships. The newly elected Conservative government restricted the ability of local authorities to spend, and reigned in public sector spending more generally (Parkinson 1990: 248). Derek Hatton contrasted the ways that Merseyside's problems were addressed in 1979 as completely inadequate when contrasted with the success of the 1945 Direction of Industry Act:

> It was the start of the Thatcher years and no city the length and breadth of Britain was to feel the impact of her policies more keenly than in Liverpool. A once great city was already in decline and had been neglected even by Labour. Miles and miles of docks which had once bustled with life stood idle as a testament to the

shift in world trade. Industry was moving away and the dole queues were growing. There was to be no help from Thatcher for inner city Liverpool. Under Margaret Thatcher's policy of 'free market forces' there was to be no pump priming. The new sunrise industries from the world of high technology would not be directed to areas like Liverpool to solve its problems. Instead they were to be allowed to go where they would, grabbing the best grants and cash handouts. (Hatton 1988: 42)

With the advent of private sector led urban regeneration under the Conservatives, the squeeze on public sector spending would be keenly felt, particularly in terms of unemployment and its associated social problems. Jimmy Rutledge remembers:

I think you could describe [that time] as 'a guide to the ruins'. More so for people who weren't intently political, just this sense of hopelessness because factory after factory [closing down]. Some employers had been in the city for decades, some for centuries, and been long term employers; generations of the same family had worked there. The docks, Tate and Lyle's, Taverner-Rutledge, Meccano; one by one [they were] like collapsing dominoes. Of course, apart from the immediate impact of the loss of jobs, you had that ripple effect because people don't have disposable income so then local businesses suffer, leisure facilities, shops, service industries are all going to suffer as a result. (Jimmy Rutledge interview, 2012)

As mass job losses began on Merseyside, industrial relations worsened as workers began to fight back, as seen in the Meccano and Fisher Bendix occupations, the struggle over Croxteth Community School, and successful development of the Eldonians co-operative on the former Tate and Lyle site. These symbolised the start of the resistance in Liverpool.

For Hatton, the situation was clear:

The fat cats of the Conservative Party didn't give a damn about Liverpool, and the Tory Press painted a picture of a militant workforce whose strike record was really at the root of the trouble. (Hatton 1988: 42)

The *Financial Times* argued, for example, that

> the question that needs to be answered is why, when companies
> choose to rationalise, the blow falls too often on Merseyside? (David
> 1979)

Liverpool pride was defended by the *Daily Post* (cited by Merseyside
Socialist Research Group 1980: 20):

> Studies have showed that productivity on Merseyside is not very
> different to that in the rest of the country, and we should not give
> credence to the damaging myths about Merseyside. (*Daily Post* 22
> March 1979)

Michael Parkinson argues that the problem was that by the late 1970s
Liverpool's economy was suffering from the classic 'branch plant'
problem: its economic future was in the hands of a small number
of multinational businesses with branch plants on Merseyside,
run by businesspeople with no commitment to the city (Parkinson
1985: 12). Well before the election of the council in 1983, business
was 'abandoning the city' (Parkinson 1985: 39) – and decisions made
in boardrooms far away can have a disastrous effect on those places
that have to deal with the consequences, often wiping out years
of painful progress overnight. For Liberals like the housing chief
Richard Kemp, the solution to this problem was to keep rates low
and to encourage more middle class housing in the city to counter its
perceived plebeian character:

> Really, we ought to be building homes for rich people. What Liverpool
> really needs above all else is more wealthy inhabitants. The domi-
> nance of council tenants only fosters the ghetto mentality. (*The Times*
> 5 March 1981 cited in Taffe and Mulhearn 1988: 54)

A local middle class, the Liberals argued, would create new jobs and
businesses. For Thatcher herself, the answer lay in encouraging entre-
preneurship. She told the then Knowsley MP and future chat show host
Robert Kilroy Silk, 'The problem with your constituents is that they
don't start up their own businesses. They've got no entrepreneurial

spirit. They've got no get-up-and-go' (Kilroy-Silk 1986: 45). By early 1981, unemployment stood at 20 per cent with a mere 49 vacant jobs for 13,000 unemployed youngsters. Manufacturing output on Merseyside almost halved between the years 1974–84 (Parkinson 1985: 12). Taaffe and Mulhearn (1988: 51) describe what they had seen happen in Liverpool:

> In the first phase of resurgent Toryism, from 1979–83 various coalitions of Tories and Liberals held power in Liverpool. Contrary to their later claims, the Liberals were more than willing accomplices in Thatcher's onslaught against Liverpool. The slashing of the city's grants from central government had a devastating effect on the lives and conditions of hundreds of thousands of working people. Within months of Thatcher's victory, experts warned the government that rather than cutting local government expenditure, massive amounts needed to be pumped in, in order to break the cycle of depravation which had become so evident in the 1960s.

Between 1979 and 1984, Liverpool's job haemorrhage could be seen in the loss of almost half of its manufacturing jobs – a staggering 40,000. Liverpool became known as the 'Bermuda Triangle of British capitalism' (Merseyside Socialist Research Group 1981: 9). The closures were relentless. As Mark Campbell put it, 'As one factory closed, another shut.' With the closure of Tate and Lyle's Vauxhall Plant in 1981, 1,500 people lost their jobs in a ward with 46 per cent unemployment, despite a good labour relations history and good productivity (Murden 2006: 437). The *Liverpool Echo* reported that a loyal workforce 'in an area all too often overlooked' had been shafted: 'Their reward for this proud record? Redundancy.' In May 1981 the 'People's March for Jobs' started in the city, as the unemployed recreated the famous Jarrow march of the 1930s depression. A *Right to Work* campaign leaflet: 'Stop the Murder of Merseyside', documented the remorseless destruction of jobs and the families that relied on them. Losses included the closure of British Leyland's Speke No. 2 Plant with 3,000 redundancies; Birds Eye with 1,300 under threat and 456 already gone; Lucas Aerospace closure with 1,200 redundancies; Lucas Fazakerley 490 redundancies; Courtaulds 500 redundancies; GEC 640 redundancies and Cammell Laird 160 redundancies. The list went on. 'Stop the Murder of Merseyside' argued:

> To the government and the employers the problem is merely one of juggling the statistics. But to us its Joe, or Jim or June next door. It's our kids hanging around on street corners with nothing to do. It's the story of our old folk neglected and cold. It's the story of friends and relatives stuck on the dole sometimes too depressed even to leave the house. And who's next? ... Merseyside has a proud record on militancy ... It is that militancy that must now be organised to fight for the right to work.

Mike Hogan lived in Speke at the time:

> About 1978, I lived in Speke, and I always remember going to school we'd always be walking past a picket line, Standard Number Two plant, and so you were sort of aware of the class struggle and so on. Then they shut Standards Number Two, they shut Dunlop's, and they were the big headlines. The amount of workers that were thrown out of work on that industrial estate ... it felt like everything was just collapsing around you.
>
> It was very real, being on a working class estate with a father who was a factory worker who worked just over from where we lived in Metal Box, and he was coming home saying 'They just announced 200 redundancies ... when is it going to be our family's turn?' So you'd be hit with redundancies and know people around you who were affected by that ... you just felt like Capitalism was collapsing around you. (Mike Hogan interview, 2012)

Life for those on the dole as a result of closures was grim. Mike Henesey remembers working in the Renshaw Street Unemployment Benefit Office, later featured in the TV drama 'Boys from the Blackstuff':

> It had been a dance hall and a roller skating rink and was where they recruited for the army during the war. [...] The roof leaked. We had wire grills in front of us. There were only windows in the roof; you had no windows you could look out of.

We were at one end of the building and the grills and the counters went on three sides. When the door was opened in the mornings you could literally hear the thunder of footsteps, people running down to sign on at a certain time and if you didn't, you had to refer somebody to the supervisor.

We had the police in there on almost a daily basis picking people up or watching people when they were going out. We had every walk of life. We had guys who came in and spent the day in there because they had nowhere else to go.

We were only there to sign people on. ... It was a soul destroying place for people to come into. There was nothing in there, there was very little done to help them get jobs, and quite frankly there weren't any. ... There was often fights, and families coming in where someone had run off with someone else's giro. (Mike Henesey interview, 2012)

Mike remembered vividly the despair in the unemployment benefit office after one of the regular closures:

[on] Monday morning after a close down you'd be inundated with new people making claims. I remember people coming in who had never signed on before – you could see them totally lost and bewildered ... Those images have stuck with me all the way down the line, of people's faces coming in, the despair and [expression] of 'what the hell happens next?'

Economic devastation spread to the city's infrastructure. Jerry Spencer went on to work for the city's regeneration company, Liverpool Vision. He remembers visiting Liverpool for the first time:

It was a basket case. You'd had the wave of closures of the factories; Dunlop's, Meccano, all that sort of thing and those were relatively recent. There were huge swathes of the city that were not rebuilt. ... The whole waterfront was derelict at the time. I wasn't prepared for the reality of cities like Liverpool that had been left to rot for so long. (Jerry Spencer interview, 2012)

John Flamson worked for Merseyside Urban Development Corporation (UDC). He recalls the state of the city in the late 1970s and early '80s.

> By the time you got to the late '70s you're actually dealing with the devastation of the depopulation of the city. So not only was it economically poor it actually looked ravaged. It was a hurt city. If you look around the city centre ... there was this air of stagnation over the centre. Many of the buildings hadn't been cleaned up, [...] they were black. But the one thing pictures [images] will not show you is *it stank to high heaven*. Down by the docks – because the Mersey Docks and Harbour Company had removed Brunswick Gates onto the river effectively – the south dock system had become tidal from 1972 and the silt was the depth of two London buses one on top of the other. So it was a tidal estuary in effect right up to the edge of the city centre. It stank because you had these algae so it wasn't a pleasant seaside smell and this was right at the heart of the city centre. It was almost as if the Albert Dock became a symbol of a past greatness and of current impotency. (John Flamson interview, 2012)

Peter Kilfoyle, later MP for Walton, recalls:

> Not only were there a lot of closures but there was a sense of hopelessness around. There was an article [...] called the Museum of Horrifying Example ... . It encapsulated the sense of [...] I won't say desperation but almost resignation that pervaded in Liverpool at that time. It was a very, very sad time and a very desperate time. (Peter Kilfoyle interview, 2012)

By the government's own admission, 'it took a riot' for Westminster to respond to Liverpool's problems. Michael Heseltine, then Secretary of State for the Environment, spent three weeks in the city and toured the disinvested areas with a coach full of business leaders. Heseltine argued that 'those who enjoy the privileges of capitalism should accept the responsibility of the well-being of the community' (*Daily Post* 4 October 1989).

## Enter Heseltine and the Merseyside Task Force

Michael Heseltine became the 'Minister for Merseyside': He recalls:

> Alone, every night ... I would stand with a glass of wine, looking out at the magnificent view over the river, and ask myself what had gone wrong for this great English city. [...] The Mersey, its lifeblood, flowed as majestically as ever ... Its monumental Georgian and Victorian buildings, created with such pride, still dominated the skyline. ... The Liver Building itself, the epicentre of a trading system that had reached out to the four corners of the earth, stood defiant and from my perspective very alone... everything had gone wrong. (Hernon 2011)

Heseltine's tour led to the establishment of the Merseyside Task Force composed of 12 civil servants and 12 seconded managers from large private companies. Heseltine argued:

> As the days passed it became more and more clear to me that there were projects that should, in the main, long have been undertaken and that now lay within my capability. At the end of my visit I was able to call a press conference. I was able to list thirteen initiatives. (Michael Heseltine 2000: 225)

He visited the city every fortnight between 1981 and 1983, working with the Task Force. As part of the Conservatives' critique of Liverpool as slow, lethargic and lacking any 'get up and go', Heseltine encouraged a 'can do' atmosphere in the Task Force. Mike Henesey went on to manage Merseyside's European Programme. In the 1980s as a young civil servant, he remembers the atmosphere:

> I remember vividly Heseltine had his list of 30 projects that ranged from some of the stuff around major housing schemes. It also included things like Wavertree Technology Park but it also included other schemes like YTS [Youth Training Scheme].
>
> The thing that really struck me about the Merseyside Task Force was in the benefit office when the senior people came it was 'tug your

forelock' almost. ... I remember the only decision I was making really was whether I allowed somebody to sign on early or late. Everything else, every other eventuality was covered in a code, so how much you paid them was in a code, whether you paid them or not was in a code, whether you penalised them because they'd left a job was set out in a code. There [was no] opportunity to actually make what I would call real decisions.

All of a sudden I went from that to an organisation that was top heavy. The director was the most senior civil servant in those days outside of London. They didn't put a Grade 3 outside of London. It wasn't heard of. But he'd been put in. I remember just thinking 'I'm dealing with senior grades on a day to day basis' and having to report back and I remember that took me six months to get used to. It also took me six months to get used to making decisions in an odd way. I never forget I came out [of one meeting about an information technology project] and I got in the car and I sat there for about quarter of an hour thinking 'what have you done, you've just approved £25,000 without any real guidelines like there was in the benefits office' ... I sat there thinking 'you've just made that decision'.

What was also interesting was that in the Merseyside Task Force every Friday there'd be a get-together and we'd go through these 30 projects and the thing was that it was everybody. We'd all meet in the conference room and you'd go in there and you had all the senior people and it took a while really to feel comfortable within that. The other thing that we did was usually Friday lunchtime you'd find almost the whole of the Task Force in what was The Queens, the pub on the corner, it's now All Bar One.

The reason I say that is because it was amazing how much (I don't like to use the phrase because in those days it didn't even exist) 'networking' we did when we went in there. You'd have a good few pints, you'd talk, talking across with all the team and that included the director and you found out what was going on, you talked across what was happening and just generally about what was going on and mostly got more out of those sessions on the Friday in the pub than spending ages trying to make links in other ways. And that was something that really struck me.

It was very much about making things happen and cutting red tape and there were funds there to do things. It was a light touch to make things happen.

Murden (2006) argues that the Task Force created 1,500 jobs, particularly through the Wavertree Technology Park, but it endured problems attracting private funding: it spent £170 million to get in £25 million from the private sector. Merseyside Council had its own view of the Task Force:

> The government's developing approach to urban problems rested heavily on an attempt to bring forward private sector finance. Mr Heseltine, early on in his role as 'Minister for Merseyside', took the Chairmen and Chief executives of many of the nation's largest financial institutions on a much publicised tour of Merseyside. The underlying message was that financial power should be tempered with responsibility, and enlightened self-interest could lead to profitable investment in the cause of urban regeneration. But the Financial Institutions Group ... has yet to produce a single project anywhere in the country that its institutional sponsors are prepared to support. (Merseyside County Council's Agenda for Merseyside 1985: 7)

Furthermore:

> Merseyside Task Force has itself failed to realise its original far reaching brief which was to do with the overall deployment and effectiveness of public resources on Merseyside and the need to modify resources or switch resources between government departments. This focus was soon lost in a plethora of local initiatives which Merseyside Task Force have pursued on a project by project basis. While these special initiatives are important in their own right, they have not been a substitute for the better co-ordination of policies and programmes [...] or the search for fundamental solutions to Merseyside's problems. (Merseyside County Council's Agenda for Merseyside, 1985: 7 cited in Couch 2003: 114)

Parkinson and Duffy (1984) comment on the lack of influence the Task Force had over the private sector:

Neither the Minster nor Task Force has acquired any real purchase over the decisions of the private sector. As its Director admitted to the Select Committee, if a firm were thinking of leaving Merseyside, the Task Force would try to ensure that it was aware of all the support it was entitled to and might advise it of prospective developments which might affect its future. At the end of the day, however, it is inevitably influenced by the general thrust of Government policy, which is that it is for companies to take their own commercial decisions. Moreover the Task Force does not really have the ability to anticipate private sector decisions. The supreme irony in this respect was the behaviour of the United Biscuits Company. It seconded to the Task Force a manager who was generally regarded as one of its most successful members; two months after he left, the company announced the closure in Liverpool of one of the most modern food-processing factories in Western Europe with 2,000 redundancies. (Parkinson and Duffy 1984: 82)

Mike Henesey is more charitable about the Task Force's success:

We used to have ministers up once, twice, three times a week. Things had started to happen with Heseltine and there was some particularly noticeable stuff that was going on. He had his coach tour round, he brought in the private sector and there was senior people from some of the banks and the building societies in those days who were involved in the likes of the Commercial Business Training Centre (CBTC) and a few of those sorts of things. Girobank was a major employer and it was linking in with the CBTCs. Some of the initiatives like Wavertree Technology Park involved Barclays and eventually they put one of their Barclaycard centres on there. The Garden Festival clearly was another one. (Mike Henesey interview, 2012)

The Task Force supplemented the Merseyside Urban Development Corporation, which bypassed the local authority and employed Thatcher's 'market-oriented and property-led approach to urban regeneration' (Murden 2006: 438). The UDC, along with London docklands, one of the first of the Urban Development Corporations, was created to redevelop derelict areas like the docks for residential, industrial and commercial use. Its focus was the Albert Dock, which became the home to Granada Television, the Merseyside Maritime Museum, a host of shops, offices, flats and restaurants. In a deliberately provocative call to action, Heseltine wrote about the Mersey in 1983:

> Today the river is an affront to the standards a civilised society should demand of its environment. Untreated sewage, pollutants, noxious discharges all contribute to water conditions and environmental standards that are perhaps the single most deplorable feature of this critical part of England.[3]

In August 1981 the Speke Enterprise Zone was declared and whilst seen as developable, it attracted little private sector investment, relying instead on investment by English Industrial Estates Speke. The Speke Enterprise Zone received £20 million between 1981–1989, whereas Manchester's Trafford Park received £40 million, nearby Salford £100 million and £170 million was awarded to Gateshead. At the end of its ten year life much of the land remained vacant (Couch 2003: 113). Regeneration initiatives then were based on a Thatcherite approach to deregulation, which assumed that a newly liberated private sector would step into the gap, rather than centred on partnership and planning. A private sector-focused approach had obvious limitations in a city suffering from mass disinvestment. Consequently, although regeneration efforts did many good things, they did little to dent the long standing 40–50 per cent unemployment rate in the dock areas and Speke (Murden 2006: 539). Critics of Heseltine's initiatives, in particular the Garden Festival, were unimpressed. 'We want jobs, not trees,' they argued, 'Heseltine came, they planted a few trees amongst the rubble, and went away again' (GEC striker cited by Stack and Watson [1985: 10]).

The creation of the Garden Festival led to criticisms that this was not enough to create jobs and the slogan 'jobs not trees' epitomised this. Between 1984 and 1985, around 4 million visitors went through the Garden Festival gates (Murden 2006: 446), but unemployment during this period went up remorselessly from 47,165 (20%) in 1981 to 61,123 (28%) in 1985 (Merseyside County Council 1985: 7).

Criticism of the undemocratic nature of the UDC rested on claims that it imposed plans on the city without consultation or willingness to work with the council. This led to claims that money used here was at the expense of the city as a whole. Thus, far from aiding Liverpool, it left it worse off and represented 'just another phase in a long line of urban policies tested out on Liverpool'. The problem with such initiatives was that they were too *ad hoc* and they often stopped before they made an impact, or changed track (Murden 2006: 445–447). Heseltine conceded 18 months after the riots, that 'the weight of the recession has been devastating' (author unknown 1985). That is not to say that, for many, Heseltine had good intentions. Peter Kilfoyle argued 'Heseltine showed you could actually do things – and he deserves credit for that'.[4] Margaret Thatcher paid him a backhanded compliment:

> He made a great impression ... For the most part, though, his efforts had only ephemeral results ... I would not blame him for that – Liverpool has defeated better men than Michael Heseltine.[5]

It would take many more millions and many more years of European funding to make a difference.

For socialist critics, then, the government's response was inadequate. They argued that the government's free market ideology prevented it from adopting an interventionist role in economic development and was 'sceptical about assisting risky enterprises in the inner city' (Merseyside County Council 1985: 7), which meant it was not able to respond to the wave of closures, particularly of multinationals, that gulfed the city after 1981. Too much aid had gone to too few large multinationals like Ford and other manufacturers which provided around 20 per cent of the city's jobs and little support was given to service industries that provide approximately 75 per cent of jobs locally. It was argued that a regional policy was needed that was sensitive to economies like Liverpool's that would be prepared to subsidise jobs (Merseyside County Council 1985: 7). The private sector, socialists argued, had been decimated and the local authority must take up the slack. By 1985, the public sector provided 33 per cent of the city's jobs (Merseyside County Council 1985: 9). Socialists argued, and many agreed, that a more radical solution was necessary: a socialist council prepared to fight the government for more resources. Former councillor Jimmy Rutledge remembers:

> It was just so absolutely bleak, which was bad enough, but what seemed to compound it was that there wasn't a shred of sympathy from central government. The old Tories might have wrung their hands and said, 'well we'll see if we can come up with some form of scheme to alleviate the suffering'. But the hard face of Thatcherism and this sort of new injection or revival of laissez-faire capitalism and economic liberalism; it was just so bleak. In a sense that filtered through to people who weren't overtly political; probably your average Labour voter who voted because of a class instinct or because of family tradition and who thought, this is really, really serious. (Jimmy Rutledge interview, 2012)

## 'militant' or 'Militant' Liverpool?

Liverpool in the early 1980s was, then, a city in crisis. For some, it was tragic that throughout the 1970s the city suffered from a triple crisis: an economic crisis in common with the rest of the country that saw manufacturing and port employment decimated; a geographical crisis that left a largely derelict city marooned on the wrong side of the country; and a political crisis as the city's leaders failed to rise to these challenges. In 1991, Peter Kilfoyle who won the parliamentary seat for Labour in Liverpool Walton (following the death of Eric Heffer) reflected on the political conditions that facilitated the coming to power of a council dominated by the left, including members of the Militant Tendency:

> [it] is the story of consistent failure of political leadership in one of Britain's great cities for more than 20 years. Liverpool at the end of the 1960s was enjoying a brief Indian summer, as the success of its bands, its comedians and its football clubs masked the serious and long term decline of its industrial and commercial bases. Its city fathers were, with one or two exceptions, oblivious to these real conditions [...]. The council Labour group was [...] not only divided

but lacking in ideological coherence. Incapable of providing a political lead, its only driving force was unenlightened self interest. Into this vacuum moved the partisans of the Revolutionary Socialist League, a Trotskyist grouping far better known as the Militant Tendency. (Kilfoyle 2000: xix–xx)

Kilfoyle accurately portrays the political leadership that left the city tragically defenceless at a crucial time in its history. Through the 1970s and into the 1980s the economic decimation of the city sat alongside weak minority Labour and Liberal administrations as they traded places year on year, with little being done. For some, the imposition of the Merseyside Task Force (MTF) and the Merseyside Development Corporation (MDC) was recognition that local government was failing the city. John Flamson worked at the MDC and recalled a council debate in the early 1980s about the corporation: was it an unwelcome and undemocratic imposition on the city? Some thought so. Others felt that at least something was being done to deal with the city's deep seated problems: the council was doing nothing, they argued, in what was the heart of the city. John remembers one councillor, who will remain nameless, and may well have been using Liverpool's famous wit, saying: 'I know nothing's happening but if nothing's happening we want to be the ones who are doing nothing.' Perhaps that summed up the malaise. Michael Parkinson argues that the failure of any administration to deal with many of the city's most pressing issues contributed directly to the crisis of the 1980s as many of the city's services were both inefficient and expensive (Parkinson 1985). Reform was badly needed. Across Liverpool, for many years left wing members of the Labour Party with deep roots in the city had been developing an alternative to the Heseltine approach. In May 1983, the Labour Party won a comfortable majority on Liverpool Council ending years of weak leadership.

Consequently, opponents and friends of the Council that was elected in 1983 recognised that the new administration was a new broom. It represented a new determination to overcome the malaise and do something about the city's problems. While the validity of what was proposed is of course hotly disputed, no one disagrees that 'something needed to be done', and that the council elected in 1983 showed a new determination to overcome the stagnation of the past 15 years. It is also important to recognise that the council of 1983 to 1987 was dominated by left wing councillors, but it was a *Labour*, not a *Militant* council. Of the 47 councillors disbarred, only 13 were members of Militant. Peter Kilfoyle, no friend of Militant (his job was to clear them out of the Liverpool Labour Party), argued:

> One point that ought to be made of course is that the Liverpool Council was not a Militant council; it might have been [militant] with a small 'm'. It was often portrayed by people that it was jam packed with members of Militant Tendency, it wasn't. There was a hard core who provided a drive, an impetus behind their political stance, but the majority of the members of that group were not actually members of Militant. It [Militant] became shorthand for a council ... let's be fair, we're not even talking about the council, we're talking the Labour group, the majority group on the council and we're talking about a group that was heavily influenced by the Militants in their midst. But I would never say that they were absolutely dominated or run along the lines of some kind of Trotskyite organisation. ... But you can't ignore the impact that those Militants had on the thinking within the group and in steeling them up. (Peter Kilfoyle interview, 2012)

Senior members of the administration, including leader John Hamilton and finance chair Tony Byrne, were never Tendency members. Liverpool's left wing networks were wider than Militant and in particular included a strong Communist Party with a strong presence in the unions. The press – understandably perhaps – focused on the Militant, and in particular on Tony Mulhearn, Ian Lowes and Derek Hatton, and claimed that they were the real power behind the throne. The reality was that the councillors saw themselves as Labour Party members. Outside the Tendency, Militant found both supporters and opponents. But to call the council a Militant council is a misrepresentation, at best lazy media shorthand, though their influence is not disputed.

# CHAPTER TWO

# LIVERPOOL RESPONDS
# TO THE CRISIS

S ocialist politics came late to Liverpool. In the hundred years
between 1850 and 1950, Liverpool's political history was
controlled by Tory elite, many of whom remained independent of
London and, basing their wealth on trade with the Empire, saw little
need to invest in the city itself. Manchester by contrast was characterised by Liberal free traders such as Cobden and Bright, who also
invested in libraries and other institutions aimed at the betterment
of the lives of the working classes who had helped to create the city's
wealth (Hunt 2005). Liverpool's wealth was made elsewhere, and while
the gateway to the city around Lime Street Station and on the waterfront boasted a suite of world-class buildings, one mile away the slums
of north Liverpool were ignored. While elsewhere the Labour Party
emerged to champion the working class, in Liverpool a clear sectarian
divide saw the Tories securing the Protestant vote, while Irish repub-
licans secured the Catholic vote. Liverpool Scotland was represented
by Thomas Power O'Connor, an Irish Nationalist MP, up to his death
in 1929. The city would have to wait until 1923 before the first Labour
MP was elected for Edge Hill, and longer still before Labour secured a
majority of MPs in 1964, including the MP for Huyton, Labour Prime
Minister Harold Wilson (Kilfoyle 2000: 2).

This is not to say that working people did not organise in Liverpool. In 1911 the city was paralysed by a transport strike. Elites sent word to London that the crimson flag of anarchy held sway over the city, and the cruiser Antrim was moored in the Mersey (O'Brien 2011). The docks and life in the slums bred a city of fighters. While socialists began to organise in the city from the 1930s onwards, it was not until 1955, after nearly a decade of Tory dominance in local elections, that the Tory stranglehold was finally broken. Liverpool's political landscape now began to change as Labour took power for the first time. Between the mid-1950s and the early 1970s, control of the city was shared between Catholic focused Labour (in the shape the Braddock machine) and the Protestant orientated Conservatives (Parkinson 1985, Kilfoyle 2000). Many argued that the dominance of Catholicism in the Labour Party manifested itself in 'a politics of personality, patronage, corruption and bossism' (Parkinson 1985: 18), exemplified by the Braddocks, but which continued long after (Crick 1984: 147; Kilfoyle 2000: 6) and which bred passivity. Labour Party organisation was intentionally poor to keep out the 'wrong sort of candidate' (Taffe and Mulhearn 1998: 36): anyone trying to join Labour this time would be told it was 'full up':

> Getting into the Labour Party proved a little bit difficult. You could see Gillmoss Ward Labour Club from where I lived and a couple of times I went over and was more or less turned away at the door. One time the guy at the door went and got somebody involved in the political side of the ward to come to the door to speak to me, and it turned out it was Councillor Eddie Roderick who came out and said 'it's alright son, there's no vacancies at the moment'. So I was turned away on the fact that there were no vacancies within the Labour Party. (Tony Rimmer interview, 2012)

Malcolm Kennedy moved to Liverpool in the 1970s. He was no 'bedsit Trot', later becoming a leading opponent of the Tendency. He too had to fight his way into the party:

> I actually tried to join the Labour Party, I think, about 1975 and applied to Huyton, but never heard anything more from the local organisation there. I always say the word 'student' on the application form at that

time probably put them off. It was Harold Wilson's constituency and they were fairly fierce opponents of Militant and I think that some constituencies would try and keep potential Militants out of membership in order to not be overtaken. I think 'student' might have been a clue. As it happens, I was far from being a member of Militant, I'd joined the Labour Party to avoid all of the Trot groups that I'd come across as a student. (Malcolm Kennedy interview, 2012)

## Militant Merseyside

In the 1930s the first Trotskyites in Liverpool – Tommy Birchall, Jimmy Deane and others in the Deane family – began to put down roots in the city (Taaffe and Mulhearn 1988: 33). By the early 1950s Walton Labour Party had become a hub of far left politics within the Labour Party, with the selection of Militant founder Ted Grant as parliamentary candidate in 1955, followed by George McCartney (a supporter of the *Militant* newspaper's predecessor *Socialist Fight)* in 1959. Although neither was successful in winning the seat, Militant's ideas appealed to trade unionists, youth groups and others on the left, and not just in Walton but nationwide. Militant argued that the far left groups such as the Workers' Revolutionary Party, The Socialist Workers' Party or Tariq Ali's International Marxist Group were often based on intellectuals and students. In contrast, they argued, Militant on Merseyside was proletarian from the start, and more deeply involved in the unions as well as the Labour Party. Through the late 1950s and early '60s, Militant members in Liverpool, Brian Deane and Pat Wall, became councillors for County ward and Walton Labour Party Youth Section began publishing *Rally* at the end of 1957 (Kilfoyle 2000; Taaffe and Mulhearn 1988).

During these early years, Militant activists became heavily involved in industrial action, including the national apprentice strike in 1960 which won higher wages for apprentices: Militant's Terry Harrison was Secretary of the Apprentices Committee on Merseyside (Taaffe and Mulhearn 1988: 38). It was during this time (1964) that both Ted Mooney and printer Tony Mulhearn were drawn into the Walton Constituency Labour Party following another apprentice strike in Manchester and Liverpool, and the *Militant* newspaper was launched as a means to propagate and agitate for socialist and Marxist ideas, initially within the Labour movement, and later the Labour Party (Taaffe and Mulhearn 1988: 38). The basis of the organisation then was firmly rooted in the organised Labour movement on Merseyside, rather than intellectuals and students who might have been attracted to such ideas. Militant supporters were not 'bedsit Trots' moving into industry or a new town, then attempting to build socialist ideas in an environment where, as seen in the previous chapter, it felt like capitalism in general and Liverpool in particular was imploding. Militant's solutions seemed to make sense to many who joined the Tendency, whilst others remained sympathetic and supportive from outside. Mike Hogan joined the (Militant-controlled) Young Socialists:

I went to a Young Socialist meeting, I was attracted by it. I tried to join the Young Communist League, then I tried to join the Young Socialists […] I went along with a friend of my step-brother to a meeting and I just started going the Young Socialists, and got recruited into the Militant.

Militant's very strong in Liverpool and with the accents […] it was like a Scouse mafia at 't'Militant' [laughing] and people used to joke about that. I mean Militant wasn't only in Liverpool, but Coventry, but even early on in Brighton, South Wales and stuff like that. The difference in Liverpool was the base amongst the working class. We were known within the Labour Party in Walton [through] a phrase at the time, a 'Walton resolution' […] a resolution that ended up demanding the nationalisation of the top 200 monopolies under democratic control [chuckles].

But it had deep roots, people were respected, known within the working class and was, if you like, an organic part of the Left within Liverpool. In discussions about the rates and the deficit budget it was a recognised platform within the Labour Party because the people advocating it were Labour Party activists with deep, deep, deep roots within the Labour Party.

Militant was not just the left wing but it was a socialist/Marxist organisation […] and to be honest with you [there was] a kind of arrogance:

'We know what's going on. We also know what needs to be done'. That's it then, it's solved! [laughs]. I always thought that communist, socialist ideas, [were] going nowhere on their own, so what we need to do is be in the Labour Party, it's our party, so that's why I joined.

These were proper socialist ideas, [no] messing about, [not] 'let's nationalise part of the economy and let's hope that'll cure the problems'. It was 'take over the monopolies and we'll run it, the working class can run it – why can't working class people run things? They know what needs to be done'. So I came from it from that point of view. ... I was already convinced about Socialism and what was happening around me just convinced me more. It was Socialism right. (Mike Hogan interview, 2012)

For Derek Hatton, Militant seemed serious, focused and committed to change:

I suppose when I joined the Labour Party [1972] I met a number of people ... and the one with most influence on me was Tony Mulhearn. ... At that age and being the type of person I was, I wanted to get things done and I was not the sort of person that was prepared to sit back and go through the processes of getting from A to B. I think probably in Militant you saw a much clearer black-and-white and less shades of grey. It fitted in a lot more with what I was thinking at the time. (Derek Hatton interview, 2012)

Many people, non-Militants, valued their contribution to the wider Left in the city. Jerry Spencer recalls:

I think there was a developing sense that if we are going to change this then we're going to have to do it ourselves, we can't look to the government to do it [...] it has to be done from below. 'We can't go on like this anymore' was the general feeling that was starting to grow ... a lot of the old politics [was] still around – the living wage, the classic stuff about the struggle against poverty, against discrimination, those sorts of things, that the Labour Party had always centred itself in. But there was also a lot of discussion about how do we regenerate the city? What should a city be like? Stuff like that was starting to be talked about.

That depended on a whole new politics being put in place. That's why I was, in a sense, glad Militant was around; it provided a challenge to the old politics and the old structures. It sought to mobilise, to harness the latent power of the working class, working people, ordinary people in the city, listening to them. There was a great deal of listening going on as well as a lot of teaching and instructing and dictating, there was a lot of that. And out of that, I think, came a new vision, a new kind of politics and a new kind of vision of what cities might be like, how they might work for ordinary working people.

These ideas were being developed by others, but I think what Militant did, and people on the Left who in the early days worked in partnership with them, was creating the possibility. They created hope, there was a sense that actually by capturing this ward here and that constituency there and building a movement, that actually some of these ideas might get going, we can sweep some of that away, get rid of the gridlock that just seemed to be that kind of sleeping municipalism. Build the houses, reorganise the schools, these sorts of things. (Jerry Spencer interview, 2012)

Militant then, was and is part of Liverpool's history and heritage. As Derek Hatton puts it:

Militant on Merseyside is unique. Elsewhere in the country Militant supporters may be accused of being Johnnie-come-latelies, but in Liverpool the Left has had Militant working from within as a component part for twenty-five to thirty years. Peter Taaffe, Pat Wall, Tony Mulhearn, Ted Mooney, Terry Harrison – Militant activists from the early days – all come from Liverpool backgrounds.

That's why I still laugh when I hear the nonsense talked about Militant's entryism into the Labour Party. No matter what you think of the politics of it, the fact is that the Derek Hattons, the Tony Mulhearns, were born and bred on Merseyside and so was Militant. We hardly tunnelled in or parachuted down. (Hatton 1988: 31)

Even the *Liverpool Echo*, no friend of Militant, could characterise Militant supporters as 'young, unsmiling, radical [...] but not infiltrators'

(*Liverpool Echo* 24 December 1979: 9). So yes, Militant was part of Liverpool, but, for some, not necessarily a part to be celebrated. Militant opponent Malcolm Kennedy puts forward an alternative view:

> I was very, very convinced by the Labour Party and also very convinced that the people that were members of the local branch that I'd joined had very little to do with what the Labour Party was about. They'd spend most of the time arguing for policies which weren't Labour Party's policies. They spent the rest of the time trying to get rid of Labour Party members out of representative positions. ... I went to the Houses of Parliament with Militant and their whole conversation was about 'how do we get rid of right wing Labour MPs?' (Malcolm Kennedy interview, 2012)

Militant was based in the Liverpool trade unions, but unlike the other local socialist authorities of the 1980s, it struggled to engage with the new 'identity politics' of race and gender that emerged elsewhere throughout the 1960s and 1970s. It focused very closely on the traditional, overwhelmingly white, manual working class. Kennedy recalls:

> I saw them as ... having a very narrow view of what the working class was [...] and of whose support you needed to gain to form national governments. They seemed less bothered about that, they were much more focused on the industrial struggle and the downfall of capitalism and this wasn't the Labour Party in reality. They seemed to hate the Labour Party, basically, and were there to undermine it rather than to support it.

> I just thought that they had a different agenda from the Labour Party; totally ignored the realities of the world economic situation in the seventies, the impact of the oil crisis and ultimately helped pave the way for Thatcher... Totally ignored what people actually voted for.

> I'd decided at that time that they were wrong, they were determined to destroy the Labour Party and the big battle for me was being involved in the long term salvation of the Labour Party so that it could get to a point where we could win general elections again and we could reverse the impact of Thatcherism on Liverpool.

> It was simple as far as I was concerned. I was Labour Party, they weren't [...] they were infiltrating the Labour Party. Nothing to do with the Labour Party, as such, they were just trying to undermine it. (Malcolm Kennedy interview, 2012)

For Malcolm Kennedy then, Militant made the election of a Labour Government that could help solve Liverpool's problems, less not more likely. Others were sympathetic to the council's struggle, but could not join the Tendency. Mark Campbell worked at the heart of the council's publicity unit, but never joined Militant. He explains why:

> It politicised me. It was a privilege in some respects to sit in that office and listen to people who had seen it and done it and all the rest of it and I was like, naïve, wet behind the ears and trying to absorb as much as I possibly could whilst still remaining with a degree of distance from that. I was always scared of becoming a supporter of the Militant Tendency because I'd hear other people from other factions of the Labour movement, you know, decrying them.

> Part of me wanted to because they were making all these noises that, in my head, were right. Yeah, I'm a young, working class man and why should we have £30 million spent on the Garden Festival for a few months when there's people who haven't got somewhere to live and decent living standards etc. So, they ticked all those boxes.

> But I held back because other people whose knowledge, experience and views I valued, I listened to them. ... I also didn't like some of the tactics that they employed. It seemed a bit juvenile at the time. ... there was a lot of 'us and them' within the Labour Party ... I remember there was a buzz word of 'you're a PB' – Petty Bourgeois, and that was directed at other sympathisers and supporters ... The Militant Tendency people very much looked down upon people who I looked up to. Certainly [this happened] behind their back and occasionally to their face and publicly try and undermine their importance and their involvement. (Mark Campbell interview, 2012)

Other sympathisers felt, on balance, despite there being much about the Militant that they disliked, the struggle against the Government ultimately determined which side they were on. John Airs, again never a Militant supporter, argues:

In the Thatcher years I realised I had to join a party, so we joined Labour, which in Aigburth was a very small ward, we had a Labour MP but not councillors. At first I didn't like [Militant's] take on politics generally in that they seemed to be arguing that if you could get the class war sorted out everything else would fall into place so they weren't interested in the woman's cause, black cause, any others.

So I joined a Broad Left group who were caucusing across the city against them ... we caucused quite seriously against them, to make sure that whenever something came up in the local constituency that we were there to oppose them.

Then when I began to think about it, I thought, this is ridiculous! (we got to the point when there was only Liverpool and Lambeth opposing Thatcher) we should be fighting with them, not against them. I knew quite a few of them, I knew Felicity Dowling. ... Tony Hood was an interesting character. He was not a Trotskyist, but he said, 'we've got to work with them' so I said, 'OK, let's do that', and a lot of people in the area began to think the same, we built up and built up until we had in this ward 400 paid up members! (John Airs interview, 2012)

The council was then 'militant', not 'Militant'.

## Stroppy scousers?

Viewers of Johnny Speight's comedy 'Till Death Us Do Part' (which between 1965 and 1975 attempted to satirise the views of character Alf Garnett – a working class, right wing, Enoch Powell-loving racist) will remember the 'Scouse git', played by Cherie Blair's dad, Anthony Booth. Booth played a socialist firebrand who mocked what he saw as his father-in-law's craven submission to the ideas that kept him poor. He encapsulated Liverpool's reputation for militancy, the reputation that Malcolm Kennedy saw as so unhelpful. Even Prime Minister and Huyton MP Harold Wilson argued in 1968:

From the day when as President of the Board of Trade I scheduled Merseyside as a development area, the full power of the state was thrown behind the drive for full employment in this area, an area which has not, in living memory, previously known anything like full employment. And the response? Strike after strike frustrating the effort of government; signalling a question mark to those industrialists who are attracted to the inducements and are considering establishing themselves here. (Murden 2006: 432)

Huw Benyon's analysis of life in the city's Ford factory in the 1960s and 1970s encapsulated how many socialist-orientated working class Liverpudlians saw life. One Ford worker recounted why he became a shop steward:

Three years ago this place was in a very bad way. Ford's controlled everything. We had no steward on the line at the time. The lad who'd taken it on broke down. The frustrations and pressures were too much for him. ... So I stood. Someone had to do it. I didn't want to stand to be a shop steward. That's the last thing I wanted when I came to this place first. I wanted to get on a bit. But I could see all the injustices being done every day so I thought I'd have to have a go. It wasn't right that they were having to take all the shit that Ford's were throwing. (Benyon 1973: 191)

For Tony Lane, localised issues at Ford Halewood began to be used as a way to label the whole city:

The docks apart, it was events at Ford's, which more than anything else helped Liverpool acquire its militant reputation. Ford workers were translated into *Liverpool* workers and so when, for example, the press discovered an exiled Liverpudlian at the head of the Pilkington strike in 1970, a front page headline shouted 'SCOUSE POWER'. (Lane 1987: 153)

Peter Kilfoyle argues that Militant in Liverpool was a reflection of a longer tradition of working people trying to get jobs and then keep some control over their terms and conditions, as well as gain access to council services through their trade unions:

You've got to look a little bit more deeply. For example the council workforce, very well organised particularly through GMB and T&G branches and they had a vested interest in terms of their jobs. The unions, as organisations, had a big interest in terms of nomination rights for those jobs. There was nothing new in this, the council was always the place that if you wanted a permanent job in Liverpool you went to work for the Corpy, as we used to call it, because you were guaranteed a job when all the other jobs appeared to be casual in the area. So they systematised this tendency in Liverpool to look after members of your family and whatever. (Peter Kilfoyle interview, 2012)

Lane (1987) argues that while strikes in Liverpool cannot be doubted in terms of frequency, at the same time this was not that different from any other region at the time. Rather, what attracted attention to Liverpool's industrial relations was the *style* of Liverpool's trade unionists compared with others, captured by a local culture of swagger and mocking of authority: 'It was the militancy of Militant that impressed, not the deep-laid, apocalyptic strategies' (Lane 1987: 155). By the late 1970s, Militant had established itself in:

several of the more degenerate ward and constituency Labour Parties in the city [...] and this helped give it legitimacy and credibility with younger trade unionists who had grown up in a climate of expectations where a win or a draw seemed more certain than a defeat. (Lane 1987: 155)

The crisis of the early 1970s led to a wave of factory occupations, when workers in enterprises facing closure refused to accept redundancy, arguing that under workers control and with state support to tide them through the difficult times they could become going concerns. Taaffe and Mulhearn (1988) argue that Harrison and Mulhearn were central to organising support across the city for the occupations. In February 1971, 25,000 marched through Liverpool to the Pier Head in support of imprisoned dockers.

In 1972, the Tory Government passed a housing act which led to rises in rents to market levels of 20–25 per cent, which many tenants felt were unaffordable. The bill led to a nationwide strategy of rent strikes, which many in Liverpool supported. At that time, 60 per cent of Liverpool's housing stock was in public ownership. Labour's leader in Liverpool, Bill Sefton, whilst initially opposing rent increases, on re-election then proposed rent increases of 10 shillings a week (50 pence), a 25 per cent increase in some cases. The Labour Council split. Twenty-one councillors refused to vote to raise council rents as in their eyes this was capitulation to the Tories. Kilfoyle (2000: xx) argues that Sefton's decision to back down led to a catastrophic loss of credibility in a city 'dominated by oppositionalist rhetoric'.

The unrest of the early 1970s (by no means confined to Liverpool) grew to such an extent that following strikes by miners and power station workers, the country was put on a three day week (Beckett 2010). Tory Prime Minister Ted Heath was forced to call an election posing the question, who rules the country: the government or the unions? He lost. Such working class militancy had forced out an unpopular and incompetent Tory government (Darlington and Lyddon 2001). The imposition of major austerity measures on the nation was a lesson not lost on socialists in the city. Similarly, the costs paid locally, of backing down in a struggle with the Tories, were noted.

## Pavement politics

Inspired by the youth revolt of the 1960s, from the early 1970s an energetic new wave of activists in the Liberal Party, and in particular, the Young Liberals, began to challenge the moribund Labour and Conservative machines (Hain 1975). They used a new form of 'pavement politics' focusing on identifying and meeting local needs, exposing the machines as complacent and out of touch at best, corrupt and authoritarian at worst. The Liberals seemed a breath of fresh air, and they came seemingly from nowhere to take power in 1973 in a minority administration with Tory support. For the next ten years Liverpool's council politics were characterised by coalitions, hung councils and confusion, switching between Liberal administrations with Tory support, and minority Labour administrations (Parkinson 1985). For years, the three parties failed to agree on many fundamental issues, and city centre land remained vacant as no one could agree what to do with it. Michael Parkinson argues that: 'decline would have been difficult enough to handle with an enlightened leadership: that it had to handle political incoherence was a cruel turn of fate' (Parkinson 1988: 23). The Liberals were only a minority force in the city.

The Liberal Party's strategy for the city was split between a focus on diversifying (for some) or dismantling (for others) the large public sector housing stock built up by Labour and Tories. The Liberals also sought to maintain low rates to keep the private sector in the city and to facilitate the formation of more small businesses. As we saw above, the jobs holocaust of the early 1980s put paid to that: no independent local business elite developed that had an interest in working with the council to solve local problems. Rather, the private sector contributed to the city's decline by shedding jobs or turning inwards to weather the economic storms (Parkinson 1990). The city lacked a business voice that could generate jobs and had an interest in the city's future. The lack of a private sector voice in the city reinforced a tendency for the city to seek support from government, rather than addressing fundamental problems itself. It reinforced Labour Party dominance politically, and public sector dominance economically. As they competed with each other electorally for the smallest rate rise proposals, between them the Tories and Liberals bequeathed Labour an inadequate budget settlement when they took power in 1983 (Parkinson 1985).

## The attraction of the Labour Left

Consequently, Peter Hain's radical ideas notwithstanding, Liverpool Liberals were closer philosophically to the Tories and their approach was consequently not attractive to many radicals in the city. Left wingers in Labour were as opposed to the city's machines as everyone else, but they wanted, as they saw it, to reclaim Labour as a party that aimed to benefit working class people. John Airs, a teacher in Liverpool, and part of this movement, put it this way:

> I didn't even think of joining the Liberals, it didn't occur to me. I know about Peter Hain, but it didn't occur to me. In terms of ideology, I see the Liberals as basically a capitalist organisation, whereas Labour is pretty capitalist too, but it is the story of two parties, and my interest was in a more radical way of the Labour. When I did join, I got some

great friends, lots of people I really respected, who knew lots about the world. More than I did. (John Airs interview, 2012)

By the 1970s, many people in Liverpool's leftist networks felt 'only Militant has a worked out programme and perspective that could prepare the Liverpool working class for the mighty events of the 1980s' (Murden 2006: 453). Kilfoyle (2000: 39) puts it less positively: 'as the Labour Party flirted with self destruction … Militant provided a clear and simple analysis of the political condition, together with soundbite solutions, which struck a chord with the young, the idealistic and the naïve.' Was this a conscious strategy by Militant to get people to join Labour and take it over? Militant supporter Ian Lowes disputes this:

> People came into the Labour Party at that time not because of the Tendency as such – it was going to happen anyway – but the Tendency were able to capitalise on that. The new people who joined the party would go to meetings and be impressed by what was said by the leading lights of the Tendency.

> Some say that there was this wonderful plot by the Tendency to go out and get people to join the Labour Party in order to take it over. Well it wasn't like that. People came to independent conclusions. They thought that the Labour Party was the party of working people and that the only way you were going to change it was from the inside. (Cited in Kilfoyle 2000: 49)

Peter Kilfoyle argues that often the Labour Right deserved to be challenged. They had become seriously out of touch. He cites Ian Lowes:

> They'd never been called to account. They'd never been asked to explain why they'd done this or done that. A lot of them were older, and if younger people were coming into the party they would insult them by saying 'you've only been here for five minutes. I've been in the party for thirty-five years and a councillor for twenty-nine: so what right do you have to tell me what to do'. (Ian Lowes cited in Kilfoyle 2000: 42)

On the other hand, Militant found it easy to take over moribund wards: a few committed individuals who made the meetings drag on with rather formulaic motions soon made the faint hearted leave. Some say 'undisguised ruthlessness' and 'objectionable' behaviour was part of the process (Kilfoyle 2000: 50). Through this, and through affiliated unions, Militant built its strength on the District Labour Party. Before long, Kilfoyle argues, the DLP became swamped with new delegates and subject to a Militant take over, forever passing Militant-inspired 'model resolutions' (Kilfoyle 2000: 80–85).

By 1978 there were seven Militant-supporting councillors on the council. An attempt to depose Labour's non-Militant left wing leader John Hamilton by two right wingers led to uproar, and Militant and the Left defeated the attempt. By now Militant was seen as a powerful force on the District Labour Party, but, it must be argued, the Left more generally was in the driving seat. The DLP used its power to select council candidates. From 1978, Liverpool Labour Party policy was that Labour councillors would implement policies developed at the DLP. For some, this was seen as a way to keep councillors account-able and give more people an input into policy making. The Labour Left wanted to move away from personalist 'boss' politics through which councillors distributed largess to their supporters without challenge. They wanted to avoid what they saw as 'sell outs', such as that made by Sefton on housing. Then DLP chair Tony Mulhearn puts it his way:

> In the old days before we took the council you had Jack Braddock, Bill Sefton, who made very radical statements. When they were elected to power they proceeded to break them, and when they were challenged, particularly Jack Braddock they used to say 'well I am carrying out policy', he said, 'but the constitution says we should carry out policy but the timetabling is the responsibility of the council'. Bill said 'we'll carry out your policy but not just yet'. So they would go on and on, rent would go up … We came in, we were totally different and that is what horrified the establishment. They said these people are making promises but not only that, they are carrying them out. It horrified them. (Tony Mulhearn – workshop interview, 2011)

On the other hand, opponents would argue that councillors were elected by their ward, were legally responsible for their decisions and accountable to their ward. They could only be thrown out by their elec-tors. None of this was true for a delegate to the DLP. The DLP saw the councillors as its delegates rather than representatives (Kilfoyle 2000). Further, Militant's opponents argued that in time the DLP executive, not the DLP itself, began to set the agenda, often (they argued) through emergency meetings called at short notice and at random times, against standing orders, and in an atmosphere of crisis. Kilfoyle (2000) argues this was how Militant dominated the council.

In May 1980 Labour was hit heavily in elections as a result of having set a rate rise of 50 per cent the year before with tacit local Liberal support. Militant supporters argued that this was a crucial mistake (a factor picked up later). Between 1980 and 1983 the Liberals took charge of the city from 1981 onwards, following DLP policy, and Labour called for 'no cuts in jobs or services', or rate increases, and for the mobilisation of the unions for a battle with the government. Through the early 1980s Labour's rhetoric radicalised to the extent that the Liberals began to campaign against what they condemned as a 'Marxist Labour Party'. For example, one of their leaflets featured an image of a gravestone with the legend 'Liverpool Labour Party: died 1980 from Marxist Infiltration', with the ex-Labour Liberal candidate arguing that voters 'don't want to be in the hands of a Marxist-dominated city council or government in Britain' (*Daily Post* 24 April 1980: 6). The *Daily Post* described this as 'McCarthyite'. In an article entitled 'Hard Left is Hard Fact', the *Liverpool Echo*'s Peter Phelps quoted Derek Hatton arguing 'we would ... like to see the local authority taking over as municipal enterprises those firms that are closing down, and making redundancies'. Asked how he would pay for it, Hatton responded:

we would make the case to the government. ... Last year, of £73 million paid to the moneylenders – the banks, finance houses and big business – £60 million was pure interest. Capitalism generally has milked the working class over Liverpool for long enough. As far as we are concerned that would be a start in terms of non payment of interest. ... we believe that only through mass action of the trade union movement, the Labour movement, and the working class generally will this sort of struggle be victorious.

If the government refused to pick up the bill there is no way we as a Labour group would put on the backs of the working class of the city further rate bills, which in real terms would simply be asking the people to compensate for the Tories' actions of lining the pockets of the rich and big business.

There would obviously be a conflict between ourselves and the Government, and we would look to the working class of this city to support us. Pressure would be so great from Liverpool it would act as a beacon to many other local authorities to follow suit which would result in the bringing down of this Tory Government and the return of a Labour Government pledged to socialist policies. (Phelps 1981: 6)

Asked why he held these views, Hatton argued 'It's because I believe there are only two alternatives facing mankind: nuclear annihilation, or Socialism. There's no other road left now, as society collapses around our ears.' An editorial comment on the same page argued 'if the militant socialist ambitions, spelled out on this page, look like coming to pass, many people would want Whitehall overlordship as a permanent feature' (*Liverpool Echo* 10 December 1981: 6).

The commitment to break with a perceived past of Labour Party 'sell outs' and introduce meaningful changes was something shared by many Labour councillors and is expressed below by Jimmy Rutledge:

If you harp back to the Braddock's era, which I regard as a form of Tammany Hall politics, there was a deep rooted impression [amongst] working class Labour voters that you vote for them [councillors] and they say they're going to do this and they'll put that on a leaflet and they'll say there's a manifesto. But once they got in they'd come up with a million and one excuses saying, 'well that's not practical'; 'no, that can't be done at this particular point in time'; 'well, we'll look at that for the future' and all the promises were just hot air.

There was a feeling that this time that if we made a commitment we'd actually stand by it. [I was asked by DLP], if elected in pursuance of the council policy as framed by the District Labour Party policy, what would you actually do if it brought you into conflict with the government or the wider establishment? I just said, 'well I'm standing for election under this banner and that's the priority, that's the commitment'. It's not to say the same old stuff; 'well I wanted to do this but I couldn't, you know'. I think that filtered through collectively, which

I think was quite radical for the Labour Party. So that's probably why that particular era and that council stands out, [there was a sense that] we'll go as far as possible, we'll deliver. I think the council did that as far as was possible. (Jimmy Rutledge interview, 2012)

Tony Rimmer, a former Liverpool councillor, felt compelled to do something during these years:

We were all just so incensed by the attacks the government were putting upon the working class ... workers' rights were changing, opportunities were being lost ... industry was being decimated, and the slogan that we used in my particular case for the election [to the council] was 'enough is enough'. ... We needed to put a stop to it if we could. (Tony Rimmer interview, 2012)

A Labour defeat in council elections in 1980 and the rise of the newly formed Social Democratic Party (SDP), composed of former Labour party members who were opposed to what they saw as Labour's drift to the left, cleared many right wingers out of Labour. Militant Terry Harrison was picked to fight Edge Hill against Liberal Jeremy Alton. Tony Mulhearn was picked for Toxteth, Terry Fields for Kirkdale and Derek Hatton for Wavertree (then a Tory seat). In the final event, only Terry Fields stood in the 1983 election as a result of boundary changes in which Liverpool's seats were reduced from eight to six, a symbol of the city's continuing depopulation. In the May 1982 council elections, Labour stood on observably Militant policies, while the Liberals campaigned on the slogan 'Marxists out, Liberals in'. Labour gained two more seats. In 1983, while the rest of the country voted heavily against Michael Foot's Labour Party and for Margaret Thatcher (who basked in the glow of victory in the Falklands), Liverpool's voters went against the national trend and elected a Labour Council pledged to confront the Tories.

## Lessons of the 1970s

The election result of 1983 did not come out of the blue: it was the culmination of decades of work by the left in Liverpool, both Militant, and its sympathisers, supporters and fellow travellers. Harry Smith joined the Tendency in 1974, and became a councillor in 1980. Harry argues:

> What you have to realise is that it was not 49 people who just turned up one day and happen to be in a room together and vote. The District Labour Party and the trade union movements over many years had built up people into a Labour group who gave certain undertakings that they would not make the cuts, they would not do the rent rises. So everyone that was there had given an undertaking. You did not come from another planet ... The Labour group was a big selection of people from all walks of life who [had] given an undertaking. (Harry Smith – workshop interview, 2011)

Dave Lloyd argues:

> It started decades before. Particularly though it started in 1978 to 79 when the Militant really got organised and influenced people like myself, who were totally committed to the trade union movement and thought my energies were best fighting for the jobs there. ... We had little meetings of people who felt this way inclined and then we got a list of people who were really committed to stand for the council. From 1978 onwards they went to the DLP and said, 'I'm going to do that'.

> You know you get a football team that develops over six years and you get all the right people in it and the right structure behind them it was similar to that. We had our disagreements ... but we had no difference [in] what it meant to getting them houses built, getting those schools sorted out.

> The proudest thing my child said to me 'Dad you have never sold out'. We can look back in history and we can say that we have stood our ground. We would have been prepared to be bankrupt, it was not idle chatter and the wonderful thing is there were many, many people who had lots of political ideas and thoughts but that moment when the vote was taken in the council nobody shirked, everyone put their hand up and everybody knew the consequences. And when I see councillors now who are part of the machine, they are part of the

system. Just get it done, we would all be responsible. We would not be in just an ivory tower enjoying the perks and the luxury of being a councillor.

We all suffered for it. Lot of us lost our jobs, I did. But it was a wonderful time to be with committed people who were determined. Life was giving the working class a bad deal and we were going to stand firm and say 'no'. It is a wonderful thing when you're 66 years old and my son can say, 'Dad you never sold out.' (Dave Lloyd – workshop interview, 2011)

This was a group committed to doing what they said they would do. John Nelson argues:

One of the proudest things that ever happened to me when I actually came onto the council [was that] I fell amongst some people who actually meant business. Who actually [were] about to go out and do something, step up to the plate, put themselves on the line and they meant what they said. ... 49 people actually stood up and said they are prepared to go to jail prepared to do this. (John Nelson – workshop interview, 2011)

Another driving force was anger at the way working people in Liverpool had been treated. Paul Lafferty, one of the 49, recalls what drove his father, Bill, also a surcharged councillor:

He had been on the council for several years and was an old-fashioned councillor in some respects, he loved the people that he represented, he did the limited amounts that he could ... but he did it in a sincere and honest way and sometimes in an angry way because he was angered by the way working people had been treated and continued to be treated. (Paul Lafferty – workshop interview, 2011)

James Dillon wanted to fight for what he believed in:

I have always been of the belief that if you believe in something you fight for it, depends on how hard you believe in it. I believe that if you go, you go 100 per cent. I knew that we would end badly, that we would

get thrown out, but that does not stop you fighting. (James Dillon –
workshop interview, 2011)

Paul Lafferty recalls the realisation that this time Labour would not,
as he saw it, 'sell out' hit home:

I remember Derek Hatton coming to see us when I was at work
before the election and we sat down and he told me what would probably happen, what we were going to do. It came as a bit of a shock. I
thought about it and agreed with that because I had been brought up
by betrayal from trade union officials from MPs to councillors, insin-
cerity was rife. No wonder people say 'well, politics is all bullshit'. ... I
think for the first time we actually didn't [sell out], that surprised
people. (Paul Lafferty – workshop interview, 2011)

Labour went into the 1983 election arguing that the Tory Government
had treated the city badly. It had penalised the city in deciding how
much support the city should have, based on the low rates settlements
implemented by the previous Liberal administration. As a result of
this, Labour argued that £23 million had been unreasonably withheld
by Government, and they should give it back. The council resolved on
confrontation to provide the resources it argued the city needed.

# CHAPTER THREE

# THE ELECTION OF 1983

I n May 1983 Labour did not expect to take power as comprehensively as it did: the feeling was after one more push the party would be in a majority in 1984. Recall that the SDP had won the Crosby by-election, which returned Shirley Williams to Parliament, only eighteen months before. The Falklands had been retaken, and in May 1983 Margaret Thatcher won a majority of 144 seats to retain power. In Liverpool, things were different. The many years of building the Left in the city over the previous years (discussed in chapter two) paid off.

Labour was elected on a wave of militancy in the city. A major focus was the dispute at Croxteth Comprehensive (see Hatton 1988: 45–55). No one disagreed that Liverpool's secondary education system was in dire need of reform. The Secretary of State demanded it. After two years of delays, in July 1982 Liberal education chair Mike Storey decided that Croxteth Comprehensive should be closed in the face of falling rolls, but he failed to consult teachers or the community to win support. Closure plans came as a bolt from the blue. Locally, there was a strong feeling that Croxteth, a deprived ward in the city (with an unemployment rate of 40 per cent), needed a school, and this would be a major blow to the community. The Labour councillors opposed closure, and the parents and sixth formers established a Parents Action Committee which engaged in a programme of civil disobedience, blocking roads and staging demonstrations. Visiting Education

Secretary, Sir Keith Joseph, and later Michael Heseltine, were pelted with eggs by Croxteth School supporters. Eventually parents and teachers, with the support of the local Left and the unions, occupied the school and from September 1982 ran it as Croxteth Free Community School. For the Left, this was a cause celèbre: for example, the actress Vanessa Redgrave appeared in the city as a fundraiser. However, a lack of resources for teaching, a break in, and limited electricity and heating oil made it a hard winter in the school, and some pupils drifted away. In February 1982, just before the elections, the Liberal Council sent the parents committee a rates bill of £27,000, and threatened to send in the bailiffs. In response, supporters worked hard in the unions to provide money for the school, identifying Liberal wards and turning them Labour with the slogan 'Vote Labour to keep the school open' (Kilfoyle 2000: 79). The battles over Croxteth School, alongside a dispute over sexual harassment at the 'Lady at Lord John' shop in the city centre and a council typists' strike, all contributed to a feeling of militancy in the city which fed into Labour's victory – and the salvation of the school.

## A tough campaign

The election campaign was in many places bitterly fought. Paul Luckock recalls unseating a sitting councillor, and then enduring a sectarian campaign by his opponents:

> It was fascinating for that moment because in the '83 election for example, the Liberals who ran against me in Vauxhall, it was like going back to PJ Kavanagh the Irish Nationalist MP and all of that, they actually had a leaflet and on the front of it, it had a picture of the Pope saying do not vote for this person he is the anti-Christ. In fact, one of the questions they asked me [at selection] was 'Are you a Catholic?' And I said 'No. Actually I was brought up in the Church of England but I'm a non-believer you know, I don't really have a faith'. So that was the sort of [issues that came up]. But I won hands down with 89 per cent of the vote so I got elected. (Paul Luckock interview, 2012)

Tony Rimmer recalls his selection against a veteran right winger:

> I found myself being invited to go and address the Ward along with
> the sitting councillor, which as it happened was Eddie Roderick, the
> person who had turned me away at the door a few years before saying
> that the membership was full. So come the night of the selection
> meeting, I addressed the members [...] and I actually won by just one
> vote. I think the headline in the *Liverpool Daily Post* the following day
> was 'One vote ousts veteran'.
>
> From there the campaign began and we were all just so incensed by
> the attacks that the Tory Government were calling upon the working
> class and workers' rights that were changing, individuals rights
> were changing, opportunities were being lost, industry was being
> decimated [...] and the slogan that we used during the election was
> 'enough is enough'. We used every particular topic, unemployment,
> workers' rights, housing, education and highlighted the various cuts
> and attacks that the Tories where doing and kept repeating 'enough
> is enough' ... we needed to put a stop to it if we could. (Tony Rimmer
> interview, 2012)

Tony remembers legal attempts to disqualify him:

> Come election time, the following May, there were one or two obsta-
> cles put in the way of my right to stand as a candidate in the election.
> The day before the election there was a knock at the door of the
> Telephone Exchange where I was at the time, which was Bootle [...]
> although I lived outside the Liverpool boundary, my qualification to
> stand was the fact that I worked in Liverpool. The knock at the door
> turned out to be a woman from the Tory Party who advised me that
> they were challenging my right to stand as a candidate in the election
> and asked me to withdraw. They obviously knew things weren't going
> well for them.
>
> I explained to her that I had every right to stand as a candidate in
> Liverpool. I was employed by the Liverpool Telephone Manager [...]
> and under no circumstances would I be withdrawing from the election
> the following day. I told her to go ahead with her legal challenge if she

wanted and that I had nothing more to say to her and closed the door and went inside.

When I went back into the building, the very minute I walked back, there was a phone call and it was Radio City asking to speak to me. The caller introduced himself as Paul Rowley, the Local Government/ Political Reporter and that they believed that my right to stand as a candidate had been challenged. [...] Nothing more came of it, they were obviously using every political ploy that they could, and we just carried on as normal and got on with the last minute work we had planned. (Tony Rimmer interview, 2012)

## Election night

In the 1983 June General Election Britain swung 3.9 per cent *from* Labour, while Liverpool swung 2.4 per cent *to* Labour. The city now had no Tory MPs. Militant supporter Terry Fields won Liverpool Broadgreen on a 4.8 per cent swing to Labour. To its astonishment, Labour won 23 of the 33 seats it contested and took power with 46 per cent of the vote, 51 seats, the highest number to date. Only 9 of the 51 Labour councillors were paid up Militants. The Tories and Liberals together secured 48 seats. Derek Hatton recalls:

There were massive, massive changes that were happening. The build up to '83 and the campaign, we never actually expected to win in '83, we all thought we were going to win the year after, we had built something in our minds.

For Derek Hatton, the election of Jimmy Hackett in Warbreck was an early sign of major changes afoot:

Jimmy Hackett was Johnny Hackett's brother and Johnny Hackett was a comedian. Jimmy was a cracking fella, a great lad. He was very supportive of us. ... He got selected for Warbreck [where] Reg Flude was the leader of the Tory group. Reg was like an old fashioned working-class Tory [but] I personally got on much better with him than with any of the Liberals. You knew exactly what he was and if we had a gun in the revolution we would shoot each other but other than that we would have a pint. He was popular in Warbreck (so it was not a ward we expected to win).

On the night of the election I went down to Netherley for the count [...] I was going over the flyover towards Dale Street and all the results were coming in. All of a sudden they announced we have a result for Warbreck and it is a Labour gain. Well I promise you I nearly drove over the edge because that meant three things: it meant first of all that Reg Flude was out, secondly it meant Jimmy Hackett was a councillor and thirdly it meant we had taken control of the city, because if we took control of Warbreck we took control of the city. It was that moment driving over that flyover towards Dale Street that all of the sudden we knew that everyone's life was going to change. It was – we were taking over. (Derek Hatton interview, 2012)

Jimmy Rutledge recalls a feeling that something was in the air:

On the night of the elections, when obviously people were ringing around and the news was coming in – Labour had swept across all the usual working class areas of the city centre and maybe some of the outskirts. But also [they had] taken the odd seats which had been traditionally Tory; the sort of leafy suburbs which had been Tory since time immemorial and you thought, this is something different. So there was a real surge of elation and of course hope, that maybe we'll actually have the numbers and the commitment to achieve something this time.

It would be unrealistic to put it down to a sudden ideological awakening of the working class vote, because it's simply not like that. You know, the average Labour voter, without being dismissive of them in any way, tends to be a traditional thing. I'm working class, my family's working class, I basically live in a working class area and you vote Labour. My dad voted Labour, my mam voted Labour, my grandparents voted Labour.

Obviously the Labour Party in the run up to that election had been saying, let's actually sort something, this council has just drifted for years and it's been Lib/Tory, Labour's been the largest party, [it] couldn't take control, but Labour's been tied and they've had the deciding vote. So I think even the people who weren't overtly political picked up a sense that something needed to change and I think they made the extra effort in turning out to vote. (Jimmy Rutledge interview, 2012)

Labour's manifesto had argued for no job losses or rate rises. The government, Labour argued, had 'stolen' £270 million from the council, and the people needed recompense (Wainwright 1987). The dispute arose from a change in the block grant system of central government funding for local authorities. This was supposed to provide needs-based transfers of funding through central government from more wealthy to poorer local authority areas. Between 1971 and 1983 employment in the city had fallen by 33 per cent in contrast with a national figure of 3 per cent and in 1983, the city's unemployment was 24 per cent: double the national average (Parkinson 1985). Needs in the city were growing. Yet while in 1980, central governments contribution to Liverpool's finances was 62 per cent, by 1983, it provided just 44 per cent of the council's budget (Parkinson 1985). The change had come about through the recalculation of the block grant based on what Labour argued were deliberately deflated 'low rates, low spending' policies of the outgoing Liberal administration. The Liberals, Labour argued, had bequeathed a deliberately inadequate budget to the incoming administration, in which they would need to raise rates by 170 per cent to meet manifesto commitments, and by 60 per cent just to stand still. Derek Hatton argues that the response was clear, non-negotiable and obvious:

We established that principle from the very word go that we were not going to put the Tory cuts on to the backs of ordinary people because we had hammered the Liberals in the past for doing it, so we were not going to do that. That was a fundamental principle, it was not something that we sat round and discussed. [When we were talking] to Islington or the GLC or Sheffield or whoever we just went in and said that. It is like you walking in and saying 'yes I have got a striped shirt on', you don't have to think you've got a striped shirt on. That is the point. We went in and that was us, the politics was already well established. (Derek Hatton interview, 2012)

Tony Mulhearn recalls a feeling that the task ahead was immense, and Labour's proposal would be opposed:

> When we took control in the previous seven years 65 per cent of the Liverpool economy had collapsed. We had no illusions about the scale of the task. In all our election material we said that is the situation – 65 per cent of jobs have been lost hand over fist. I was made redundant three times, I am sure other people were. I was an activist within the trade union. We had no illusions at all and we said to the people this is the scale of the problem and this is what we intend to do.
>
> In addition to the concrete proposals, housing etcetera, we said we will campaign to get the cash back from the government and that was a key element of the campaign and we were the only council that succeeded in getting the equivalent of 60 million back into the city that allowed us to carry out our electoral programme. We had no illusions that once we did that they would declare war on us. (Tony Mulhearn – workshop interview, 2011)

Feelings on election night ranged from apprehension to immense pride that the councillors had an opportunity to make the changes they felt necessary. Harry Smith recalls a sense of foreboding about the battles to come:

> We were in the Labour club on Childwall Valley Road, it was absolutely chocker after the 1983 vote and we had Radio Merseyside on the speakers, and it was coming over we have won this seat we have won that seat. And when we took overall control being a member of the Militant, being a delegate to the District Labour Party, I knew what that meant to me as an individual and I could tell you my heart sunk when I knew where we were going. I had no doubt whatsoever that we were going to be done for illegality and ... I said to my wife 'this is where it begins'. If I could predict other things as good as that I would make a lot of money in a betting shop because I knew that we were not going to be tolerated as a Labour group carrying out the policies. (Harry Smith – workshop interview, 2011)

James Dillon recalls feeling the responsibility:

> The first day that I got elected I was on a taxi stand and someone came over, in Penny Lane, and they said 'You are wanted on the phone down there'. I said, 'Who is it?' they said, 'Liverpool Echo'. They said, 'You are the new elected councillor ... what are you going to do they asked, what are your hopes?' I said that 'We promised things which we are going to do like nurseries, housing and build 5000 houses in Liverpool. We're going to knock down flats and try and make life bearable for the people of Liverpool'. 'Okay thank you' and they put the telephone down. ... I am glad to say that we built those 5000 houses. (James Dillon – workshop interview, 2011)

Tony Rimmer recalls a feeling of satisfaction about the Tory attempt to unseat him:

> Throughout the election it was a very well organised campaign, thanks to a fellow called Phil Knibb who was my Election Agent and the hard work put in by the members of the Gillmoss Ward Labour Party. Nothing was left to chance and following the challenge to my candidacy from the Tories we had work to do. We managed to get a leaflet produced that night telling people what the Tories had done, we got the leaflet distributed to every house in the Gillmoss Ward on the morning of the elections. Something like five o'clock that morning we were out leafleting.
>
> After a very long day of leafleting, canvassing and getting people to the vote, we managed to get 'me' elected. I think we worked it out that Gillmoss had the largest Labour majority in Liverpool. There were so many good things put into the work that we did each day to get our message over. The commitment during the election campaign from the Gillmoss Ward Labour Party members was really excellent. So that was it, then I was a Liverpool City Councillor. (Tony Rimmer interview, 2012)

This would be a new broom. Derek Hatton recalls:

> I remember sitting around on the first morning and obviously all of a sudden as it happened [...] we knew certain people who would do

certain things, Tony Mulhearn was not elected in that year. We knew he was still going to be looking after the District Labour Party. We knew I was going to take a certain lead in certain things. We knew who was going to the finance; we knew what we were generally going to do. I always remember the Broad Left we had after the election was just a fascinating meeting, there were no big battles but I was aware the real decisions were taken. (Derek Hatton interview, 2012)

The first job was to ensure that the officers understood what was planned. Derek Hatton explains:

The day after we got elected, Tony Byrne and I got all the officers together and we emphasised the spirit on what we had been elected on, we made it clear to them that we had been elected on certain things. We told people that we were going to do these things and believe you and me we are going to do these things [...] you will know exactly where decisions are going to be taken and they will be taken, but equally there are a lot of them you're going to find very new and different. You have got to understand that and if any of you are not happy about it then [...] if you want to walk out of the room please walk out of the room and do not be part of us. That is the way we are going.

I always remember Arthur Evans who was then the Director of Personnel, oh boy, lovely man I had been working with him for a few years, so he knew what we were going to do. He just whispered to me, 'Derek, just remember, you are now the chairman of the board that employs 30,000 people'. Well if ever there was a statement that stopped you in your tracks that did. We knew we were running the council but then that reality hit home – there is me a hairy arse fireman suddenly in a position where I was chair of the board. You cannot start to think about the total transformation of your thinking, in terms of what you're going to do.

In all fairness I have got to say most of the officers were actually brilliant, they actually fitted in – you would never have expected it, [...] we thought that half the officers would walk away. We thought that we were going to have a real clear out and we would have done that, but it was quite amazing that we did not have to. ... Most stayed and if they had not been prepared to accept us then they would have gone. We were very, very pleased about that. With hindsight what a good thing that was because they did know the mechanics and they were very good at helping the mechanics. (Derek Hatton interview, 2012)

## The budget

The council drew up a budget with a £30 million deficit. It demanded that the Government should provide more money to replace that which it had 'stolen' from Liverpool. The council made seven demands on the Government:

1. Recognise that the Rate Support Grant system is inadequate, and that it had deprived Liverpool of £120 million since 1979 (up to 1984).
2. Recognise that the spending targets discriminate against Liverpool. Manchester has a target £30 million above Liverpool, average for cities that size.
3. Recognise that the penalty system for spending more than the Government had set, the rate cap, further penalised cities like Liverpool unfairly.
4. The Government should disregard some essential spending like temporary accommodation for the homeless, grants for clothing and footwear for schoolchildren from deprived homes etc. Spending on this should not attract penalties.
5. The Government should recognise Liverpool's appalling housing situation and give an additional allocation. Housing spending has been cut from £61 to £38 million.
6. More Urban Programme money, for urban problems, is required.
7. Recognising Liverpool's unique problems, there should be a housing subsidy for flat demolition.

There were wider issues. Derek Hatton describes the Labour Group as composing of a broad spectrum, from the more pragmatic Tony Byrne on one hand, to the more strategically confrontational Tony Mulhearn on the other:

There will be differences of emphasis amongst a lot of people, ranging from Tony Byrne on the one hand to Tony Mulhearn on the other hand. Tony Byrne would argue that it was very much houses, houses and more houses. Tony Mulhearn would have argued we want houses, we want schools and we want everything else and that was simply a platform to raise political consciousness...

There were all sorts of lines in the middle. I was nearer to Tony Mulhearn than Tony Byrne but none the less, I understood and argued very vociferously that there was no way in this world that you could even start to talk about the revolution unless people did get houses, unless people did get good schools, and that people did get their bins emptied. You cannot get elected and not do those things. (Derek Hatton interview, 2012)

Whether the group was focused on the pragmatic task of winning more resources from Government or in confrontation with the government as a way to raise the socialist consciousness of the working class, the stage was set for confrontation. At this stage, many who were neither close to the council or the Left in general felt that the council had a case. The rate support grant had been based on historically low spending, and did not represent a fair settlement. Louise Ellman (MP for Liverpool Riverside), then Leader of Lancashire County Council, felt:

Liverpool suffered very badly. Liverpool City Council's stand was seen at the beginning, as legitimate, trying to defend Liverpool [and that] the Tory government was anti-public sector and anti-public services. They were also opposed to any organised power outside of central government. That is why they attacked both local government and the Trades Unions. (Louise Ellman interview, 2012)

John Flamson, then at the Merseyside Council, felt:

When the Militant administration came in, it wasn't necessarily a surprise and there were some people at the time who were hostile but by and large I would say that people were reasonably supportive, more supportive than historians might think of the Militant council, because they didn't think it was a Militant council. That's the label that we use now. They thought of it as a radical Labour council actually.

We need to get that in our heads. People are not daft, in fact they're very savvy in Liverpool about politics, so they knew about Militant Tendency and so forth but they know that there are all sorts of tendencies and all sorts of political parties, so that wasn't a big issue. It was more about 'are they going to address some of the big problems?'

Maybe the people understood that there was a fight waiting to happen with the Thatcher government but actually a lot of people in the city wanted that fight. They didn't necessarily agree with every political tactic, to sort of bring the city to its knees or something, to force an issue, but they agreed with the fight because they were seeing what was happening in other industries across the country as well so I think in that sense there was probably more support. (John Flamson interview, 2012)

Even opponents understood the motivation for confrontation. Anti-Militant councillor Malcolm Kennedy feels:

Well we all hated Mrs Thatcher, there's no doubt about it, in as much as everything became personalised in a sense [...]. But certainly Mrs Thatcher was a real hate figure. I mean it's clear since, that Mrs Thatcher saw the future of Britain as de-industrialising and forging a new kind of future in the world economy. For Liverpool ... we were all anti-Europe as well, because everything had moved towards Europe and the ports down south were improving, while ours was disintegrating or seemed to be disintegrating. Certainly, much less important was a source of employment. The Labour Party was really having a defensive action, up to that point. It was Militant that put them onto the attack, in a sense. But it did seem a bit like the Charge of the Light Brigade. Might've been very brave, but the cannons were from the Left and the cannons were from the Right. (Malcolm Kennedy interview, 2012)

Michael Parkinson echoes others we spoke to who argue that the city needed to stand up and fight back:

I think it meant a lot of people in both the public and private sector say, 'Look we can't go on like this, we can't drift, we've got to get our act together,' so in a certain way actually the shock of all of that changed people's attitudes. When we now sit here X number of years later and say 'the place is different', which it is, and the politics are different, which they are, and the culture's different, it's because they partly went through the fire of all of that. And that's life, we probably, we shouldn't have needed to do that but that's what happened …

There was a line in the book I took from the survey we did [it said] 'I can't stand the Militant but at least somebody's standing up to the bitch'. I've never asked the question what would have happened if it had never happened? I don't know, would the place have been different? I think in some way it was cathartic and it did slightly frighten people and it sort of meant that a decade later when the market boomed and cities were back Liverpool had spent ten years vaguely getting its act together politically so that they were in a position to respond. I think 'never again' was one of the things. (Michael Parkinson interview, 2012)

Other comments from the time include 'You've got to understand: we were not all Militants, or Militant Fellow Travellers' (Wainwright 1987). John Bohanna, senior shop steward at Ford's told Hilary Wainwright:

It's our city that's under attack, that's how most people I talked to saw it. Every Scouser loves Scouseland, they regard it as *their* city. That's what was at stake: our city, not the Labour Party, not Militant. (Wainwright 1987: 130)

For many then, this was a necessary fight, forced upon them. Over the coming two years Liverpool City Council would engage in a number of battles and confrontation with the Conservative Government to secure more resources.

# CHAPTER FOUR

# BUDGET CRISIS 1984

T he services provided by local councils – schools, roads, street
lights, bins, libraries – are vital parts of our lives. We do not
often think about who provides them or how to pay for them, except
when they fail to work well or are cut back or even withdrawn. Many
of these services are taken for granted. The playwright Alan Bennett,
born and brought up in Leeds, was an enthusiast for the services
his council provided which he felt enabled someone like him, from
a poor background, to do well. He talks movingly about the impor-
tance of the 'Leeds City Council' crest on his school books, about the
council library and art gallery, about how these services, provided by
the council, made him feel part of a community. Crucially, he writes
that such services did not arise from the benevolence of the rich and
powerful, but that his parents' generation earned them through the
blood they spilt in the Second World War. He sees these services as
his, and our birth right as citizens. 'We are *entitled* to them.' (Bennett
2005: 512–3)

The post war settlement where councils saw their role as providing
services to their residents began to unravel under the shocks of the
stagflation of the 1970s. Famously, on 29 October 1975, President Ford
delivered a speech in which he denied that federal assistance would be
provided to spare New York from bankruptcy. The front page of *The Daily
News* the next day read: 'FORD TO CITY: DROP DEAD'. In a speech in

Manchester Town Hall in 1974, British Environment Secretary Anthony Crossland told the country that the party was 'over':

> For the next few years times will not be normal. Perhaps people have used the words 'economic crisis' too often in the past. They have shouted 'Wolf, wolf!' when the animal was more akin to a rather disagreeable Yorkshire terrier. But not now. The crisis that faces us is infinitely more serious than any of the crises we have faced over the past 20 years ... With its usual spirit of patriotism and its tradition of service to the community's needs, it is coming to realise that, for the time being at least, the party is over ... We are not calling for a head-long retreat. But we are calling for a standstill.

What this meant was that cities could no longer expect central government to provide them as of right with the resources they needed to solve their problems. Rather, in what British Geographer David Harvey (1989) called the move to 'urban entrepreneurialism', cities now had to compete with each other to win the resources they needed from foot-loose global capital. Their focus should be on winning business, not providing services. They should encourage inward investment, invest in transport infrastructure, keep local taxes low and regulation light so as not to put off business, encourage tourism and shopping. They had to do what Liverpool has done since the turn of the twenty-first century, through the Capital of Culture, Grosvenor Estates' Liverpool One shopping centre, and the *Echo* Arena and BT Convention Centre. Note the private sector sponsorship: this is not the *Liverpool* Arena, but the *Echo* Arena. Cities like Manchester had waited in vain for 'the cavalry to come to the rescue in the form of a Labour Government', but in the end, local business people:

> got together with the City Council and began to say 'let's stop dabbing our eyes at the loss of these manufacturing industries and see whether we can't do something to get to terms with what Madam called the enterprise culture'. (Quilley 1994)

Harvey's 'entrepreneurial agenda' was that of the Liberals: treat business well and jobs will be created. Liverpool, as we saw, was a place that businesses were abandoning, before the election of the Labour Council in 1983. Consequently, Liverpool believed that recovery should be public sector led. It opted to fight for more resources to achieve this. Critics of entrepreneurialism argue that for a council to attract business it needs to spend money that might go to provide roads, schools and libraries or things business needs: convention centres, sprucing up city centres, supporting plush restaurants and coffee bars. In doing this, are they not transferring resources from the poorest to wealthy multinationals? Is this a form of 'corporate welfare'? Can the poorest realistically compete for new jobs, many of which are part-time, poorly paid service ones that replace full time, unionised and highly paid manufacturing jobs? Do we end up with uniform, identikit-type cities, with the same large shopping centres dominated by the same chain stores that kill off, through competition, smaller local shopping centres? Are there alternatives? Many socialist councils in the 1980s thought so (Boddy and Fudge 1984; Shennan 2008). They tried to forge another way, by trying to ensure that local residents were supported through the economic changes of Thatcherism which now with hindsight, involved far reaching transformations of the economy, particularly from manufacturing to a more flexible, service based economy. As David Blunkett (later Home Secretary) put it when Leader of Sheffield Council in the 1980s:

A realisation developed in local Labour Parties that local government might develop, once again, into a tool for change that had been so effective in the late nineteenth and early twentieth centuries. (Blunkett and Jackson 1987: 88 in Lansley, Goss et al. 1989: 6)

So, for example, the Greater London Council under Ken Livingstone supported training programmes to help people get the new jobs, rather than leaving it to the market (Mackintosh and Wainwright 1987). They, and other Labour Metropolitan and city councils like Sheffield, Manchester, the West Midlands, Lambeth, and Islington supported co-operatives and created enterprise boards to support small local businesses, the decentralisation of service delivery to be closer to communities, cultural and community events, and projects working with black communities and women's groups. They argued that a weak private sector could not be expected to show the way out of the crisis: recovery should be led by the public sector, and driven locally. Councils should intervene to save jobs and help local businesses reorganise themselves and should not just be left to go to the wall. When councils helped private business, they insisted on 'planning agreements' which gave the public sector and trade unions a say in the company's future as well as input into pay and conditions: they wanted this to be more than 'corporate welfare' where a private company receives public support but has to do little for itself. They also identified wasted assets, land, people and plant and tried to bring them back into use.

Such councils also campaigned actively against unemployment and central government cuts, and declared themselves nuclear free cities. The GLC displayed London's unemployment rate on the roof of Country Hall in figures large enough to be read from Parliament across the river. Its 'Fares Fair' campaign involved public transport users in campaigns against fares increases. The councils adopted a campaigning stance in relation to their residents, informing them of and involving them in campaigns through newsletters, demonstrations, and festivals. Taking inspiration from George Lansbury's Poplar Council in the 1920s which famously agreed to 'break the law rather than the poor', many Labour Left councils agreed to stand together in fighting the cuts. They would together refuse to set a rate that meant cuts. Liverpool was not alone in this stance.

## The campaign

In July 1983, Liverpool Council told the government that it would not implement the cuts. It called a series of 'Merseyside in Crisis' meetings across the city to build support. A Central Support Unit was established. Councillor Paul Rutledge remembers:

> As well as the Central Support Unit, you have to remember that the council itself, the individual councillor, subscribed to a fund for propaganda. We actually called it, *Not the Echo* because we regarded the *Echo* as being simply the principal mouthpiece of the Lib/Tories. There are historic reasons for that as well as editorial reasons. So we consciously called it *Not the Echo* and started saying, 'Don't believe everything you read in the press'. (Paul Rutledge interview, 2012)

Following the Labour Left's conviction that the recovery should be public sector driven, Liverpool Council cancelled 1,000 job losses and created 600 more jobs. The council argued that the private sector had abandoned the city, so the only alternative was the public sector (Parkinson 1985). This encouraged greater support for the council, as many saw such action as the only time jobs had been created in Liverpool when working for 'the Corporation' seemed the only alternative. For many, Michael Heseltine's attempts to get private sector investment into the city after the 1981 riots had not made any difference, and the Merseyside Task Force had a trivial amount of money to spend, given the scale of the problem. Taaffe and Mulhearn argue that:

> The campaign, on a higher level, and touching more people than the local and general elections, drove home the facts of the situation. Capitalism had failed the population of Liverpool. The private sector, upon which the Tories strategy for rebuilding the inner cities rested, had failed. (Taaffe and Mulhearn 1988: 103)

The council, and widespread opinion in the city, concluded that central government was not serious about solving Liverpool's problems. The Tories' response was that Liverpool was expensive, inefficient and badly run, and incapable of responding to its problems. Thus Michael Parkinson argued that at the heart of the conflict was:

> the pervasive feeling among local politicians [is] that Liverpool has no place in the Conservatives' scheme of things, who simply do not care about its people or its problems. In local eyes, Liverpool is redundant politically and economically ... the place clearly needed help but felt Government was not prepared to give it. (Parkinson 1985: 17)

In such conditions, the council's actions appeared inspirational. Journalist Michael Crick found that even right wing Labour members agreed that if they themselves were unemployed teenagers they would find Militant attractive (Crick 1984: 145). Leading Militants Peter Taaffe and Tony Mulhearn (1988: 60) argued that even opponents agreed that Militant supporters worked hard on mundane tasks and stood in unwinnable seats. They quoted *The Times* of December 1981 approvingly (Taaffe and Mulhearn 1988: 64). Militant supporters,

*The Times* argued, shared a working class background and belief that people like them had been ignored and cheated by those who should represent them in politics – be they trendy intellectual left wingers, or right wingers who quickly sell out in the face of privilege.

The council organised factory gate and street meetings, mass canvassing, and printed 210,000 copies of leaflets and 180,000 copies of *Not the Echo* (Taaffe and Mulhearn 1988: 109–10). On 19 November 1983, a 20,000-strong march to the Pier Head on a bitterly cold day was addressed by Tony Benn (an inspiration to the Labour Left both then and now) and Sheffield's David Blunkett (Parkinson 1985: 42). Forty meetings were held into the New Year: the council seemed to be winning the propaganda war with the government and as previously noted, many other Labour authorities took the same oppositional stance. Labour Leader Neil Kinnock and Shadow Environment spokesperson Jack Cunningham argued that a legal rate should be set as a 'dented shield', enabling a Labour council to do what it could to defend local services at a difficult time. Cunningham argued:

> We should not become obsessed with Liverpool. Many other councils are also in difficulty. Trying to bring about confrontation is not the way forward. We will not give Liverpool a blank cheque for what they want to do without telling all the financial details first. So far they have not given us the financial information we have asked for. (Parkinson 1985: 45)

David Blunkett argued:

> We don't want to pretend we can be of help if we can't. There will be a great deal of sympathy for Liverpool. But the other left wing authorities are not in the same position as Liverpool so there is no way they can take the same stand. (Parkinson 1985: 45–46)

In January 1984, the council set up a campaign 'working party' involving 70 trade unions, community activists and council workers, with council Heads of Department in attendance to ensure that resources were available to support the working groups. In February 1984 a 'Liverpool in Crisis' meeting was held in the city to help build support. Derek Hatton argued at the time:

Obviously, we do worry about the prospect of surcharge and bankruptcy. If we all stick together, though, especially if we have a national campaign, the Tories will be powerless to act. This is not a fight conducted by and on behalf of 51 councillors – it is a fight for a whole movement and must be conducted by the movement … Our programme to begin to tackle Liverpool's programmes has been described as the work of 'Mad Marxist loonies', our answer to that is – look at the disaster inflicted by the bosses, Tories and Liberals in Liverpool – who are the real loonies? (Taaffe and Mulhearn 88: 112)

Non-Militant Labour Party member John Airs reports on the atmosphere on the campaign:

The atmosphere on all of the meetings, […] demonstrations, it was the fact that the streets were *absolutely packed*. You couldn't see the end. I remember on one demonstration saying, '*How far back does this go?*' We were trying to see the end of the thing. Terrific sense of all being in it together, definitely that. And the people on the side, who didn't join in, looking enthusiastic about it too. … You had that sense, people were with you. I felt the city was *politicised*. (John Airs interview, 2012)

As the perception grew that perhaps an injustice was being done to Liverpool, Labour's Jack Straw looked at the books and concluded:

The problems facing the city council are not of their own making … they need more money, not Government penalties. … The picture that I was given of the inheritance left to Labour last May by the previous Liberal-Tory administration is worse than I expected. (Taaffe and Mulhearn 1988: 116)

## Meeting Patrick Jenkin

In late February, Labour councillors, including Deputy Leader Derek Hatton, met Environment Secretary Patrick Jenkin in London, and felt he was impassive and unsympathetic, flatly refusing to discuss more money for Liverpool (Parkinson 1988). Jenkin argued that Liverpool was not unique in having to face tough political choices and that it must follow the rules. Furthermore, he argued Liverpool Council had aggravated the problem by increasing spending and proposed the council should raise the rates by 70 per cent and slash services. Jenkin argued that Liverpool Council was 'proposing to go outside the rules and spend money it hasn't got and is asking us to go outside the rules to make it up. That is unacceptable. We must apply the same rules even-handedly to all authorities' (Parkinson 1985: 48). Derek Hatton told Jenkin: 'Everyone is being too polite. I want to tell you mate that you are for it if you don't give us our £30 million' (Taaffe and Mulhearn 1988: 117) and that demonstrations outside Jenkin's London home could not be ruled out. Hatton felt such tough talk was justified given the scale of the problem and given that the Tories threatened Liverpool councillors with bankruptcy and surcharge. Jenkin was quoted labelling Liverpool councillors as 'a very nasty lot', and Tony Byrne as 'a hard Trot' (Taaffe and Mulherne 1988: 117). The *Daily Express* (1984) revealed what it called 'one of the most chilling insights ever into the violent nature of left wing extremism'. Hatton's reply to the press was:

> The only violence we know about is the violence being shown by Patrick Jenkin and the rest of the Tory Government against the people of Liverpool. It is the violence against those on the dole, those without houses and hopes for the future. None of us spoke to him in threatening terms. What we said was that if the government continued along the lines they are going now, there will obviously be a time when young people will react. (Taaffe and Mulhearn 1988: 118)

It was clear that confrontation was inevitable. Jenkins agreed that the city had 'exceptional social problems', but the councillors came back from London empty handed. In the face of what looked like a lack of response from the Government, the campaign gained intensity. David Sheppard, Bishop of Liverpool, called the council's policies 'a cry of pain' (Wainwright 1987: 128) . He argued that some in the city:

> are trying to persuade people not to abandon the rule of law and peaceful processes of change. But, if we are successful ... what will happen then? Will prosperous Britain heave a sigh of relief and forget about Liverpool again? Make no mistake, we are wasting the

God-given resources of the nation by leaving three million on the dole and we are breeding a dangerously bitter spirit. (Parkinson 1988: 53)

Throughout the conflict Sheppard and Archbishop Warlock kept the lines of communication open between the Labour Council leaders on one side, and Thatcher and Jenkin on the other. The city seemed to be standing behind what was until then an unusually cohesive Labour group on the council until in March 1984 the Labour Group split. A group of seven emerged, opposed to the deficit budget. One of the seven, Roderick, was reported as saying: 'There's no way I'm going to vote for an illegal budget. Do you think I want to end up on the dole like you lot? I'm not that bloody stupid' (Taaffe and Mulhearn 1988: 125). They became known as the 'scabby' or 'sensible' seven, depending on how their perspective was viewed.

The councillors met Labour Leader Neil Kinnock in Parliament, and he again suggested the 'dented shield' strategy – it is better to comply with the Government's cuts and do the best you can to preserve essential services, rather than continue with opposition and be thrown out of office by the District Auditor. In contrast, Liverpool Council leader John Hamilton argued that Liverpool's desperate situation was threatening its fragile social cohesion, was in danger of breaking down. The councillors argued that struggle could win new resources for the city: for example, the Tory Government of the 1970s had put money into the Upper Clyde shipbuilders after a work in, and had similarly provided £20 million to Liverpool after the 1981 riots. Why then, Hamilton asked, were their demands so unreasonable? Militant's perspective was explained in their pamphlet – 'Liverpool fights the Tories':

The collapse of private so-called 'enterprise' has been aggravated by Tory policies. Yet now Thatcher and Co. want the Labour Council to 'balance the books' so big business and the banks can go on collecting their rent, interest and profit from the people of Liverpool. There is only one way to avert the city's bankruptcy. To force concessions from the Tories through the pressure of industrial action and mass protest. (Militant 1984: 3–4)

At the time Hatton argued:

> We persuaded people that it wasn't just a battle over what happened
> to the city council, but it was a battle over the very survival of the city.
> So on 29th March ... a lot of factories shut down. There was almost a
> general strike in the city. (Waddington 2011)

On 12 March 1984, the National Union of Miners began what became
a twelve month strike. Liverpool's battle was now part of a wider
conflict with the government.

## 29 March 1984 – Budget Day

On 29 March 1984 the council met to set its budget. Outside the Town
Hall a mass demonstration filled Castle Street, supported by a council
workers' strike. A contemporary pamphlet produced by Militant
painted the following picture of 'Petrograd-on-Mersey':

> 40–50000 workers and young people packed the city centre. Castle
> Street, facing the town hall, was jam packed with demonstrators
> shouting support for the councillors inside.
>
> Roars of approval followed the socialist speeches from the Town Hall
> balcony. The crowd sung in football style: 'Labour Council, Labour
> Council, we support you ever more'. Postmen, firemen, water workers,
> printers, car workers, builders, seamen, dockers, hospital staff, civil
> servants, office workers, miners, ferrymen, shop workers, railwaymen,
> these and many other sections joined the masses of council workers.
> Community groups and thousands of unemployed and housewives
> further swelled the numbers ... and many thousands more would
> have joined the march but for the transport difficulties caused by the
> magnificent decision of the busmen in all three companies to strike.

Militant supporter Mike Hogan recalls the scene:

> I spoke from the top of the Town Hall. ... I had a job to do, we all
> did. We met early in the morning, all the activists around Militant,

[...] raising money for the Young Socialists, raising money for the campaign, selling the Militant, giving out leaflets and so on [...] it was just enormous. Biggest demonstration I've ever been on. And then getting up and speaking. I think I was overawed by it all. [...]

It's kind of daunting, but being involved in the movement and being an activist in the movement, the other people on the platform put you at ease, the likes of Eddie Loydon who spoke as a Liverpool MP, Bob Parry, Tony Mulhearn was there, all those people put you at ease and look after you and all the rest of it. [...]

I spoke as a Young Socialist speaker [about] youth about unemployment and about the fact that in Liverpool for the first time since the late '70s here was a *growth* in employment [at a time when] this is closing, that's closing, [but the council's saying] 'We're going to take on a thousand young people' and 'We're going to take on people as council workers' and it seemed to me that the first time in my short life there was kind of a growth *and we were doing it.* I spoke about youth unemployment and [the way the] council was prepared to fight and do something about it rather than just talk around the issue and say 'Isn't it horrible?' (Mike Hogan interview, 2012)

Mark Campbell was a member of the council's Campaigns Unit, and supported the council's strategy. He recalls his feelings on the day of the demonstration:

It was euphoria, it was the culmination of all the hard work that we'd done ... We got through all the earlier rounds and this was our Cup Final and it was two fingers up to anybody who was in opposition to our views. It felt like the whole city was fully behind what we were trying to achieve, because at that stage I was very much embroiled in it and probably boring my mates in the pub who weren't as politicised as I'd become. One of our jobs was getting the publicity material done, stickers. So every time I saw an 'I support Liverpool Labour Council' red sticker on someone's chest, I was delighted. (Mark Campbell interview, 2012)

Labour councillor Paul Rutledge recalls:

> I was actually on the march when it started and it was considerable and
> the Labour group went in to the town hall prior to the council meeting
> and someone said, 'You've gotta see this', because often when you're on
> a march you don't get the full perspective because you're in it. So I went
> upstairs and I managed to get onto the balcony, facing down Castle
> Street and I managed to squeeze in amongst the luminaries. It was just
> so impressive. [There were] trade union banners, community groups,
> neighbourhood councils. Just absolutely solid. Liverpool's certainly
> never seen anything like it since. It just indicated the extent to which
> the support was there. Obviously they'd turned out on a Thursday at
> some point and put an X against their name, but to actually see people
> go beyond that and from every walk of life, you know, labourers,
> teachers, health workers, housewives, the unemployed, pensioners'
> groups ... it was just really so impressive. It actually forced you to think,
> 'Well yes, we're doing something right'. (Paul Rutledge interview, 2012)

Steve Munby later became a Labour councillor and cabinet member
for neighbourhoods. At the time, he was a left wing opponent of
Militant and believed the confrontational approach was misplaced,
but conceded that it was popular:

> The defiance strategy dominated Militant's campaigning style. It had
> enormous support, I disagreed with them profoundly but I'm not
> going to pretend for a moment it didn't have enormous support in
> the city. ... There were big demonstrations in the city and there was
> rage against the Tory government. Lots of people saw this as the only
> game in town – remember we'd just lost the '83 election, catastrophic
> moment for the left on top of the Falklands War.

He also perceived a slightly unpleasant tinge to some of the
demonstrations:

> I went on the demonstrations. It was very noisy, a bit, if you weren't
> part of the fan club, it was a bit unpleasant at times. There were jokes,
> bit exaggerated by critics but there was a touch of the Nuremburg
> Rally about some of the stuff outside the town hall and the style of

Hatton and other people there I think that is over the top, the real parallel for myself was with the communist take over of Eastern Europe in the late '40s. (Steve Munby interview, 2012)

For eight hours the council debated the budget in a heated exchange, with charge and counter charge, and the roar of the demonstration outside. Militant-supporting councillor Pauline Dunlop argued:

> It is not us that creates chaos but capitalism ... There are people dying unnecessarily whist firms like GEC announce record profits and lay off 1000 workers. We want an alternative: a planned socialist society where people can fully develop ... Listen to the people inside and outside the council chamber. They are saying *no* to a policy of despair. (Taaffe and Mulhearne 1988: 130)

A budget of £267 million, £55 million above the Government's target, was proposed. At this stage, the Tories hoped that Liverpool voters would turn against the 'intransigent' council in the May elections. Jenkin attempted to get the Liberals to put together a viable coalition, but in reality the Liberals and Tories could not collaborate. Moreover, with the level of support for the council on the streets, they worried about the potential electoral cost of seeming to side with the Government.

On the day, chaos reigned. The council failed to pass the deficit budget, and as expected, six of the seven Labour rebels combined with the Liberals and Tories to vote it down (Parkinson 1985: 55). Jenkin hoped the rebels (along with the Liberals and Conservatives) would vote through a legal budget and offered a sweetener in the form of Manpower Services Commission funds if they did so. For the seven, this was a step too far: they were not, as they saw it, 'traitors'. The council also voted down the Liberal proposals of £40 million less than Labour's. For Michael Parkinson (1985: 56), the Liberals were 'hardly statesmanlike'. Proposals for an emergency committee and for a new budget meeting on 11 April were also voted down by the Liberals. It seemed that the 'pursuit of partisan self interest which had marked the lost decade' (Parkinson 1985: 56) still dominated the city. The meeting was abandoned; the city was left leaderless and without a budget. A second budget meeting in April also failed to come to a resolution and ended again in disarray. Jenkin accused the city of committing 'hari [sic] kari': did the city have the right to buy even a postage stamp? Nationally, Labour's Jack Cunningham argued 'I don't believe a Government can be blackmailed into giving extra resources by making a city bankrupt – it's the worst course of action to choose' (Parkinson 1985: 56).

On the other hand, it began to be clear to many that the council had a large amount of support in the city. Labour began to see if negotiations were possible. Even the *Sunday Telegraph* argued 'it is idle to say the problem is to get Liverpool to live within its means. Within those means, what sort of life?' Archbishop Warlock criticised what he called 'extremism', but also said 'Is it out of the question that discussion and even negotiation should take place?' (Parkinson 1985: 74)

## The May 1984 elections – vindication?

Patrick Jenkin's hope that Liverpudlians would quickly tire of their 'recalcitrant' council was quickly dashed. In the May 1984 elections the turnout was 51 per cent, 20 per cent up on 1983. Labour won 46 per cent of the vote, increasing its majority by six, neutralising the power of the six rebels. Opinion polls showed that 46 per cent of Labour voters supported the deficit budget approach. After the election, an NOP poll showed 70 per cent support for an occupation of the council offices in the event of job cuts, and 55 per cent support for a general strike (Wainwright 1987: 129). On 4 May, the *Daily Post* argued 'the size of the triumph was a major boost to Labour Party confidence and an enormous 'thumbs up' from the electorate over the fight with Thatcher and the Government'. Liberal leader Trevor Jones said 'the Labour Party in Liverpool has raised the consciousness of the people ... that's why we had such a high turnout. The council believed it now had a "double mandate" for confrontation.' (Parkinson 1985: 72)

Press coverage began to get more supportive of the city. The *Liverpool Echo* started a 'Save our City campaign'. In a leader, the *Liverpool Echo* argued that it was the Government that was being intransigent: 'The Inner City deprivation which all Northern cities suffer from is more widespread in Liverpool – and the blame for that cannot be laid at this council's door.' It argued that the problem could be solved with the sort of creative accounting that Ministers do all the time for their 'pet' projects. The Tories began to realise that they had lost the argument. A strong anti-Government, pro-Liverpool strand of opinion had begun to emerge in the city, including significant support for direct action against the imposition of commissioners to run the city (Parkinson 1985: 63).

NOP polls suggested most people at the time thought the city was not getting a fair deal, and believed it should. Despite threatening to send in the commissioners, in reality government officials did not believe that they would be able even to leave the motorway as Edge Lane would be blocked by mass demonstrations. Nor could they expect co-operation from council employees, and doubted they would have the capacity to govern a modern complex city using dictatorial means. 'Liverpool against the Tories' (Militant 1985: 5) cited an adviser to Patrick Jenkin arguing: 'The caretakers have to unlock the doors, the computer has to be set up. There are 25 things that have to happen before you can sit in your grand office and pretend to run the city.' The Government felt it could only go in when the council had completely broken down.

Given the election result, Kinnock called for negotiations to find a way to give more money to the city, while Cunningham entered talks with councillors, MPs and civil servants to find a solution. Jenkin for his part agreed to a joint task force of local officials and civil serv-ants to examine Liverpool's books. This met for six weeks in May and June 1984. The failure to find a way to balance the books prompted the headline in the *Liverpool Echo* (11 June 1984): 'Whitehall Whizz Kids stumped' (Parkinson 1985: 104). Through the middle of 1984, the argument appeared to be going the council's way.

## Jenkin visits the city: and is 'visibly shocked'

On a previous visit to the Garden Festival, Patrick Jenkin had refused to view the poor quality housing stock at the heart of Liverpool's problem, but said he would at a later date (Parkinson 1985: 75). He visited the city on 7 June. The following day, the *Daily Post* (8 June 1985) ran with the headline 'Jenkin says Liverpool's slums "very grim indeed"'. What Tony Byrne called a 'visibly shocked' Jenkin, was apparently horrified by what he had seen, famously saying 'I have seen families living in conditions the like I have never seen before. ... They are very grim indeed' and conditions do 'beggar description'. It seemed the Government really did not realise how bad the housing situation was in Liverpool. Derek Hatton recalls the visit:

> In real terms, it was a Tory who had never seen anything like that perhaps saying something that he should not have done. Let's be honest, he had never seen an area like that, he had never seen conditions like that. Nobody was surprised that he never seen that. Maybe we were surprised that he said it, because normally they don't. All they do is to employ people from areas like that. They don't have to go and see them.
>
> I must admit I don't often smile at Ed Miliband jokes but I was just driving here now and I was listening to his response to the Budget and he said someone should tell the Chancellor of the Exchequer that Downton Abbey was a serial drama, it was not a fly on the wall documentary.
>
> It was the same here. There is no way that Patrick Jenkin would have seen anything like that other than on the telly or in pictures, and, all of a sudden, he can smell it, he can taste it and just opened his mouth and he said 'I have never seen anything like this before'. Well obviously he hadn't. The likes of Thatcher or someone more organised would not have opened their mouth. (Derek Hatton interview, 2012)

Councillor Tony Rimmer recounts an anecdote that, true or not, indicates the gulf that Liverpool's Labour Leaders felt existed between them and Government Ministers who, reasonable or not, did not understand the depth of the city's problems. Tony recalls a conversation after the tour between what he called a 'fairly reasonable' Patrick Jenkin and Council Leader John Hamilton:

> When the tour around the city had finished we went back to the town hall and discussions went on there, and one of the stories that got told was they broke for a cup of tea and some sandwiches, they were having a chat. It was, I think a Friday and they were talking about what they were going to be doing for the weekend. Patrick Jenkin said he was off to his farm for the weekend, and he turned round to John Hamilton

and said 'do you farm John?' So that was a misconception that these people had of us you know. John Hamilton was quite an imposing figure you know, always wore a suit and a tie and quite often a trilby but he certainly wasn't a farmer! [laughing] He lived in a terraced house in Anfield, but this guy thought he'd had his own farm to go to for the weekend. As I say they were in a different world to us.

Jenkin then was sympathetic, some even said reasonable, but he also argued that the answer to Liverpool's problems did not lie in purely municipal schemes, reminding the city of the initiatives open to it. He mentioned housing co-ops and housing associations, and argued for a mixed approach: 'a combination of resources from the private sector and local authority to give a better service to tenants'. He suggested talks with the Task Force leader, Eric Sorenson.

In July 1984 Byrne, Mulhearn, Hamilton and Hatton met with Patrick Jenkin in London, and a breakthrough was finally achieved. A settlement allowed for some 'flexibility' in the £3 million of Urban Programme spending that would otherwise be funded by the rates, and an additional £17 million for other support, including a subsidy for demolishing flats and environmental improvements. Overall, the settlement provided an extra £20 million of the £30 million needed to balance the budget (Parkinson 1985: 115–116; Wainwright 1987: 129). Jenkin intonated that the settlement next year would understand Liverpool's special problems, but no specifics were given. He said:

> I can give you an assurance that I will do my very best to ensure that the allocation to Liverpool under the Housing Improvement Programme, and the Urban Programme, taken together, will enable the council to make positive progress in dealing with the city's severe needs. (Parkinson 1985: 121)

Tony Byrne took that to be a commitment to future support and agreed to 'capitalise'[6] spending on housing on that basis, which balanced the books. He thought that the government would provide him with the money he needed for his housing programme in the future. Later, Merseyside Task Force would deny that any specific commitments had been made. Jenkin also argued that there was a need to improve quality of repairs services, and for the council to work more closely than it did with housing associations and community groups. He argued that the offer of more money was dependent on the city diversifying its housing strategy: an approach which obviously clashed with the council's socialist, municipal, public sector focus. When this became clear, Tony Byrne accused the Government of reneging on the deal.

## 'Here we go!'

Parkinson argues that Government expected Liverpool to keep the deal secret until it was ratified by the full council, then each side would claim victory. In the event, the jubilant councillors quickly proclaimed victory, emerging from discussions to clenched fists and the battle cry 'Here we go'. For some, they needlessly rubbed the Government's noses in it, reneging both on how and when the settlement would be made public (Parkinson 1985: 107–108). Derek Hatton recalls the scene when the councillors returned to Liverpool:

> When we got back to the T&G [in Liverpool] it was just an unbelievable feeling that we got, because not only was the room inside chock-a-block there must have been 1000 people outside. We said that 'It is a great victory here and this is what we have got'. That is when Patrick Jenkin made that famous comment that I was walking all over his grave or something like that. I cannot think that he would be so naïve to (a) think that we would not say that or (b) that no one else in the room would not have said it. He had obviously been told by Thatcher that we will do this we will only give them this year while we sort the miners out. We will not give them next year: you make sure that you keep it quiet. (Derek Hatton interview, 2012)

John Hamilton claimed the concessions were worth £50 million. Derek Hatton claimed the Tories had 'bottled out of confrontation' and that:

> There is no way even Thatcher can take on the might of the working class of this city. And this is just the start. Next year will see not only the defeat of rate capping, and the plans to cut the metropolitan

councils, but we will start to see the kicking out of Thatcher herself. (Parkinson 1985: 108)

Militant's perspective of these events is given by Taaffe and Mulhearn (1988: 147) who argue that the working class of Liverpool had, through mass action, inflicted a major defeat on the Tories. Thatcher had been forced to beat a tactical retreat for only the second time since she had been elected (her accommodation with the NUM in 1982 being the first time).

The Tories were furious with Liverpool claims of victory since for them, Labour had trapped the Government into becoming involved with Liverpool's problems. Additionally, Jenkin accused Liverpool Council of 'dancing on his political grave' by exaggerating the deal. The Government vowed not to be caught out again. In his autobiography, Derek Hatton (1988: 85) recalls Teddy Taylor, Tory MP for Southend, telling him 'You do realise that we had to tell Patrick to give you the money. At this stage we want Scargill. He's our priority. We'll come for you later.' Michael Parkinson comments:

I think Derek just wanted to exploit [the situation] politically. I knew Eric Sorenson [the Director of Merseyside Task Force, a very senior civil servant] at this time [and he said] 'Over our dead body – there'll be rats eating babies on the streets before we do anything to help Liverpool' – certainly before we send in the commissionaires as they were called because he said 'We're not going to give in. We would burn and that's that'. (Michael Parkinson interview, 2012)

Today, Derek Hatton argues:

In the first year I think the government did not particularly want to take us on at that stage. I had been involved over the years in different discussions with different ex-Tory ministers from the time and it was quite common for a number of them to say to me, 'the reason why you got away with it in '83 to '84 was because what we did not want is any distraction from defeating the miners, what we did not want was a major problem in a major city at the same time that we were taking on the miners'. There are a number of ex-Tory ministers who told me in different television discussions something like that, off the record and stuff like that. (Derek Hatton interview, 2012)

Taaffe and Mulhearn (1988: 151–3) reported the press reaction. The *Daily Express* (10 July 1984) condemned 'a shoddy and cowardly deal', while *The Times* (11 July 1984) contained accusations of 'Danegeld in Liverpool to buy off Militant'.

## Reflections on the 1984 campaign

Did the Labour councillors make a major tactical error through their vociferous claims of victory? Could they have been more subtle, magnanimous in victory, building their opponents a 'golden bridge'? Councillor Tony Rimmer thought so:

In the discussions Patrick Jenkin apparently declared the words something like he'd seen housing that day that he never thought existed in Britain. So he was prepared to discuss and talk, carry on talking with us and see what he could do and he did say that his door would always be open to us. So there was an agreement reached and there was a way forward. Now one or two people then used that and there were some comments made that we'd given the Tories a bloody nose. That upset one or two within the Labour group that we shouldn't be saying things like that and that's really what I felt as well that we shouldn't really go upsetting them if he's wanting to keep his door open for us to go back maybe the following year. Anyway I think because of that, what happened was Patrick Jenkin lost his job and I think eventually he was replaced over that year by Nicholas Ridley and when we went back the following year to knock at the door it was firmly shut and Thatcher had obviously got rid of Patrick Jenkin, didn't agree with the settlement that he'd reached with us. (Tony Rimmer interview, 2012)

In contrast, Derek Hatton (for some, the culprit) puts it like this:

When we came back to Liverpool and told everybody from the steps what was happening, I do not remember ever saying that we weren't going to say anything. We might have used tactics to get the money, but honouring part of the deal that you made with the Tory government was not as important to us as honouring the deal that we had the people of Liverpool.

There was no way that that number of people could walk out of the room and keep it quiet. That was just nonsense. It made me laugh the way people used to say to us 'Why did you do it?' 'You blew it there'. But there must have been about 30 people in that room as if those 30 people are going to walk out and all say we are never going to say a word about what was decided today. It was an absolute nonsense.

We all decided on the train back, we said we are going to go back [and] there will be thousands waiting for us and there was. What do we do here? We said that we have to be honest and we said 'Look this is what we are going to do'. I do not remember there being one objection to that by the way. (Derek Hatton interview, 2012)

Fellow councillor and non-Militant Paul Luckock did feel that the councillors, and in particular Derek Hatton, got carried away: but he did not think any benefit would have been gained by a more conciliatory approach. The Tory press would have condemned any victory from the Left as a defeat for the government. Paul put it thus:

Derek, he's a lovable wide boy, he's undisciplined, nobody could control Derek, Derek was Derek. He was under siege day in, day out from a range of people.

I think there was a compromise because both sides were looking for a resolution, that was a reality. And OK, we were able to celebrate because in a sense their compromise was bigger than ours [because] Jenkin said 'Oh, you've rubbed my face in this' and the Tories then said 'Oh, next year you're on your own'.

Politically if we hadn't talked up the situation you know, there would have been very little political benefit. If it had just been a hush, hush would the media have made much of it? *The Times* the next day said the Tory Government has paid *Danegeld* to Liverpool and all that sort of stuff. [So] I don't know whether tactically it was a mistake. (Paul Luckock interview, 2012)

Paul Rutledge, then a councillor and now a member of the Socialist Labour Party, argues:

I never, ever imagined that it was a huge final victory. I thought it was a decent result for the time but it was never going to be set in stone. I personally wouldn't have trumpeted it as a huge victory the way it was, but given what was going on in the country, there was a feeling that we have to fly this as a banner to encourage the rest, to encourage the others and even to exaggerate the level of victory, whether in financial terms or political terms. Being a socialist I can see the virtue of that in its own way, even if it's not a total reflection of reality ... So as a sort of beacon and a PR exercise I could understand it.

I don't know how much you could say that [Patrick Jenkin had] his nose rubbed in it because I think even though he was on the wet wing of the Tories, he's still a Tory and I don't think that would particularly affect him. ... I think the Tories were driven by hard economics and I think you could've been really thankful and you could've grovelled and they'd have said, 'good'. But at some point they'd have come back to try and recoup. (Paul Rutledge interview, 2012)

Looking back on that year, Mike Hogan recalled that what was important was the mass support for the council in 1984:

We achieved a massive majority within Liverpool. If you look at the voting figures at that particular time, they were the highest voting figures. ... Labour achieved something like 90,000 votes within Liverpool. From about 1980 it had doubled the Labour vote, an absolutely massive vote, particularly in working class wards. What it also did was polarise because there was the biggest Liberal vote at the same time: there was a massive polarisation within the city around these two camps. One upshot of that and the campaign was that the Tories completely vanished as any kind of force in the city. (Mike Hogan interview, 2012)

For Tony Mulhearn, the media's emphasis on the role of the Militant Tendency was misplaced. This was a wider movement:

> The key for me was the mass movement that was the key to the whole situation. The mass meetings that we had at the St George's Hall they were incredible, they used to pack the place out. We had speakers, Tony Benn, Eric Heffer, ourselves, of course. I was in the chair. It was fantastic testament due to the correctness of our policy and the demonstrations that we organised, again 25,000, 30,000 and one time 60,000 in Castle Street, supporting the policies of the council. That is not the work of a tiny group which the press love to and Kinnock loved to attack. This was a mass movement led by people with commitment and courage who said 'That is what we promised and that is what we are going to do'.

> Everybody in the Labour group should have had a gold medal for them; they should not have been attacked. There were great moments and the number one lesson for me was it is important, as any shop steward will know, you have got to take your members with you. You have to take the rank and file with you, you have to educate, inform the rank and file that is what we did. We informed, if you recall we put out bulletins once a month. We used to get 50,000 bulletins printed that went to most houses in Liverpool explaining the policies of the council. We had public meetings all over the city everybody was given an opportunity of contributing to that debate. ...

> I would make the point that being in that chair and seeing the way that movement developed, being part of such a great team who all made their contribution. There are people who got their name in the papers and so on, but everyone's contribution was equal. It could not have happened without the support of everybody involved. (Tony Mulhearn – workshop interview, 2011)

Opponents felt that the council misunderstood, and failed to capitalise on, those members of the Government who were more sympathetic to the city's plight, such as Michael Heseltine. Malcolm Kennedy, now a senior Labour councillor and Cabinet Member for Regeneration, was at the time a Labour Party opponent of the confrontational strategy. He argues:

> I can remember one of the Conservative ministers coming out, who was actually sympathetic to the city ... there were people like Michael Heseltine who was sympathetic to what was happening in the city. Okay, I'm not going to say they were opposing Mrs Thatcher's policies or whatever, but the fact is, they took him round, it was almost as if Militant were embarrassed if they gave the City Council some money. Then, they would be rude and objectionable and shout even more. From my point of view, it was the worse it got, the better Militant liked it. That's how it appeared to me.

> And the people of Liverpool made their judgement. During all of those fights, Labour continued to do worse and worse on the national scene. We lost the heaviest general election in '83 at a time when unemployment was at its worst. ... You had to oppose what the Conservatives were doing, you had to demonstrate, you had to make your point of view, but you also had to negotiate. It's like being on the ground in a boxing match and coming out arms flailing. You have to do a bit of dodging as well as swinging the fists.

> Even I wanted to go doing my bit of shouting and going up to Glasgow and marching through Liverpool. It wasn't that I was saying well, Mrs Thatcher's doing everything right, at all. I can understand why people did what they were doing, but there was a sense of realism there in people like David Blunkett. This wasn't necessarily going to be what won you the battle. When it came down to Liverpool, the tactics were horrendously wrong. (Malcolm Kennedy interview, 2012)

Mark Campbell broadly supported the council's strategy, but he felt opponents were very badly treated: in particular the 'scabby' or 'sensible' six:

> The six Labour councillors who didn't go down that road, when they started throwing their two pennyworths in and getting treated disgracefully. These were senior members of the Labour Party who probably had done or tried to do an awful lot of good for the city. But,

they were treated disgracefully because they didn't go along [with] that ... They were still members of the broader Labour movement and all the rest of it. As a compassionate person I didn't like the way they were treated. (Mark Campbell interview, 2012)

Mark remembers a feeling of events running away:

You were carried along, for want of a better word, because they ticked all those boxes that I wanted ticking. They said the right things and they were determined, there's no doubt about it. ... It wasn't a roller-coaster because I don't remember too many downs until later on, it was constant up. ... It was all the public meetings, it was all the rallies that were called, it was the trade unions got behind it. There were very few dissenters, we were all in it together and Derek often exaggerated the numbers, but the numbers were very impressive irrespective of what he said. I remember him saying about 100,000 people at Castle Street and the rest of it. Well, you know ... (Mark Campbell interview, 2012)

Paul Rutledge takes this view:

There was the cliché in advancing the working class and socialism that you'll take two steps forward and one step back, but don't take that other step back. So it's an incremental advance. But certainly, given the nature of the Tory government, I never, ever imagined that it would be a clean sweeping victory. The mere fact that there were concessions, it was a compromise because I think Thatcher, being an astute politician as well as evil, she's aware of everything that's going on around. There's widespread discontent and not just from cities like Liverpool because obviously that recession's sweeping everywhere – factories are closing, people are concerned about their jobs, there's pressure on wages. All the time she's looking, she's got to have one eye on her party and her government stands. I'm sure the first thing she would've said was 'Stamp them out'. But then if you've got this issue here, maybe an industrial issue or a major social issue and we've [the government] got this local issue; do we do this now, placate them now while we look at this broader issue, and when that's under control we start reining them in? I think it's the nature of government. (Paul Rutledge interview, 2012)

Tony Rimmer recalls taking a call from the Labour Party nationally, to find out how the council had reached a settlement:

> The day after that trip round the city, I was in the Labour councillors' room in the municipal annex and one of the secretaries outside, said there was somebody calling from the Labour Party and they wanted to speak to somebody about the settlement. Now, as I say, I've not been involved in the discussions, but there was nobody else about so the call got put through to me [laughing] and I don't know who it was I spoke to. Could have been Peter Mandelson for all I know [...] But they wanted to know how we'd gone about reaching a settlement with them because they could then pass it on to other Labour councils, which we were talking to anyway but it seemed strange that they were quite pleased that we'd reached this settlement and wanted to know how we'd done it and in only a matter of months or within a year later you'd got Kinnock on the platform at Bournemouth really criticising us. We got no support from him at all. (Tony Rimmer interview, 2012)

Gideon Ben-Tovim was a Labour Party opponent of the confrontational approach. He recognised that it was popular, seen as a struggle for socialism against an unpopular government: but in the end, he argues that what he regards as 'serious' politicians need to make tough decisions about priorities within the limits of the system they are working in. He argued:

> I think some Labour Party members did feel this was a fight for socialism and for the working-class against a reactionary Government, and that's probably a fair comment about how some people felt at the time. [...] that was part of the appeal for some people: that the Labour Party in Liverpool was standing up to the Thatcher government, and it was indeed building houses and sports centres, it was trying to create and save jobs, and it carried through a comprehensive school reorganisation.
>
> I think there is a simple choice – if you are involved in mainstream politics or do you want to go to the barricades and take no notice of the structures that you are in? In my view if you are in the real world, if you are in mainstream politics, if you are in the sort of democratic

society in which we are, then you have to either get out of it because you do not like being involved in politics and in the difficult issue of allocating resources and deciding on priorities or, if you choose to stay involved, then you have got a responsibility to serve citizens to the best that you can in a difficult environment. (Gideon Ben-Tovim interview, 2012)

Many said that if Galtieri could not defeat Thatcher, what chance did Liverpool have in the long term? After the victory of 1984, should the council have adopted a more pragmatic approach? Defending the Militant approach, Taaffe and Mulhearn (1988: 102) put it like this: 'To paraphrase Napoleon, "first engage in struggle – and then see what happens".' Going for only what is 'practical' is an 'arid concept of history'. Who is to say what is practical?' Michael Parkinson recalls: 'Tony Byrne said there isn't a solution. Either the government give more money or we go bankrupt. So I think it was a game of chicken and some people got killed.' (Michael Parkinson interview, 2012) The stage was set for further confrontation into 1985, to be followed in time by bankruptcy and disqualification from office for 47 councillors, and the expulsion from the Labour Party of many members of Militant.

# CHAPTER FIVE

# BUDGET CRISIS 1985

## The battle against rate capping

The struggle over the 1984 settlement had taken so long that Liverpool was into conflict with central Government over the 1985 settlement almost immediately. Having won concessions from the Government, Liverpool believed it was in a strong position to do so again, in alliance with other local socialist councils. The council knew that it would have to continue to campaign hard to keep together the movement it had built up. Mike Hogan was a member of the central campaigns unit. He recalls the feeling at the time:

> The Conservatives capitulated at that time, and everything seemed to be settled around a compromise and we were there to fight another day. Well, we knew that we had to fight another day. I was one of those who was involved in the campaign unit which was set up specifically to campaign amongst private industry workers.

> We were visiting Ford's, visiting factories to explain the situation because there was a little bit of a history of council workers within Liverpool … we'd just come off the back of the Winter of Discontent

and there was a real campaign against council workers and public sector workers amongst private sector workers so we thought we have to counter this, we have to explain to people what we're doing on their behalf as residents of Liverpool and so on. So that's what we set out to do within the campaign units.

We were very well received by the activists and then we'd speak to some meetings, but it's hard to gauge how we were received by the shop floor. The activists understood what we were doing, were members of the Labour Party, so we were well received there. (Mike Hogan interview, 2012)

In contrast, the Government, believing that it had lost the propaganda war with Liverpool, was anxious not to be drawn into specifics again. Patrick Jenkin refused to meet any delegation which included Derek Hatton, arguing (according to Taaffe and Mulhearn 1988: 186): 'I can see no basis for a meeting on the terms that you propose. ... you appear determined on a rerun of the disruptive and damaging campaign you ran last year.' Seemingly, Government decided to let Liverpool Council 'stew in its own juice'.

However, despite claims that the Government had agreed to look favourably on Liverpool's housing situation, money allocated for this suffered an alarming cut. Council leader John Hamilton described himself as 'shocked and disappointed'. The Government prepared a new tough line, stressing Liverpool's 'Municipal Stalinism' and 'inefficiency'. Patrick Jenkin argued that the city was being run in an unacceptable way: with officers not knowing what was happening, and power centralised in the hands of a few leading councillors: Hatton, Byrne and Mulhearn (Parkinson 1985: 124). He argued that the Labour leadership of the council 'spend their entire time abusing one, attacking and criticising. They can't expect us to put up for it forever' ... and that it was ... 'increasingly difficult for me to sell the need for additional support for Liverpool when all they do is turn around and kick us in the teeth.' ... There comes a time when people say 'Look, why are you wasting your time and our money on an unappreciative part of the country?' (Parkinson 1985: 126)

Liverpool's Labour councillors believed they would be looked upon by many as heroes when they attended the September 1984 Labour conference. In contrast, Kinnock saw them as a liability: arguing that urging people to break the law would alienate voters. Hatton was of the view that a gulf also existed between what he saw as working class Liverpool councillors who fight for their constituents in a class battle (not unlike the Tories who fight for theirs) and more middle class leftists in other local Socialist councils who funded groups based on identity politics. For Hatton, what alienated voters was the real 'Islington' 'loony left' that focused on what he perceived as more middle class concerns such as the title of the person chairing a meeting – 'chair', 'chairman', 'chairwoman', or 'chairperson', or funding special interest, political or cultural groups rather than paying attention to the basics – housing, parks, leisure centres and the like.

Conflict with the government consequently intensified. In October 1984 Liverpool councillors refused to stand to shake hands with visiting Prime Minister Thatcher. Reportedly, she had to stoop down to meet them, and was observably livid. As a parting shot, Derek Hatton asked her 'By the way, there are 37 lads who are stuck in jail because of your attitude to Cammell Lairds: what are you going to do about it?' Thatcher replied: 'As far as I am concerned Mr Hatton, if I had any respect for you before today – which I don't think I had – then it would certainly be gone by now.' (Hatton 1988: 87–88) In November 1984 Tony Byrne demanded assurance that the Government allow Liverpool a borrowing allocation for the capital budget for housing of £130 million for the period 1985/6, arguing this had been agreed in July. The Government responded by stating it had only agreed to look favourably at Liverpool's housing allocation if it diversified its housing strategy, which it had not.

According to Michael Parkinson, by now Liverpool was engaged in a battle of wills with the Government. Who would blink first? The council argued that the recent settlement had only been possible on the basis of government taking steps to solve the structural revenue problem. This was based on the unrealistically low spending budgets set by previous administrations that had led to a deficit of £96 million by the 1985/6 financial year on a budget of £374 million. Penalties that Government would impose on Liverpool for setting a budget this size would wipe out any government grant, and worst still, the council would have to raise rates by 220 per cent to balance the books (Parkinson 1988: 140). Thus Liverpool attempted to persuade

Government to reopen debates about the fundamentals of funding for cities, and get across their arguments that Liverpool was being treated particularly unfairly.

The Government's response was to argue that there was no point trying to negotiate under these circumstances. The council, it argued, should understand that government would not respond to what it called 'blackmail'. After November 1984, there was no more contact between Liverpool Council and central Government. Focusing on Militant, Jenkin argued that the council is 'living in cloud cuckoo land ... It is clearer than ever that responsibility is not an issue that the Militant Tendency understands' (Hatton 1988: 93). In December 1984 the Government cut Liverpool's housing allocation by 20 per cent, arguing this was because the city would not diversify its housing programme to involve co-operatives and housing associations. Byrne believed Government had reneged on a promise to support Liverpool's housing aspirations. By December of that year, the City Council had signed contracts for housing construction for £88 million, £11 million more than it had. Michael Parkinson argues that for Tony Byrne, the housing programme (the fundamental *raison d'être* for the council's conflict with Government) was by now so far down the line that it could not be stopped, even by bankruptcy. The programme was a *fait accompli*. The houses would be built in the face of Government opposition.

Government proceeded to further cut national housing budget allocations, and introduced new restrictions on what councils could do with capital receipts from council house sales. There was national uproar. Liverpool's housing budget was cut from £46 million in 1984/5 to £37 million for 1985/6, a bigger cut from Liverpool than that imposed on the other Merseyside Local Authorities. Spendable capital receipts were cut from £21 million to £13 million. For Tony Byrne this was a declaration of war on Liverpool, given that six months previously, Jenkin had promised to help. By January Liverpool had housing contracts for £96 million. Was the city overstretching itself? Jenkin thought so, and in February 1985 the minister invoked the little known power in the 1980 Local Government Act to stop Liverpool spending the £96 million. The city was given 14 days to reply, or from April all spending on housing would have to be approved centrally by Jenkin. The *Daily Post* reported 'It must be very clear to Liverpool's

Labour chiefs that this year Mr Jenkin is ready for them. He will not be caught this spring.' (Parkinson 1985: 134) On 8 February 1985 Jenkin rehearsed a by now familiar refrain on Radio City:

> you always want special privileges on Merseyside ... always clamouring, always clamouring for special treatment ... I can tell you the rest of the country is getting sick of the raucous clamour from Liverpool always asking for special concessions.

Liverpool Council responded by stating the city was not seeking special favours, but justice. The council's newsletter, *Liverpool Council Worker* (issue 2), said the city wanted the '£350 million stolen from Liverpool back'.

## The banks to the rescue?

Through February 1985 the economic news was unrelentingly bleak. On 14 February Liverpool crashed through the '100,000 jobs lost' barrier since the Tories came to power in 1979. Derek Hatton argued 'This is a milestone of misery and deprivation. Since we came to power we have saved 1,000 jobs and created another 1,000. Those 100,000 jobs are 100,000 reasons why people should never again vote Tory or Liberal.' (Taaffe and Mulhearn 1988: 204–205). A report on Liverpool's economy argued that 32,000 more jobs were under threat. At a council meeting Tony Mulhearn argued 'The report shows the failure of private enterprise. We have in Britain the most corrupt, effete, degenerate capitalist class in the world.' The *Liverpool Echo* argued that 'if trends continue by 1990 we may have no industrial base at all in an area which was once the main port of the empire and a great commercial and manufacturing centre' (Taffe and Mulhearn 1988: 206).

As the March Budget Day approached, on 22 February 1985 Tony Byrne announced he had secured £30 million from a consortium led by nationalised French bank Banc Paribas. The council sold its interest in mortgage payments being received for 7,000 sold council houses. Byrne argued that the council could call £9 million of this a capital receipt, to spend on housing, although the council also had a theoretical requirement to buy the mortgages back in seven years (making it a loan, not a receipt). This meant that the council now had £73 million of the necessary £96 million. The council also assumed a slippage of £10 million (the new houses would not be built as quickly as it hoped, so £10 million of the budget would not actually be spent), and therefore still needed to resolve the shortfall from £73 million to £86 million to balance its books. The council further argued that £11 million of the housing budget was for repairs, so should not be counted (Parkinson 1985: 135): thus the council argued that the books were now balanced.

Derek Hatton argued the council had found a way to fund housing that others should follow, whilst Tony Byrne criticised Jenkin for not understanding local government finance. He argued Jenkin 'has it in for Liverpool ... He became gripped in his desire to seek vengeance on the people of Liverpool and didn't bother to look at the figures.' (Parkinson 1988: 136) Again, Liverpool seemed to have pulled off a propaganda coup. Byrne's claims that he wanted to build houses, had found a way to do it, and was not interested in confrontation for its own sake, were true. The dynamics of the conflict had changed and the city now had new pressures on it: to protect its housing programme and avoid a financial collapse. The Government believed Byrne would crash the city if he was prevented from building the houses he was committed to. Consequently, while Government lawyers doubted that it was legal for a council to sell its mortgages and call it a receipt, Jenkin allowed the deal to go through. He also legislated against any anomalies or uncertainties to prevent others in the future following Liverpool by breaching government spending limits through innovative local financial arrangements. At the back end of February, the council held a series of meetings with council workers and community meetings to explain the deal.

## Services or confrontation?

Through February and March 1985 the council paid close attention to its accounts, and through monies coming in, finally got the deficit down to £5 million. A new focus on sorting out service delivery meant the council no longer looked like it was bent on confrontation: rather it focused on reorganising secondary education and housing, and improving the organisation of the council's workforce. The council talked to the unions about 'rationalisations' and a new committee structure attempted to get to grips with the problems. However, for opponents this smacked of increased centralisation into the hands of Hatton, Byrne and Mulhearn and tensions emerged. As socialists confronting a Tory government, they believed what they were doing was part of a wider battle for socialism. The question was how best to do this; by running the city better than their opponents, or by confronting the government in the hope of winning new resources? Could it do both without compromising everyday service delivery? Some rank and file Militant members preferred confrontation and pushed the councillors towards that avenue. Moreover, local opposition emerged over some of the good governance re-organisation, especially over secondary education. Additional problems occurred over refuse collection and litter. Labour claimed the problems were the result of years of under investment, while Jenkin argued Liverpool's problems were the perfect example of restrictive practices and an inefficient council. At times services seemed to have collapsed, and litter and refuse piled up for months. The councillors realised they had a problem asking people to defend local services as bad as this. The unions were unhappy, and council services seemed demoralised, expensive, and badly managed. Tenants were fed up with poor services. Was conflict wearing people out? Derek Hatton thought that people did get weary, but they also felt that the council in other respects was doing a good job:

> I think with any campaign if you are fighting for the same thing over and over again people start to ease off, particularly when they start to see things happening. If we had gone into a campaign in the second year and no houses had been built and no jobs had been created and anything else then I think people would have [raised questions] ... I think what was happening in '85, there was a feeling that we are actually not doing a bad job. (Derek Hatton interview, 2012)

### Refuse to set a rate, or set a deficit budget?

7 March 1985 was Budget Day. Taaffe and Mulhearn (1985: 196) claimed 50,000 demonstrated in support of the council (the *Liverpool Echo* reported 8,000). Liverpool Council resolved that as it needed

£265 million and only had £222 million 'It will be impossible to set a rate'. In the run up to April, local socialists in Liverpool, London, Sheffield, Manchester and the West Midlands all agreed to set 'no rates' budgets that would not involve cuts. It is often forgotten, especially after Kinnock's speech demonising Liverpool as the epitome of the 'loony left', that Liverpool's struggle against the cuts was but part of a wider movement. Derek Hatton recalls:

> although there were differences [...]. I must have stood on platforms with the likes of Graham Stringer, David Blunkett and time and time again I went to Manchester, I went to Glasgow, to Sheffield and even Newcastle.

> I spoke at meetings and there were thousands at those meetings and we got a name in Liverpool and I went to all these meetings and I stood on the platform with them and I did my bit. Although they didn't say it the way I did, there was a great response. People forget … people think that all the anti-Liverpool was during or before Kinnock's speech. Before Kinnock that never happened, there were some differences but the anti-Liverpool thing never came until after Kinnock. (Derek Hatton interview, 2012)

The central campaign group's Mike Hogan recalls:

> I went down to London to speak to mainly public sector workers around London. I can remember speaking to the London Fire and Defence Authority NALGO branch as it was then. We spoke around those sorts of branches, because we wanted to spread that struggle out.

> In 1985 we were part of a national struggle, involved with people like Ken Livingstone, David Blunkett, Margaret Hodge, such luminaries of the left. Those people were all involved in it. (Mike Hogan interview, 2012)

The GLC settled on 10 March, but 25 other councils met on 12 March to continue the battle. The councils debated setting no rate, or setting a rate that would mean a deficit budget. Liverpool councillors argued for the latter, believing that the 'no rate' strategy was misguided, too complicated and too negative. They doubted that it was possible to rouse people into a battle based on doing nothing – *not* setting a rate. Setting a deficit rate, they argued, would mean avoiding both cuts and rate increases, and would be founded on demands for the government to give cities the resources they said they needed. After all, it would be difficult to explain why the council was not setting a rate, a rather complicated argument. Hatton posited: how can you get people to support you by sitting back and doing nothing? (Hatton 1988: 90) Liverpool councillors argued that a clearer argument would be 'You have stolen (x) million from us that we need: give it back or it will cost jobs and services.' While Liverpool was very unhappy with the 'do nothing' position, the city would have been isolated and seen as sectarian if it had gone its own way. But here, Liverpool felt 'the battle was lost before it was even fought' and set a deficit budget. A London mandarin reportedly told Mullhearn 'London was pure theatre: Liverpool is serious' (Taaffe and Mulhearn 1988: 184).

Hatton further argued that the alliance with the other local socialist authorities complicated matters. This was no longer a simple 'Liverpool versus Thatcher' fight:

> This year we are doing it not only against the backdrop of last year, where certainly the government gave us the money before we had to go over the brink. But on top of that there is confusion about it not being just Liverpool. Last year it was Liverpool who started it, Liverpool who carried it out and Liverpool who finished it.
>
> It has had a big psychological effect on workers in the city when they see they are part of a national campaign. This year they see the crunch coming in London or Sheffield. They don't see Derek Hatton, Tony Mulhearn or John Hamilton blasting away on TV or Radio. They see Ken Livingstone or David Blunkett. In some ways Liverpool is seen as a bit provincial in all this. (Stack and Watson 1985: 8)

Consequently, in April 1985 no rate was set and Liverpool Council moved into illegality. The District Auditor and officers warned councillors that every day that passed made bankruptcy and disqualification more likely. In the event most local socialist authorities backed down at the last minute. By the end of May, only Liverpool, Camden, Southwark and Lambeth had refused to set rates. On top of this, another blow further isolated Liverpool. On 29 May the Heysel Stadium tragedy saw the death of 39 Juventus fans with 600 more hurt at the hands, the press said, of Liverpool fans. Liverpool as a city was labelled as feral, Neanderthal and barbaric. The city felt ever more isolated. In June Camden and Southwark set a legal rate, and only Liverpool and Lambeth remained. A new tough line District Auditor said he was not going to rehearse the arguments: he simply threatened the 49 Liverpool councillors with heavy fines and banishment from office.

The city's economic problems were still huge. The *Liverpool Echo* of 7 June reported:

> Almost 32,000 Merseyside youngsters will be chasing just 112 careers' office jobs this summer – 280 candidates for every job, 1300 for every job in Knowsley. In Liverpool city, it's 12,000 unemployed youngsters for 24 careers office vacancies, 100 YTS places. By 1985 53% of the registered unemployed in Liverpool had been out of work for over a year, compared with 39% nationally. (Parkinson 1985: 83)

On 11 June Liverpool Council again asked to see Jenkin, but was again turned down. Nationally, Labour set a deadline of 14 June to set a legal rate, with only Liverpool and Lambeth still holding out. Liverpool debated 9 or 20 per cent rates increases. Was it better to confront the Government then, or wait till the city had run out of money later in the year if a rate of 9 per cent was set? Grassroots Militants rejected what they dismissed as a 'massive' 20 per cent rate rise. Questions of justice remained: a Labour backbench councillor argued at the time: 'I'm not a Marxist: I don't even believe in all this political stuff. I just don't think it's fair. I won't vote anything but a 9 per cent rates increase.' Many remembered 1980, and wanted to avoid being seen as akin to the seven 'traitors'. One councillor, a successful solicitor, who would be bankrupted and ruined, was offered a dispensation, but refused. Any differences between Militant and non-Militant council-lors were erased. No agreement could be made through the DLP for a 20 per cent rate rise, necessary to balance the books.

Michael Parkinson argued that the councillors were by now psyched up, like troops going over the top. Then councillor Paul Luckock agrees:

There was a group of people which I'd have put myself with – whether you call them reckless or a bit gung ho, people were saying 'you've got to carry it through now, we've come this far, you've just got to keep going' And I think also from a personal level it had reached the point where almost whatever they threw at us by this time it couldn't be any worse. [And] on a personal level myself and my wife decided we couldn't risk even buying a house together even though we were two professional people, we couldn't even get married. We'd had a child by this point.

There was another group of people I think in a different position to some of these, and some of these were Militant supporters as well, who were deeply anxious about their own personal financial circumstances, you know losing houses … So there was a lot of anxiety about that.

Tony Byrne's view was – we've come to the end, but we've got to carry it through, there might just be an option if we do this, this sort of tactical manoeuvring, we might get a bit more time. … There were people in the trade union movement arguing very strongly for the tactical [manoeuvring] [but] I think some people in the group [were] desperately just trying to find a way out.

In the final meeting, the most articulate and passionate opponent against this tactical move, was a councillor called Bill Westbury. Bloke in his late '50s, early '60s, stayed with us all along, traditional, not a Militant, [but] left of the Labour Party, always been on the left, history as a trade unionist. … Everybody had respect for him, ordinary fella but sound as a pound, trusted your life with him. He was the person I would say out of the Labour group who articulated the best opposition into it. He said 'We should just carry on. We should just carry on. Let them do their worst. We don't have to do our worst. Ordinary people on the street won't understand the finer points of this'. (Paul Luckock interview, 2012)

Time then ran out unexpectedly fast. The new District Auditor announced that he was moving against the 49 immediately for losses he argued that the council had made between April and June by refusing to set a rate, irrespective of what any future decision was. This galvanised the rather shocked councillors even more: 'We might as well be hung for a sheep as a lamb', they felt. Councillor Jimmy Rutledge recalls his feelings at the time:

> I was unemployed and I was a council tenant, I was still living in a tenement and I'd no assets. I had nothing to lose, got no car, got no stocks or bonds ... I never had the real fears some of the people had. For me personally, it was quite abstract, it wouldn't have affected me. What you going to do? Going to take my Giro?

> For me the only impact was purely political, which was that emasculation of the council's latitude to try and do anything. You're unceremoniously kicked out of office [without a] care [about] what the people think who voted for you. I still say they should've voted me out [as opposed to be kicked out] and that's the bottom line really. (Jimmy Rutledge interview, 2012)

Former councillor Heather Adams recalls:

> I sometimes look back on my time on the council and think, it's a bit of a cliché to say, that it was the best of times and the worst of times. There were bad times, I remember coming home and telling my husband what the consequences were going to be and he said, 'You're bloody joking!' and I said 'I'm not!' (Heather Adams – workshop interview, 2011)

At what was described by Michael Parkinson as a very sombre meeting on 13 June, Liverpool Council set a rate rise of 9 per cent, which resulted in a deficit of £117 million. The council argued this was an illegitimate Government surcharge and it challenged its validity. It would only have taken three Labour rebels to defeat the proposals: but there was none.

# The backlash begins

The Government again considered imposing commissioners, but it still did not look feasible. The Chamber of Commerce and the Liberals discussed a high court challenge. On 14 June the District Auditor required the council to explain why the councillors should not be surcharged and disbarred. The council argued that the city had structural problems with the levels of government financing that needed to be addressed with more government money. Moreover, this was a reasonable thing to debate and negotiate on. They argued that the District Auditor had accepted this argument in 1984, and should do so again. In July, the District Auditor said that by September the council must cut spending; go to court to quash the rates level set, and set a balanced one or sack its 30,000 employees (Taaffe and Mulhearn 1988: 279).

The council debated ways to solve the problem by capitalising housing spending, but Tony Byrne preferred to defend the housing programme than see public sector salaries paid for a few more months. He argued this would condemn working class people to unfit housing. The council stopped demanding from government its £30 million lost rate support and asked for permission to borrow £25 million to keep the city going. If they did not get this permission, officers told councillors, they would have to issue redundancy notices to all staff or they could be sued for breaking employment law. Plans were drawn up for very basic services to be maintained: everything else would cease. This came as a huge shock to the councillors. They thought they would be able to start again with a clean slate in the new financial year. It also came as a shock to the unions: up to now there had been no mention of redundancies and in time differences between the council's responsibilities as a campaigner and as an employer blew the campaign apart. On 29 July 1985 a letter from Derek Hatton and John Hamilton to council workers denied what it called 'mischievous rumours' that 32,000 redundancy letters had been printed, that vacant posts could not be filled, and spending must stop. The policies of the Labour Council were clear; they argued 'We will never issue a single redundancy notice. We were elected to protect and create jobs, not to sentence people to a life on the dole.'

# The turning point

However, on 6 September 1985, as the cash crisis deepened the council announced it would issue redundancy notices to all workers and their jobs would cease to exist from December. It saw this as a tactic, as an accounting trick, a way to put pressure on the Labour Party to back them against the government. Former councillor James Dillon argues 'This was a cunning thing you know. It was a ploy anyone who had ever played cards, poker or anything like that would know that it was a bluff. We tried to bring pressure on.' (James Dillon – workshop interview, 2011). Derek Hatton argued the council needed to do it to stay within Employment Law: 'Not that we ever intended on sacking anyone, and let's remember that we didn't.' (Hatton 1988: 99) However, he went on to argue that the council 'unleashed an animal reaction we could not control. We had badly miscalculated. None of us thought the reaction would be so vicious, but the truth is that the trade unions no longer had the will to battle with us with Whitehall to get more money.' The council was 'paying for the months of inactivity when we went along with the London line of refusing to set a rate' (Hatton 1988: 99). Taaffe and Mulhearn (1988: 281) called the decision 'a major tactical error'. Predictable headlines included 'Happy Christmas: Get your cards' (*Liverpool Echo*) and '30,000 workers sacked by rebel city' (*The Sun*). The headlines all made it look like council workers had *actually* been sacked. The response from the unions was immediate. On 7 September the unions refused to accept any redundancies. White collar members, in particular, were worried that if they were sacked and the Liberals came to power, they would not be re-employed. Now the money would run out in weeks.

On 8 September the District Auditor rejected the councillors' defence, imposed a £106,000 fine, dismissed them from office, and disbarred them for five years, a decision the councillors would fight for the next two years. Sheffield's David Blunkett commented that the surcharging was a:

> totally unnecessary and vindictive attack on individual council-
> lors who are doing their best to defend local communities and vital
> services ... the penalties of surcharge and disqualification do not fall

on businessmen and MPs, or indeed others in public life, but fall selectively on councillors who now face financial ruin and disqualification. (Cited in Taaffe and Mulhearn 1988: 411)

More recently, Tony Mulhearn has condemned what he calls the District Auditor's undemocratic actions, but feels with retrospect that the council could have fought back more effectively:

The DA said that we were responsible, the amount was peanuts and on that basis we were removed from office. That is the greatest criminal injustice against a democratically-elected council probably in the history of the British labour movement. To this day I believe it was one huge frame up. Something that will live in infamy.

Where I think we erred was that we did not prepare for that, we should have called a strike throughout the city, but it caught us unawares, we were not really prepared for that. We talk about social justice, but that had nothing to do with justice because the DA's [decision] was purely a decision based on his opinion and his opinion alone. (Tony Mulhearn – workshop interview, 2011)

Could a strike have been called? Was the council that popular? Views about how ordinary Liverpudlians viewed the growing confrontation predictably vary. Former councillor Paul Lafferty recalls a strong political mood in the city:

It was like the Paris commune in some respects, people were politicised, you go into a pub and you talk to the barman about the political situation, house building and what is the budget these days. They would actually know about it and that was a proud moment, you could have a reasonable discussion about what we were doing, what we were not doing.

But if you went 20 miles out of town, you are all being surrounded by militants, bullyboys – they are all bullyboys, you're forced into doing what you do. Course the further you go into town into Liverpool the more people understood what you are doing. I think that was quite a noticeable difference. (Paul Lafferty – workshop interview, 2011)

More problematically, however, the Central Campaign Unit's Mike Hogan recalls union officials who had not taken their members with them or had failed to engage them and make them feel part of the debates about the ongoing struggle:

> We were coming across council workers who didn't fully understand what was happening with the council, and unfortunately weren't properly informed by their own trade union branch. We went and spoke to a lot of them. ... we had trade union branches like Branch Five, like some of those union branches who kept their members fully informed, and were as blunt as blunt could be. There was this thing at the time about the money running out because obviously if you set a deficit budget and then obviously the money's going to run out. ... we were quite clear that meant, either we just let the money run out and the council would collapse, or we had to do that as part of a struggle. We had to build the struggle, and part of that was a campaign building for the September 25th strike and the demonstration that took place on that day. It was going to meeting after meeting and explaining the importance of that.
>
> There was a split that developed later on because NALGO and NATFE split away from the joint shop stewards' committee. They originally supported what we were doing, but then moved against it. Unfortunately some of those who said that they supported what the council was doing, I don't think they were fully clear with their members what the consequences were. I think they were frightened of those consequences.
>
> I think that those comrades like myself within Militant would go out and blatantly say to people [what the consequences were] because we had this philosophy that you tell people the truth because if you don't tell people the truth you'll be found out. That wasn't fully explained. (Mike Hogan interview, 2012)

In part, problems were founded on rather patriarchal values of some union officials that they held towards their mainly female membership:

I think there was a big element of sexism within that because we had a branch of I think four and a half thousand members, I think four thousand of them were women. And we had about twenty-five stewards and about four of them were women. So it was quite clear. There was myself and another comrade and we were told bluntly by the convenor 'Don't go out and spread those ideas amongst the women' because we were told they were right wingers, they wouldn't understand those things and all the rest of it, which wasn't our experience. That was something that we had to fight against. (Mike Hogan interview, 2012)

On 16 September the unions occupied the Town Hall and refused to let the councillors implement any redundancies. Asked what the alternatives to a deficit budget were, the white collar unions argued for capitalisation. The blue collar unions were more accepting or understanding of the redundancies tactic, and called for an all-out strike. They agreed to put the vote to members, and Derek Hatton guaranteed no redundancies would take place. The strike call was voted down. Many union leaders did not argue for it. The alliance between the council and unions had split: now the unions fought against each other (blue collar unions being more supportive, white collar unions now opposed), and against the council (Parkinson 1985: 168). Some union members felt they were being treated as a stage army, called out on strike to put pressure on the government. In *Marxism Today,* Steve Munby (now a senior councillor) argued at the time that any 'political strategy based on the financial manoeuvres of a local council ... will exclude the mass of people' and give 'pride of place to the actions of a small number of councillors'. In time the council would be left high and dry as other councils backed off as the time to set a rate loomed (Munby 1985). An October 1985 review of the struggle in Socialist Workers Party's *Socialist Review* argued that:

By winding people up to expect a fight, by leading them on to prepare for a fight in which they would be key players on the stage, the council did more harm than good. The price to be paid only became clear this year. 'The campaign does not have the same bubble' said one council worker, 'because a hidden crock of gold was found last year without us having to do anything more than protest, people feel the same thing can happen again'. (Watson 1985)

Non-Militant but supporter of the council, Jerry Spencer remembers a growing feeling that discussion of alternatives was becoming increasingly less possible:

It became more and more the sense that, we'd been mobilised, and we'd been marched up the hill to march back down again. I got the idea that we didn't know what to do in the face of such hostility and such pressure from government. By then I think a lot of the counter voices, the alternative voices, had been stifled or side lined. So, those of us who, in a sense, were part of that hard left, Militant-led movement, we didn't know what to do. We didn't have the forums in which to discuss it. You couldn't, in Kensington Labour Party, openly discuss 'what do we do now?' You know there was a manifesto, as it were, and we were going to stick to it. ... So a lot of us just became foot soldiers who were cannon fodder for this demonstration and that march or whatever.

But to be fair I don't think many people at the time talked about an accommodation with the government. I went to the caucuses in the Labour Party. People talked: can we actually bring an illegal budget? Would it be so terrible if we brought in an illegal budget? Would it be so bad? (Jerry Spencer interview, 2012)

Other more overt critics of the council's approach felt that while in its early days the council did have a case, perhaps it had now made it and it was time to make a deal. Louise Ellman, now MP for Liverpool Riverside but at the time leader of Lancashire County Council, recalls concerns that Liverpool was taking the battle too far:

The feeling was that Militant's approach would not work. We were dealing with a ruthless government who had a lot of power. I thought that they would carry out their threat to send commissioners in to councils that refused to set a budget.

This was a ruthless government. My view was that they should be given a very hard time, that we should use to the ultimate the powers we had and that the public should be made aware of the steps we were taking, but that we had to recognise the limits of what could be achieved. ... Many Labour members found Liverpool's stand in confronting the Tories initially exciting but later questioned where it was leading. (Louise Ellman interview, 2012)

Militant opponent Gideon Ben-Tovim argued:

For me I think it was a nonsense to go over the top as they did in Liverpool, and it is interesting that it was in Sheffield where David Blunkett was at the time where they were a relatively similar politically quite strong left wing council, they did not go that far. They came to a point in which they said 'We have made the point, we have done what we can to protest about the Government whilst trying to protect our services and citizens as best we can'. (Gideon Ben-Tovim interview, 2012)

Steve Munby argues:

When you get into a politics that says there's no spaces, you don't encourage people to think, look sideways [then options can be closed off], whereas I'm a proud advocate of 'He who ducks and runs away, lives to fight another day'.

Much as I love La Pasionara's rhetoric in the Spanish Civil War, one of the things that the '30s and my own political background teaches me, is that there is honour in honourable retreat. Sometimes it's still best to even retreat dishonourably. Sometimes, you got to retreat. (Steve Munby interview, 2012)

Doubts about the utility of continued confrontation notwithstanding, a one day strike took place on 25 September 1985. But some of the unions felt they had not been consulted and increasingly began to feel they must treat the council as their employers, not as comrades in struggle.

# The taxis

Sometimes the way things are done can matter more than what is done. On the 27 September 1985, the threatened redundancy letters were issued to all workers with a covering note from John Hamilton and Derek Hatton explaining the situation. The council argued this gave the Government three months to come up with a solution: if this materialised, the letters would be withdrawn. Some notices were given out at work, but some were infamously delivered in taxis. Derek Hatton argued that the use of taxis for important post that could not be given out at work was in fact a regular occurrence. Jerry Spencer, not a Militant supporter, recalls that the place of the redundancy letters in the wider scheme of the battle with Government for more resources was widely understood within the Labour movement in Liverpool:

> My recollection is ... it was pre-figured, it was debated; it was generally understood as a tactic. I think the council was forced into it ... simply because there was a great deal of brinkmanship going on, but it was understood, it wasn't a shock at all. (Jerry Spencer interview, 2012)

Nonetheless, it caused a furore. Perhaps things were not so widely understood outside the Labour movement. Mark Campbell recalls:

> I thought at the time it was a mistake. I understood why they were doing it and I sincerely believe it was a tactic, wasn't it, to heighten public awareness and bring matters to a head? But that was when the wind turned, I think. It gave other people the opportunity to criticise and also sow the seeds of doubt in an awful lot of people's minds, who had been supportive up until that point. (Mark Campbell interview, 2012)

Mike Hogan recalls the impact of the redundancy letters from the perspective of a Militant supporter:

> Around that time, we had the redundancy notices which were sort of like a bolt from the blue. I think that was part of the same element of panic ... because it was something that we, that the council was

advised to do if they wanted to stay legal, stay on the right side of the law. And as far as we were told within the Militant, it was something that Militant argued against and said 'This is not what we should do' but we had to maintain left unity so we went along with it, and in going along with that meant you've had to take the consequences ever since.

I mean ever since then when you used to appear with the Militant, it would be, 'You gave me a redundancy notice!' and 'You gave everyone a redundancy notice!' and you'd say 'It was never enacted upon, nobody was ever made redundant' but it was still a big stick to beat the council with.

I think in discussions, afterwards we see it was a mistake, it was a clear mistake. With these campaigns you always found the ruling class are trying to force you into something. And all along the line people say 'We must do this, we must do that' and then it comes to you and you either say 'No', or you have to go along to maintain unity. So we were pushed into that. (Mike Hogan interview, 2012)

Anti-Militant Malcolm Kennedy was at the time married to Jane Kennedy, later MP for Liverpool Wavertree and Northern Ireland Secretary in the 1997–2010 Labour Government. He recalls the debates at the time:

I can remember Jane, who was branch secretary of the NUPE branch which represented Liverpool City Council workers. She actually asked me, she says, 'What should we do?' And I said, 'Well look at it.' I said, 'just think of the logic. No cuts, no rate rises, no job losses; at some point they're going to run out of money. What are they going to do when they run out of money? Well, they're going to have to sack people. Well, when they sack your members, what are your members going to say?' And it was clear, clear as daylight right from the beginning that what happened with the taxis scuttling round the city was going to happen.

There's a lovely story in *The City Dared to Fight* when they described Jane being surrounded by angry NUPE members because she wouldn't give them a vote on whether to support the council. They totally ignored the fact that all of the NUPE members had turned up because they thought she was going to support Militant and they were determined that she wouldn't. She never had any problem at all with leading NUPE members in Liverpool against what Militant did, because they knew they were facing job losses. (Malcolm Kennedy interview, 2012)

Speakers at all three party conferences attacked Liverpool. *The Sun* asked: 'Will Kinnock keep his mad dogs at bay?' – and Kinnock obliged with his famous speech. The same day as Kinnock's speech the council revealed it had negotiated a £30 million facility from London stockbrokers to help with house building and repairs (Taaffe and Mulhearn (1988: 299).

Opinion polls still showed strong support for the City Council. If there was an election, 55 per cent would vote Labour, 34 per cent SDP/ Liberal Alliance and 11 per cent Tories. Fifty-five per cent of those polled blamed the Tories for the crisis and 86 per cent said the government did not care about the city, including half the Tory supporters. Eighty-eight per cent said the government should talk to the city (Taaffe and Mulhearn 1988: 296). Nonetheless, opponents of the councillors emerged in the form of 'Liverpool against Militant' which held a 4,000-strong Pier Head demonstration, with lots of union jacks waving. Liverpool Labour Left began to organise though in October, support from the churches fell away (Hatton 1988: 105). The two Bishops attacked Militant in a letter to *The Times*, and argued for capitalisation.

## Stonefrost: a solution?

In October the Association of Metropolitan Authorities explored the possibility of a £30 million loan to Liverpool. The Labour Party-commissioned Stonefrost Report argued:

Liverpool City Council is close to the point of insolvency and decisions need to be taken quickly. The critical position arises primarily from the reaction of the council to the effect of the system of grant allocations on the council's position at a time of economic and social distress in Liverpool. It is within the discretion of Liverpool City Council to avoid being insolvent. ... credibility needs to be restored. ... The options do not depend on immediate help from the Government.

It agreed that spending decisions by the Liberals disadvantaged Liverpool. Tony Byrne identified four options from the Stonefrost Report, according to *Council Worker* (1985):

1. 15% rate rise, £12m capitalisation, £4.50 rent rise.
2. 15% rate rise, £9m capitalisation, £3.21 rent rise, freeze recruitment, 2,400 sackings.
3. 15% rate rise, £6m capitalisation, £4.88 rate rise, freeze recruitment, 3,700 sackings.
4. 15% rate rise, £3m capitalisation, £6.50 rate rise, freeze recruitment, 5,000 sackings.

(all involved increased service charges).

This edition included a worrying 'Stop Press: CASH RUNS OUT ON 22nd NOVEMBER 1985'.

> As a result of the Tory Government's refusal to act in a responsible manner, the council will, on current information, not be able to pay wages beyond Friday 22nd November. (*Council Worker* 1985)

The Stonefrost Report argued for a 15 per cent rate increase on top of the 9 per cent already agreed, cuts in spending (housing maintenance and staff) and freezing vacancies. It was portrayed as '92 pence a week on the rates to solve the problem'. Kinnock argued this showed the money was there for people who wanted to find it. Liverpool Labour Left argued for its adoption. Tony Byrne however, argued against it. The council argued that Stonefrost proved that their accounts were in order, and that easy options did not exist, otherwise the council would have taken them. All four Stonefrost options required sackings and rate and rent rises. The council refused to implement these. A contemporary Liverpool Council Worker information sheet put the arguments thus:

> The council has always refused to make cuts and therefore make workers pay for the Tories policies. Many council workers have become confused by all the financial coming and going while the council have looked at all avenues to secure extra funds.

If we run out of money it will be a Tory lock out.

Provided we unite and stand firm then we can ensure that all the necessary resources to maintain jobs and services are made available by the Tory government.

The DLP voted to reject the four options in the Stonefrost Report. Militant opponent Steve Munby argues that Militant's refusal to share the Stonefrost Report with others was another contribution to the fracturing of the alliance between the council and the unions as mistrust grew. Was there a way out of confrontation? Was a solution being concealed by Tony Byrne and those characterised as the Militant choirmasters, so this could be used for their revolutionary ends? Were they, as Kinnock had charged, 'playing politics with people's jobs and people's lives?' Munby argues:

Militant sat on the Stonefrost Report, and they wouldn't let anybody see it, so the Labour Party nationally leaked it to us and the Communist Party. We organised seminars for shop stewards to explain what the Stonefrost Report said. I did it with Jane Kennedy, UNISON, NALGO, NUT, UCATT, at that point all the UCATT people virtually switched. It was partly a combination of redundancies and Stonefrost. The most dramatic one was in the T&G. John O'Brien, a Communist Party steward spoke at the debate on the redundancy notices, him and Jack Dromey against every other single steward on the convenors. John and Jack won the vote. NUPE had always been with us, NUT took legal action, NALGO had swung by that time. I think the GMB and the AEU were the only people who stayed with Militant on that vote, roughly. But there was quite a lot of work done because they wouldn't tell people. What Stonefrost showed is that there [were] other options, not great options, but deliverable options. (Steve Munby interview, 2012)

On 17 October Derek Hatton announced that the council would run out of money in two weeks. Another 'Liverpool Against Militant' demonstration was held, with car dealer Jeff Tinnion as the main speaker. A few days later, Kinnock visited the city. The councillors felt he listened apparently 'like a lamb' … 'he listened and I think understood'. Kinnock later said he 'laid down the law' (Taaffe and Mulhearn 1988: 309). Then on 29 October 1985, Kinnock published an open letter to the people of Liverpool in the *Liverpool Echo* entitled 'My patience has run out on Tendency tacticians'. Kinnock argued that at the conference he did not attack Liverpool or its people, but what he called the 'gesture generals'. Liverpool was being attacked by the Tories on one side, and on the other

> from a political grouping, which, by its dogma and by its deliberate refusal to adopt the common Labour course of setting realistic rates, has added a new level of crisis: an extra layer of anxiety to the problems already endured by the people of this deprived city. (*Liverpool Echo* 29 October 1985)

Kinnock said he sympathised with the city's problems, but that illegality would just inflict further pain on the community.

> That is why I have no patience for the dream merchants who tell me that crisis in Liverpool will result in an all-out strike that will spread and push over the Government. That is why I oppose people who play politics with people's jobs, with vital services and with the very existence of voluntary organisations. (*Liverpool Echo* 29 October 1985)

On 22 November Kinnock stated that unless the situation was resolved he would support legislation to send in the commissioners, enforced with troops. However, on 22 November a legal budget was set which included £23 million capitalisation, tempered with a £60 million loan (£30 million a year for two years) from Swiss banks. They allowed payment for housing to be deferred for two years, thus keeping the house building programme going. *The Guardian* reported 'The gnomes of Zurich have rallied to the Trotskyists on Merseyside' (Taaffe and Mulhearn 1988: 320). Views on this deal were mixed. Some critics of the council's confrontation with the Government argued that this was the deal that left the city with a debt to pay. Other otherwise critics credited Tony Byrne with having made a wise decision which enabled the council to build the houses it wanted, in a way that ramped down confrontation with the Government. Peter Kilfoyle puts it this way:

The Swiss bank loans. Again, I'm not rejecting them out of hand. I've no objection to people borrowing money, that's the way of the world, that's the way cities and governments work. So, I'm not denying it. (Peter Kilfoyle interview, 2012)

Malcolm Kennedy argues:

> I can remember one of the finance officers said to me it was the best deal that anybody ever could've got. … Certainly a dose of pragmatism was probably what Liverpool really needed at that time. But Militant, basically spending all of your money half way through the year and then having no money for the next half of the year wasn't the way to necessarily achieve your aims. (Malcolm Kennedy interview, 2012)

More radical critics were concerned that given that Tony Byrne had been working with stockbrokers to negotiate this deal since August, some council workers felt like a manipulated stage army, not comrades in a shared struggle. Again, tensions emerged, this time between the requirements of a struggle based on the technicalities of government finance (that Tony Byrne understood), and the need to involve as wide a mass of people as possible in a shared struggle. Was a 'fast one' being pulled? Mike Hogan remembers concerns about the deal from rank and file Militant members:

> [...] the conclusion we were coming to ourselves, and almost not wanting to confront,– and this showed the maturity of the leadership at the time – was that in any battle, if you go into any battle you say well, what have we got? What have they got on their side? The press, they have everything on their side. What have we got on our side? Have we got the trade unions behind us? Have we got everybody behind us? And the assessment was made that we didn't have the full support (we hoped for).

> We knew that unions like NATFE and NALGO had split away and were basically saying at the time that the council was the problem … and we don't want anything to do with the council and so on. But did we have the support of the manual trade unions? For reasons I've already said, I think that support was very weak. (Mike Hogan interview, 2012)

He remembers concerns from rank and file Militant supporters that Liverpool was being sold out, not by the London-based Tory Government, but by their own London-based leadership:

> The majority of the activists were involved in the campaigning were convinced [we were being sold out]. I can remember distinctly on the Thursday phoning somebody up saying 'you need to get down here because I think we're being sold out (laughing) and you need to get down here to argue with these people'.

> I mean to be honest with you, at that time it's one of those periods when stress makes you think ludicrous things, and we thought the leadership of the Militant [was selling us out]. We thought people were down, people would let it go, and who are these people trying to sell out our struggle? It's our movement and all the rest of it. ... We don't understand why they are doing it. So that's how we saw it. (Mike Hogan interview, 2012)

Nevertheless now was the time to make a deal.

> After discussing it, I can remember it was one of those issues where you start off being discussed with and being convinced, and then you go and start the discussion with somebody else, and you develop more authority. I'm going there discussing it with other people and saying 'we'll look at the position in branch 80, look at the position there, because basically I'm telling you now, the work hasn't been done. We've relied upon the leadership of the branch to convince its members and to bring them along as part of struggle and they haven't'. (Mike Hogan interview, 2012)

Perhaps Militant supporters were more nuanced about when to fight and when to make deals than critics have given them credit for. Opponents of Byrne's deal from Liverpool Labour Left argued:

> [The] ... deal was a disgrace. Instead of a relatively painless step of a small rate rise, it has landed the city with crippling loan repayments that seriously threaten important housing and social programmes. (Taaffe and Mulhearn 1988: 329)

Treasury officials argued that Stonefrost would have entailed a small rent rise of £3 a week, which would be paid in full or part by half the city's 66,000 council tenants with the DHSS raising £7 million of the £27 million deficit. Discretionary charges could be made for the use of swimming and sports centres, meals on wheels and school meals. More savings could be found from closing the Town Hall in the evening, retiring some teachers and ending the Christmas tree. However, Byrne's settlement was not enough to prevent the wider move against Militant on Merseyside. Jerry Spencer recalls his reaction to Kinnock's speech:

> I thought that the speech itself was unfair. What I thought was the important aspect of that was there was Derek Hatton at the back of the hall not allowed to say anything, somebody who has to shout his objections in an entirely futile way. ... I got the sense there would be payback, somebody was going to suffer ... we had been defeated. The Labour Party moved very quickly, surprisingly quickly, to punish everybody who was involved. (Jerry Spencer interview, 2012)

On 25 November 1985, the Liverpool Labour Party was suspended, and Kinnock announced that anyone associated with Militant would be expelled. He argued that 'Militant Tendency is a maggot in the body of the Labour Party' (Hatton 1988: 110). In December the campaign against Militants in the Liverpool Labour Party began, and media outcry against Hatton gained momentum as press psychiatrists put Hatton 'on the couch'. Even famous ex-Beatle Paul McCartney was reported as being angry at the 'mismanagement of his home city'. The flames of anger were further fuelled as the budget was portrayed as 'spend now, pay later', and was contrasted with what was called the eminently responsible '92 pence a week' from the Stonefrost Report.

# CHAPTER SIX

# COMMUNITY AND CONFLICT

T he level of power and control Militant wielded over the rest of the Labour Council has led to a perception that it formed a larger numerical group than it actually was. In fact Militant members formed a relatively small group of 13 out of a total of 49 Labour councillors who were surcharged (workshop interviews 2011). However, their influence during these years is not disputed. Sometimes Militant's perspectives were in tune with the wider left, sometimes not. Thus, Militant's influence meant that Liverpool never became a 'nuclear free' council (leaving it out of sync with other left Labour councils) despite wide support for this within Liverpool Council. Peter Kilfoyle explains that whilst 'there was a strong anti-nuclear element within Labour, they (Militant) believed in the workers bomb' (Peter Kilfoyle interviewed 2012). As we discuss in some detail below, there were significant differences between Militant and the Broad Left on issues of race and gender. Yet, there were many other areas upon which the Broad Left and Militant were united, including the massive house building programme. Indeed, Militant and the wider Labour council had much support within Liverpool, particularly in the early days, cemented by the wider resistance to Thatcherism. However, in time, this unity would begin to show cracks. Allegations of bullying and intimidation began to be made and controversy surrounding the appointment of fellow Militant, Sampson Bond, to the post of

Principal Race Relations Adviser in 1984, saw this unity irrevocably broken. Bond, more than anything else led to seismic splits within the Labour group and beyond, leaving a huge cavern and long-term damage in relations with important sections of supporters (notably NALGO and the Black Caucus).

The early days of Liverpool's Labour Council was marked by a sense of optimism and unity. Here was a Labour council resisting Tory cuts and savage attacks on the working class. Militant was spearheading this fight back and had broad-based support. Louise Ellman, leader of Lancashire County Council at the time remembers:

> At the beginning, Militant were seen as heroes ... Lancashire suffered a lot from the Tories and Thatcher. Liverpool suffered very badly. Liverpool City Council's stand was seen at the beginning, as legitimate, trying to defend Liverpool. (Louise Ellman interview, 2012)

Militant's strength lay in its working class roots. It was this that informed their view and desire that the working class itself should organise and lead the struggle against the Conservative Government. Jerry Spencer reflects on the working class nature of Militant:

> They were, [this was mostly the case amongst the non-university educated members], ordinary, working class members of Militant who'd lived in Liverpool all their lives, the ones who hadn't come to Liverpool to join the Party as it were, the ones who had been here the whole time, they were the ones who had the clearest ideas and they weren't sloganeering.
>
> It wasn't just a kind of 'Oh, we've got to do something for the working class sort of thing'. [It was more] 'We've got to do something for *ourselves*'. There were good ideas there, there was passion there. Not for the Party, not to beat up on the local Labour elite or anything like that, but just a real driving desire and clear ideas. That's what attracted me to Militant. (Jerry Spencer interviewed 2012)

Militant wanted to turn the Labour Party into an explicitly socialist mass party. At times this was not always done subtly, and, as Spencer acknowledges, 'More and more it became clear that it [Militant] was a recruitment vehicle'. Nevertheless, Militant was successful in mobilising support:

> It did mobilise people, it did mobilise working people. The street meetings ... I've seen some of the street meetings they organised, just knocking on people's doors and getting them out on their street; fantastic! The meetings following that, where you get 30 people, from just a tiny area of the city, turning up to a meeting and five or six of them joining the Labour Party, fantastic. So, they were really good at that and articulating, allowing people to articulate their views. (Jerry Spencer interview, 2012)

John Airs reflects on the political awareness during these years:

> My sense of what they were doing was that it was by far better than the [Liverpool Labour Broad Left] opposition [who were] caucusing fiercely against them. ... It was an amazing time: Liverpool was just so politically aware, it's never been anything like it since, I suspect you would need to go back to 1911 to get it. (John Airs interview, 2012)

Others identify a kind of 'workerist' characteristic that infused Militant thinking and became an integral part of their action. This appealed to Liverpool's working class, whose political roots in Labour were in fact quite recent. Peter Kilfoyle comments:

> Anybody who's looked at these things, is that the history of Liverpool is far less ideological, certainly in Labour terms, than any other city in the north. We were the last to have any kind of Labour council. Until 1964 we were dominated by Tory MPs and the Tory MPs were Conservative and Unionist candidates in league with the Protestant Working Men's Association. So, there was a working class dimension to their political alliance. (Peter Kilfoyle interview, 2012)

The notion of 'workerism' within Militant reflected the wider characteristics of working class culture that was not confined to those born and bred in Liverpool nor to Militants:

[Tony Byrne] was never Militant, but he was a key man because he was prepared to get on with the hard work. He was part of that 'workerist' thing, without even I think intending to be, which alienated a lot of people. (Peter Kilfoyle interview, 2012)

Kilfoyle believes the lack of any Labour tradition in Liverpool until the 1960s seems to have informed Militant's characteristics here, particularly this workerism that shaped a tendency to 'look after one's own'. A history of casualised work centred on the docks might help explain this protectionist view, whilst Liverpool's historical religious sectarianism perhaps added to this. For Kilfoyle, these characteristics then were a left-over from a local political culture based on patronage and nepotism:

I think there was a load of tosh spoken then as there is now about what Militant were. Militant in its Liverpool manifestation showed many of the features of what had gone before; a sort of protectionism towards their own, placing people in jobs. [...] you'd have relations all operating, almost as a sort of cross city cabal. (Peter Kilfoyle interview, 2012)

Trade unions, particularly before their loss of power from the 1980s onwards, have long fought to have some control over working conditions and over who gets what job. But the extent that this is progressive is challengeable: it can mean that jobs are kept in families, meaning those out of the networks are excluded. In cities like Liverpool with large minority ethnic communities, this can become deeply problematic, contributing to social exclusion. Peter Kilfoyle reflects:

I don't regard them as left; I never did.. I saw much [...] being entirely like the old right. [...] it wasn't left in the sense that it was a carefully thought through, analysed, rationalised set of propositions. A lot of it seemed to be based upon almost like a knee jerk, understandable reaction to what they would probably characterise as generations of oppression of working people and there was a great deal of truth in that. But there was no tradition in the city of that kind of real, intellectual debate in political circles; not in the Labour party, anyway.

There's a real sort of small town mentality that was prevalent at the time towards people who came from out of town, unless of course they were Militant. And there were people who were with Militant who started to affect a Liverpool accent. I found this really bizarre ... sort of ... your authenticity was reflected by how you spoke. So when I'd get up and speak, particularly as a party officer, it blew the minds of a lot of people because ... hang on, this fella's a scouser and here were people who knew me from way back, and it didn't sort of match what they said was the stereotypical Liverpool working class hero. It was a load of bunkum. (Peter Kilfoyle interview, 2012)

This 'workerist' stance has also led to charges of anti-intellectualism and may explain in part Militant's refusal to acknowledge how other forms of oppression needed ameliorative action:

Their view on single issue politics reflected the anti-intellectualism as well, [...] And it was so, so superficial; a lot of it depended on how you spoke. So if you said, 'werker', à la Tony, you're all right, he's a worker, working class [but] what's that got to do with it? [...] generally, they eschewed anything that would remotely be called an intellectual analysis. It was slogans, not trying to convince people by rational debate, but by clichés more than anything else. (Peter Kilfoyle interview, 2012)

Its critics argued that Militant appeared to focus on a narrowly defined and traditional notion of the working class that encompassed the white, male and straight sections of this group and which had little room or empathy for those who fell outside of this. This perspective could be seen at its sharpest in their refusal to understand what might be termed the 'secondary contradictions' of capitalism, namely inequalities that arise out of class society in terms of race, gender and sexuality amongst others. So, for example, little was done for the cause of oppressed groups like LGBT. This 'workerist' stance, if that's what it was, became a double-edged sword. It enabled Militant to build a strong base at the grass roots and gain the support and loyalty of many non-Militant Labour councillors. Yet, at the same time, it alienated many potential allies, with the issue of race, perhaps more than anything else, revealing the flaws in their stance surrounding single or 'identity' issues.

## Issues surrounding positive action

Militant opposed any policy that singled out particular oppressed groups (whether this was around race, gender, disability or sexuality) ,as they argued it would undermine the working class unity they felt was needed to change society for the better. Militant argued that any race and gender imbalance in employment for example, would be righted through trade union nomination rights. In this way, more women and black and ethnic minority groups could enter employment as part of a wider strategy of employment aimed at the working class more widely. The need for positive action to rectify existing imbalances was therefore not necessary. On the other hand, those who were part of the Broad Left pointed out that positive action policies were introduced despite Militant's ideological opposition. Such initiatives were seen as the beginning of a longer-term plan that was prematurely cut short as larger events took over.

Critics of both strands point out that council policy more generally failed to adequately challenge discrimination outside of the narrow class-based dimension. Positive action policies initiated by Broad Left councillors did not go far enough or were half-hearted and inconsistent, whilst Militant's 'colour blind' approach actively undermined equal opportunities policy on issues of racial equality in jobs, housing and other provisions. This proved to be divisive on a number of occasions.

The appointment of Sam Bond to Principal Race Relations Adviser in 1984, laid bare the tensions and disagreements over equal opportunities. Bond's Militant affiliations resulted in him being offered the job by fellow Militant and Deputy Leader and Chair Derek Hatton, though Bond's political affiliations had not been disclosed to the rest of the panel. The majority agreed with Hatton that Bond should be appointed (including some of those who gave oral testimonies for this work), since Bond was seen as the best candidate. Two of those on the panel disagreed because he did not support positive action policies. As a campaign of opposition to Bond's appointment intensified, it led to the splitting of the Labour group and the ultimate undermining of Militant's broader-based support.

The Bond affair epitomised for some the way Militant was able to exercise its influence in capturing the party machine and push through class-based policies at the expense of other marginalised groups. Gideon Ben-Tovim had been active in the Labour Party and had close links to the Black Caucus. For him and others, Militant operated along the lines of a form of 'municipal Stalinism' and was:

> ... a very powerful well run machine in the Labour Party where if you didn't go along with the line you were treated pretty heavily. It was dressed up in a sort of working class ideology and I think people felt if they – Militant – were challenged, they were somehow betraying the working class. I think a number of people were quiet and went along with the flow of this powerful organisation that developed in this period. (Gideon Ben-Tovim interview, 2012)

For others, concessions made in terms of positive action policies symbolised the influence of non-Militant left groups within the council and the wider Labour group. So whilst Militant was highly influential, it did not *dominate* on all issues.

Leading Militant Tony Mulhearn argues that the council and the District Labour Party had broad-based support:

> Everything was upfront the whole basis of our success was involving the broadest possible layer of the working class. The District Labour Party for instance, was made up of the trade unions, party branches constituency parties, women's organisations, the Co-ops, the YS – the youth wing, and incredibly democratic organisation. All directly elected all participated in the developments in the agreement of policy and it was that policy on which we were elected. ... this notion that it was a small group of Militants who organised and plotted behind [closed doors] is absolute nonsense. (Tony Mulhearn workshop interview, 2011)

Attitudes to the extent that Militant did or did not dominate the council, and whether this influence was positive or negative, came together over the Bond affair. For critics, this epitomised Militant 'getting it wrong', and opposition to Bond legitimated the stance that critics of Militant's line on race could not be dismissed as 'pbs' – petty bourgeois or as rightwingers. As we see, Derek Hatton was now furious with himself for making such a basic mistake, for which he took responsibility. Before looking at the various perspectives over the Bond appointment, it is necessary to contextualise these events by looking at the period immediately before Labour came to hold a majority on the council in 1983. Some understanding of the marginal position that Liverpool-born black people occupied is necessary in both understanding and framing the events that followed.

## Black Liverpool

At the start of the 1980s, Liverpool's black and ethnic community composed a number of strands. As well as first generation migrants from the Caribbean and Africa, the oldest and largest grouping composed of Liverpool-born black people whose roots in Liverpool stretched back several centuries. This longevity however did little to alleviate the marginal position and long-standing racism this community had endured. Many of the issues confronting Liverpool-born black people throughout the 1960s and 1970s had become endemic and institutionalised. Such patterns of discrimination continued to be reinforced in numerous areas of public life. As well as enduring class disadvantage in common with Liverpool's white working class, such groups were additionally subjected to racial discrimination and disadvantage in the areas of social housing, employment, policing and the courts (McNabb 1969; Humphrey and John 1972; Melish, Ben-Tovim et al. 1972; Melish, McNabb et al. 1973; Ben-Tovim 1983). The introduction of racial equality legislation seen at the time in the most recent 1976 Race Relations Act did little to challenge racism in Liverpool. Moreover, lobbying by the community itself on such issues appeared to have little impact in persuading Liverpool City Council during these decades that deep rooted discrimination and marginalisation needed to be addressed. If the solution was contested, the problem was recognised and accepted: Militant member Harry Smith reflects on the absence of black people in and around Liverpool in the 1970s and early 1980s and of the racism they had to put up with, particularly in employment:

> If you left Liverpool and you go to [other] boroughs there are a lot of black faces on the bus, but if you go to Liverpool there are no black

faces – I'm talking [about] the '70s and '80s. You go to the shops in Liverpool there is still very few non-whites. You had the police encouraging black people not to go to town so employment and the opportunities in Liverpool were chronic. That is why we thought of having an equal opportunities committee and as Ian [Lowes] was saying to redress the amount of people working for the council. What had happened, the council would not put vacancies up in Toxteth. So the vacancies would not appear, so no one applied – but they are not going to if the vacancies are not advertised in particular areas. To be fair I don't know the percentages of the people that live in the Dingle etc. who are non white but they didn't advertise the jobs.

You hear things about the Fire Brigade – 'we have to expand your chest by so much and a black fella could never do the tape' [fit the trumped-up chest size being asked for]. So they wouldn't get a job in the Fire Brigade. There were all those kind of racist things to stop [people] getting a job. We were trying to address that because we identified it. (Harry Smith – workshop interview, 2011)

The City Council's poor record of employing black Liverpudlians throughout the 1970s and early 1980s has been well documented (Ben-Tovim 1983; Murden 2006; Gifford, Brown et al. 1989) and can be gleaned from the low numbers employed during this period. The informal recruitment policy operated by the council that relied on family networks or friends, excluded all but those who already had a foot in the door and this disproportionately affected black workers. In 1978 only 225 black people were employed, increasing to 250 out of a total of 30,000 between 1980–1982 (Ben-Tovim, 1983; Liverpool Black Caucus 1986). The lack of open recruitment in Liverpool was not confined to the council and could be seen in the all-white workforce that existed in Liverpool's car factories for example.

Outside council employment, Peter Kilfoyle reflects on the exclusionary nature of employment recruitment more widely in Liverpool from the 1960s that not only excluded migrant labour but also Liverpool-born black people:

I worked on the docks going back to the sixties and on the docks you very rarely saw a black face. I remember having very comradely debates with friends of mine who were dock officials about this; dockers and dock officials. One of the things was cards, you needed a union card to be there and you got a card through your family. You didn't get immigrants suddenly having these connections within the union in order to be able to get into the job in the first place and so they were closed shops. It all evolved from a very legitimate wish to look after your own, to look after your family. Before the unions you had your family and that was just about it and you wanted your family to have jobs. That doesn't change, I think it's a basic human impulse but it's not very fair and it does exclude large numbers of people. That was true at this time for many of the jobs within the council. (Peter Kilfoyle interview, 2012)

A number of initiatives emerged throughout the 1970s within particular local authority departments but these appeared half-hearted and uneven and they did not have the full support and commitment needed to make meaningful changes. Part of the problem was a deeply held view among those in key positions that equal opportunities policy was not necessary because the position of black people (and by implication women, people with disabilities and so on) was intertwined with and indistinguishable from the position of the rest of the working class in Liverpool, and that the best way to solve these problems was through class unity. By focusing on these other disadvantages this only served to divert attention away from the real issue of class (Liverpool Black Caucus 1986: 23). Moreover, it was believed that adopting equal opportunity policies, which it dismissed as middle class preoccupations of the 'trendy' or even 'loony' left in London, would alienate the rest of the working class as such groups would be seen as receiving preferential treatment. That, in turn, would exacerbate racial tensions. Ian Lowes (Militant) explains:

On the question about positive discrimination, I oppose that. When that debate was going on we had the same debate in the trade unions as well as the Labour Party. When you take a city like Liverpool with high unemployment and you embark upon positive action or whatever you call it, that fuels [the] fires of fascist organisations like BNP, and NF. Can you imagine going to predominantly white areas such as Norris Green where there is mass unemployment saying the corporation is only taking people on [who are] black and you cannot get a job? (Ian Lowes – workshop interview, 2011)

Moreover, it was argued that the trade union movement would not lend support to such policies and had in any case been operating a 'nomination' recruitment policy whereby potential interviewees had to be nominated by a trade union. The council's stand on race equality is summed up in the following quote from the Chief Executive of Liverpool in October 1980 to the Parliamentary Home Affairs Sub-Committee on Race Relations and Immigration:

> The Council would feel that to declare itself an equal opportunity authority would certainly imply or be taken as implying that it has not been an equal opportunity employer in the past ... the singling out of a part of [Liverpool's ...] unemployed community for special treatment could lead to as much disharmony as harmony. (Liverpool Black Caucus 1986: 25)

Again, the *Liverpool Daily Post* had reflected this 'colour-blindness' two years earlier:

> ... the situation in Liverpool is simply this. There is no racial problem. There are problems of unemployment, of crime, of hooliganism. They are problems which trouble both black and white alike. (28 November 1978 cited in Liverpool Black Caucus 1986: 26)

## Establishing the Race Relations Liaison Committee (1980) and the battle for positive action

When in December 1980 one of the most important committees within the council (the Policy and Finance Committee) decided to establish a Race Relations Liaison Committee with representation from the three main political parties as well as black organisations from within the city, this was indeed a milestone. Two issues are perhaps important here for understanding this development. Firstly, this came after representatives of 16 local black groups and organisations had written to the council encouraging it to implement Section 71 of the 1976 Race Relations Act. This urged local councils to 'make appropriate arrangements' for the 'elimination of unlawful discrimination and the promotion of equal opportunity' (letter to Liverpool City Council from Merseyside Community Relations Council cited in Liverpool Black Caucus 1986: 28). Secondly, a visit by the Parliamentary Select Committee in October of 1980 had received evidence of the deep rooted problems facing Liverpool's black communities based on research undertaken by local black organisations (Merseyside Area Profile Group 1980). A clear case had been made of the necessity to develop and implement 'race' initiatives in line with national legislation and other local authorities. Liverpool appeared to be out of kilter with the rest of the country on equal opportunity policies at this time and the paucity of such policies and practice here was of some concern to the visiting Select Committee (Liverpool Black Caucus 1986).

The establishment of the Race Relations Liaison Committee in 1980 was a positive step forward in light of Liverpool's slow start on the road to racial equality. However, from its very beginning, this Committee's ability to fully commit to racial equality was undermined partly due to the inexperienced and junior status of the Liberal representatives, and partly because of what was seen as the 'intransigent, class-only approach to race policy' of senior Labour representatives (Liverpool Black Caucus 1986: 33). Moreover, Labour's reluctance to 'compromise' with Liberals and Conservatives meant this Committee lacked the clout needed to fulfil its mission.

Moreover, when initiatives were put forward relating to job opportunities for local black workers, these were often sidelined by the Labour group. In 1981, Liberal leader Trevor Jones put forward a motion that would effectively lift the moratorium imposed on Merseyside Community Relations posts, as well as other posts related to local race relations work. The motion urged the Race Relations Liaison Committee to look at ways of improving black representation in council employment sinceit was hugely under-represented here. Councillor Hatton, supported by the Labour group, rejected Jones' original motion for greater black representation and put forward the following amended version:

That the resolution of the Emergency Sub-Committee be not approved and in an attempt to increase the job opportunities for both white and black the moratorium on the filling of vacancies within the Authority be lifted and immediate discussion be held with the Local Authority trades unions as to how jobs could be created in order to improve the services of the City Council; full consultations would then take place with the black organizations in order to ensure that there would be no discrimination in the recruitment policy. (Liverpool City Council, 18 December, 1981, cited in Liverpool Black Caucus 1986: 45)

There was little room then for any positive action initiatives that would rectify existing racial imbalances and address the deeply rooted and engrained patterns of discrimination that continued to persist against Liverpool-born black people. The privileging of class against all other forms of oppression informed this view, even though the majority of those being discriminated against were in fact working class. Whilst such views were held by an unknown number of individuals within the Labour group, as we will see, it was most forcefully adhered to by its Militant members. According to one Labour Party member at the time:

Militant had this idea that you can't be oppressed on the basis of your race and you can't be oppressed on the basis of your sex. It's only capitalism and if you're middle class black or upper class black or upper class women you know [you don't suffer discrimination]. According to Militant ideology, discrimination is solely based on class. They simply refused to acknowledge that a person could be discriminated because they were black or female. (Sam Semoff interview, 2012)

Again:

They [Militant] didn't seem to have a policy on racism, they didn't seem to have a policy on feminism. In fact they argued theoretically against these things, everything could be reduced to the alienation of the workers. (Peter Kilfoyle interview, 2012)

Militant's view on gender inequality echoed similar sentiments according to Sam Semoff:

To give you an example of the sexism, we used to have discussions over a woman's right to choose. From the Militant point of view, it was only about working class women, if you weren't working class you could afford an abortion so it wasn't an issue. It was that kind of mentality and of course that carried very much over into racism. You didn't challenge racism *per se*, you challenged capitalism. If you did away with capitalism you wouldn't have a problem with racism or you wouldn't have a problem with sexism and, as I say, that was part of the key with the Bond issue. (Sam Semoff interview, 2012)

One of the 47 councillors and Militant member Ian Lowes opposed positive action and believed trade union nominations were preferable to any positive action initiatives:

They didn't need them when the unions had nomination rights. I remember the debate went on within the labour movement at the time and there were people arguing for positive discrimination. Where I was coming from on this was if you allow the trade unions nomination rights [providing the trade unions are genuine and honest and not corrupt, because the problem was always if you had a bent trade union or bent officials that were just using it as a 'job for the boys' exercise that was wrong] it gives opportunities to demonstrate that this can work and you monitor it and see what results you have, then we can prove our point. (Ian Lowes – workshop interview, 2011)

Ian Lowes explained how this worked in practice:

Trade unions went out and actively encouraged black people to apply to go on the trade union's nomination list because you did not have to be a trade union member so it was not a closed book. It was not only trade union members who could be on the trade union nomination list, anyone who wanted to, [could] apply.

You do not need positive discrimination if nominations rights went to a diverse group. When it was done through the unions we achieved results. I will always defend the fact that the trade union involvement providing it was done properly, transparent, that gets more results than any positive action programs than anyone will see.

We argued that consistently in the unions at the time. (Ian Lowes – workshop interview, 2011)

Such nomination rights were also applied in the case of women who were under-represented in traditional male occupations:

The area that I worked in was the parks and gardens, women were grossly under-represented in that area, it was seen, if you like, as a traditional male job like the bins like the road sweeping and stuff like that. Through nomination rights we were able to direct women who wanted to go into those areas. I will say this as well without fear of contradiction, more women got jobs [in] what was seen as traditional male workplaces when the trade unions had nomination rights than ever before and ever since. (Ian Lowes – workshop interview, 2011)

A diversity of views existed within the Labour Council on issues of inequality and discrimination and not all, including other Broad Left, agreed with Militant's views on positive action:

Militant had what I consider a very fundamentalist view of Marxism. Their idea was simply you defeat capitalism and you solve all the problems. The opposite to that is what I call the Bennite left [those who would agree with the views of Tony Benn] or Livingstone left and that's a recognition that you've got to challenge capitalism… For the Bennite or the Broad Left the prime struggle [was] of the working class [this] was extremely important but it wasn't limited [to] that … you can have exploitation other than on the basis of being working class. You can have exploitation on the basis of race, you can have exploitation on the basis of gender … in other words you had to challenge sexism as such and you had to challenge [racism].

To me the big difference between what I call the Bennite left and the Militant left is that the Militant left refuse to recognise the other kinds of exploitation. (Sam Semoff interview, 2012)

One Broad Left Labour councillor Paul Lafferty saw the need for positive action policies to tackle racial and other forms of discrimination and had begun to implement these before the Sam Bond issue exploded:

There was quite clearly a discrepancy between numbers of the black population and the number of jobs they had. We did a survey which I was part of to try and see how many black people were in the shops, shop workers you know and the council introduced [ethnic monitoring] through tick box forms, this was all quite new then, 20 odd years ago. We introduced that to try and get a balance but we knew things weren't [balanced] and that's what the Broad Left always wanted to try and address some of these issues.

We wanted to monitor [and] gain a picture of what racial minorities were being represented, alongside the disabled and women. We were monitoring, looking for whether it was happening or whether it was not happening. There was no question about it, it was not happening as good as it should have done. We understood the need for a proportional representation, so that there was a fair crack of the whip given and the workforce reflected the population.

One of the frustrating things is I would have liked to have gone faster and done a lot more [...]. There was a lot of racism in Liverpool, a huge amount of racism and I think we needed to address that situation. It was sad that it was stopped purely because of the Sam Bond affair ... Somehow that got mixed up with this young man. (Paul Lafferty interview, 2012)

Moreover, trade unions like NALGO had supported positive action initiatives and had won the broader support of the Liverpool Trades Council.

1981 would see Liverpool's inner-city explode in serious rioting and unrest. Police racism and harassment of the Liverpool 8 community had been a major catalyst for the unrest here. By 1982, this area became the most heavily policed in Liverpool with the infamous Operational Support Division (that had precipitated the riots) spearheading the 'maintenance of law and order', even though crime was allowed to grow. It was against this background of the 1981 unrest, the continued heavy policing of Liverpool 8, the discriminatory recruitment policy of the council, and a reluctance to embrace the spirit of national race relations legislation for equal opportunities, that organisations within the community emerged (such as the Liverpool 8 Defence Committee) and pushed for a voice within local government (Murden 2006: 460; Frost and Phillips 2011). Paul Luckock, Labour councillor, reflects on the historically 'paternalist-maternalist' attitude of Social Services in Liverpool that failed to provide adequately for all its communities and which in turn led to a proliferation of community organisations:

We'd had massive issues with Social Services on the council and because they had a very sort of patriarchal, paternalistic [and] maternalistic attitude towards their service users – adults, older people, children and young people. We were saying that doesn't reflect the city. We are a community, I'm not denying they're needy people and we need to take kids off some of these families to safeguard the children. [The reason] why we've got all these community groups and activities was because for years the City Council had not delivered effective support services for families, the disabled, the mentally ill and older people. (Paul Luckock interview, 2012)

Liverpool 8 then had begun to organise both before and after the 1981 riots in an attempt to highlight issues around racial inequality, including the need for a Race Relations Unit with dedicated staff.

## 1983 Labour victory in Liverpool

When Labour secured an overall majority in the council in May 1983, Derek Hatton became Deputy Leader and Chair of the Race Relations Liaison Committee. Soon after, the council agreed to a request for a Race Relations Unit composed of officers who could advise and provide specialist knowledge in the area of racial equality. This was in line with the practice of other local authorities but represented a concession by Militant and others who opposed positive action policies. At the same time, moves were made towards rectifying racial inequality on the employment front through trade union nomination rights rather than the usual positive discrimination avenue. Ian Lowes explains:

When the trade unions, by agreement with the council, were given nomination rights for jobs one of the things that we set about doing was trying to form links with the black community. The number of black people who worked for Liverpool City Council was extremely low and it was a question of trying to re-dress this imbalance. So we made contact with a variety of organisations in order to get names submitted we could nominate them for jobs. (Ian Lowes – workshop interview, 2011)

Part of this initiative involved the Labour Council funding organisations like South Liverpool Personnel whose job was to liaise with businesses to obtain local employment opportunities. However, initiatives like this were not without their problems:

I remember working with [anonymous] and this organisation to get names for jobs while some people did come through that organisation a lot of the names that were put forward [...] were paper names. When it came to attending interview no one turned up. In the end it got to the stage it became an embarrassment because [...] we would submit the names of people to go to interview within the council and they would not show up. (Ian Lowes – workshop interview, 2011)

Yet in spite of these problems, Ian believed that improvements in the opportunities for council jobs did increase:

It is an absolute fact that during the period that the trade unions were given nomination rights for jobs, more black people obtained employment with Liverpool City Council than had ever done before and have done ever since. When those nomination rights were removed by the Labour council that took over from us the 47, [numbers declined] if you monitored the number of black people who came into the council since then. (Ian Lowes – workshop interview, 2011)

Similar claims are made with reference to the employment of women:

What is true [about] people from ethnic minorities getting positions is also true about women and is also true about disabled people, because our unemployed registers – we deliberately went out to make sure that we had women who were interested in those types of jobs, black people, ethnic minorities that were interested in those sort of jobs, disabled people who had never had the opportunity to get into [work]. We did it, [with] the widest possible audience and it was a success until they took it off us [the Labour council that followed]. (Ian Lowes – workshop interviews 2012)

Broad Left councillors like Paul Lafferty were also actively involved in trying to set up an equal opportunities committee that would be responsible for implementing positive action policies across the board:

> The Sam Bond thing was about to emerge on the scene and blow everything out of the water. I agreed to be chair of the Race Relations Liaison Committee providing that there would be an equal opportunities committee and that we would be looking at women's rights, the rights of the elderly, rights of people who had disability. So [for me] it [was] about [having] an equal opportunities committee. We persuaded the council to have one major committee with as much power as the Housing Committee, Social Services Committee and every other committee, equal power. So instead of having eleven committees, they have twelve major committees [or whatever the number was], but it never got off the ground. There are a lot of things we could have done no question about that.
>
> It was at that point Sam Bond came in [and things became] polarised. NALGO refused to co-operate basically and we did loads of work on [gaining support for] this. It [got] stuck, stuck in a pit where NALGO said that they refused to do anything until Sam Bond was dismissed. And of course we couldn't dismiss Sam Bond because he'd been taken on legitimately with a letter saying 'You've got a job'. NALGO did not allow us to function. I thought it was really sad because they decided to sacrifice a major committee, so it was a difficult situation at that point. (Paul Lafferty interviewed 2012)

Gideon Ben-Tovim was involved in a number of community organisations including the Merseyside Community Relations Council (MCRC) and the Black Caucus and had contributed to a number of research projects that documented the marginal and disadvantaged position of Liverpool's black community.[7] He presents a different perspective – of a Labour group that was reluctant to embrace positive action policies both before and after Labour took control of the council in 1983.

One thread ran through all of the Labour group's stance [was that of] trying to stop projects that had a major influence for the black and minority communities, such as sheltered housing schemes or targeted social service support; or resisting widely accepted and indeed legally required or commended mechanisms to redress racial inequality such as ethnic monitoring or positive action schemes. These were all interconnected. Labour had a very simplistic and one-sided approach to any specific actions, initiatives, or interventions that had a race or ethnic flavour: they were just taboo because ideologically they did not fit their crude and dogmatic class only approach to politics and policy. (Gideon Ben-Tovim interview, 2012)

Examples to support this claim can be seen in moves to block initiatives within the Housing Liaison Committee (Ethnic Minorities) to provide accommodation for elderly Chinese people who had been excluded from council provision and had particular needs. Tony Byrne, a member of this Committee before Labour swept to power in 1983, had opposed any such moves in 1982:

That this Working Party is of the opinion that hostels for the elderly should be provided to meet the needs of the local community as a whole and not for any particular ethnic group. (Housing Liaison Committee, Ethnic Minorities, 26 March, 1982, cited in Liverpool Black Caucus 1986: 46)

However, the council had agreed in principle to demands from the MCRC for a host of other initiatives designed to better cater for the needs of black and minority ethnic groups. This included the development of a Multi-Racial Education Unit (funded from Section 11) and initiatives within the Youth and Community Service were acted upon. Moreover, suggestions for ethnic monitoring of the workforce were established and the need for initiatives within Social Services was accepted (for example the establishment of a community hostel in Liverpool 8, Chinese Social Work Unit, Black Social Work Project, Black Home Help Scheme and plans for sheltered housing for black elders – see Black Caucus 1986: 54–55). Heather Adams sat on the Social Services Committee and explains how there was awareness of cultural sensitivities around black and ethnic minority communities and their needs:

I think we were mindful of cultural differences, in Social Services Committee we had a special project to recruit black social workers which was quite successful and they would have priority of social work training programme. District D I think it was at a special social work office that was staffed almost exclusively by qualified black social workers and we also had a recruitment drive for black home helps. There were people in the community that specifically said that they would not have or do not want a white person in their house. We were conscious of those I think. I mentioned briefly this morning a special programme for Chinese with menus specifically tailored to their needs.

In the residential sector we tried to make sure a lot less from those minority sectors went into care, but we [also] tried to ensure that when they did that their cultural needs were taken care of, they were in an area where they had lived and links were maintained. (Heather Adams – workshop interview, 2011)

Paul Lafferty who had chaired the Race Relations Liaison Committee believed a wider equal opportunities committee should have been established to look at women's rights, the rights of the elderly, rights of the disabled and so on, alongside racial equality. He explains:

There was a need for specific policy. We forget that there wasn't a lot done in those days. It took years and years to get black footballers [...]. The benefit of hindsight is a really good thing but you have to put yourself there – there wasn't a lot done for equality in general so I thought that would be something I could really get my teeth into and bang the drum [for equal opportunities]. (Paul Lafferty interview, 2012)

Paul also reflects on the initiatives that were targeted at the local Chinese community:

I like to think I was a little bit radical in that we employed Chinese social workers because it was always a myth that the Chinese look after their own. When a Chinese man was found dead and hadn't been visited for several months we needed to do something. We took on social workers who were mostly Chinese speaking. [Another] positive initiative we had with the Chinese community was we changed the meals and Social Services to cater for the Chinese community. We created quite a lot of Chinese lunch clubs serving Chinese food. That had never been done before.

[Social workers would] help people fill in forms, help the elderly. We were doing quite radical things with Heather Adams allowing social workers to go into surgeries. Some real ground breaking stuff at the time where you could have a holistic approach to people – multi-disciplined so we were actually doing that and the irony is one of the GP's practices were one of the first to do it. I think there's a lot of stuff we did. (Paul Lafferty interviewed 2012)

Clearly then, there was a diversity of attitudes and policies towards equal opportunities and positive action more generally, with not all in the council rejecting such moves. Moreover, whilst Militant saw the use of positive action policies as divisive and unnecessary, any suggestion that Liverpool 8 did not benefit during these years has been challenged. Tony Mulhearn explains:

Let me make this final point, if you look at the money that the council pumped into areas per head of population Toxteth, Granby received more money than any other area in this city, no question about that. We took on more apprentices by the way from that community than any other previous administration. [But] all that was forgotten in the hatred of the media ... [during the Bond affair]. In terms of resources, we put more money in that area than in any other area in the city. (Tony Mulhearn – workshop interview, 2011)

However, conflicts between the council and black groups began to emerge, particularly in relation to racial harassment policy and the allocation of council housing,[8] but also around issues of ethnic monitoring, black employment (Commission for Racial Equality 1984), and the failure to fill Section 11 posts. Gideon Ben-Tovim reflects:

I was also quite involved with the members of the Black Caucus and the MCRC in producing evidence about the racially discriminatory practices that the Militant council was perpetuating.

We produced evidence after evidence, not just about housing but about employment within the City Council, about Social Services, about access to meals on wheels and sheltered accommodation, about support that the welfare state should have been providing to all citizens. We were indicating that there was a failure of the council in Liverpool to adequately and fairly meet the needs of all citizens, and we found that clearly there was a race dimension to this inequality. (Gideon Ben-Tovim interviewed 2012)

The picture emerging then is a mosaic of different and at times contradictory claims and actions during the period 1983–1985. Whilst Militant councillors did not ideologically support positive action, at the same time they were forced to compromise on occasions, through a combination of pressure from black groups like the Liverpool Black Caucus, as well as statutory obligations to implement equal opportunity policies and also because of the support for such initiatives from some Broad Left Labour councillors. Whether or not enough was done in favour of positive action during these years remains a bone of contention. Groups like the Liverpool Black Caucus claim that not only did Labour not do enough when in office, but that it actively resisted such policies because of Militant's ideological opposition. So whilst some initiatives were allowed as a concession, others were resisted or dropped because essentially, Militant disagreed with this on political grounds. Broad Left councillors like Paul Lafferty had honourable intentions in relation to equal opportunities but has argued that any progress made on this front was disrupted and even halted because of the Sam Bond affair and the subsequent action from NALGO:

All we were trying to do as a Broad Left was to recognise that there was racism and prejudice endemic within the system [and] it had to be monitored and addressed. There was an agreement and then it was put through the council that we would have an equal opportunities committee [but] equal opportunities just petered out [after that] because NALGO never allowed any of it to actually happen. (Paul Lafferty interview, 2012)

Harry Smith also comments on plans for an Equal Opportunities Committee that was halted:

It wasn't that we didn't recognise [the need] or propose the committee [because] unless you recognise that there are problems and try to address those problems [they won't be resolved]. We were frustrated in trying to address these problems, I [and others] was pushing for it. There was a constitution for it so it is not as if we did not care about it. It is just that we were blocked and to sacrifice that because of whatever you thought of Sam Bond, I thought was sad. It should not have happened, that is one of the biggest disappointments I had. It never took off, it would have been a trailblazer and it would have done a lot of good work. (Harry Smith – workshop interview, 2011)

Jerry Spencer is of the view that the Labour Council was a broad church in which different voices and perspectives could be heard and were respected, but with time its ability to implement different policies became more difficult:

There was some room early on for people to say, okay, let's get the housing going, let's do this, let's do that, let's set up the neighbourhood forums and things like that. I do get that sense. It just became less and less possible to do that. But I don't think there was any sense at all that this was a monolithic movement. I think there was a degree of respect. There was some listening that went on and a willingness to let people get on with that. (Jerry Spencer interview, 2012)

As time went on, Militant councillors with the support of Broad Left and others were able to push through policies sometimes by removing those who were proving obstructive in allowing the council to carry out its plans. In other cases, it was a case of appointing those who were Militant activists or sympathisers to key positions, as in the case of Sam Bond. Paul Luckock was not a Militant supporter but reflects on how the 'old guard' had obstructed the housing programme and how this was dealt with:

I think I was given that post [chair of the Technical Services Committee] because we had to get rid of the City Engineer because the engineering department was basically stopping [us] getting our housing priority areas done because you had to get the bloody drains in and the lights done and the roads built and the old guard officers were a nightmare. Senior officers who were unwilling to implement the policies in our manifesto should have done the honourable thing and resigned instead they did everything in their power to hold things up. There were some significant exceptions but we had to pay off a number of people who were skilfully obstructive. It was distasteful that we had to pay so much money to get rid of them. (Paul Luckock interview, 2012)

For him and others, this strategy was motivated by a desire to bring significant changes about. Luckock argues: 'I just wanted to get things done, I wanted to get houses knocked down and new ones built and nurseries built and things like that, that's what I was motivated to do.'

It is within this context that Sam Bond's 'political appointment' was framed and justified. Whilst a strategy of appointing sympathisers and supporters to key committees seemed sensible and even logical, opponents of this strategy argued that this left little room for dissenters who challenged the underlying principles and political ideology of Militant, and in particular those who advocated positive action for disadvantaged groups. It provides evidence for those who argue that the Labour group was dominated by Militant, and legitimated the opposition of many who in other ways supported what the council was doing: confronting the government and building houses. This was particularly important when the Labour Council had begun to move away from its initial concessions to such causes seen in the disbanded Black Social Work initiative and the shelving of the agreement for a Liverpool 8 community hostel amongst others.

## The Sam Bond affair – a political appointment?

The council fulfilled its commitment to establish a Race Relations Unit to be headed by a newly appointed Principal Race Relations Adviser with a number of other posts being attached to this. The person eventually appointed in October 1984 was Sampson Bond, a black Londoner and Militant supporter. Controversy surrounds the manner in which Bond was both short-listed and appointed. Critics have argued that he was only a serious contender for the position because of his Militant affiliation rather than his suitability for the job. This formed the basis for the various strands of opposition to this appointment that included black groups like the Liverpool Black Caucus, sections of the left in the Labour group and trade unions like NALGO.

The chair of the appointment panel, Derek Hatton, admits that he was under pressure from fellow Militants in London to appoint Bond as one of their own:

> When we decided to get a Head of Community Relations, all of the sudden there was talk in London amongst Militant people down there that they had this lad called Sam Bond who was very involved [and] who would be perfect for us. We used to talk to London about what we were doing, and they'd sometimes make suggestions. Sometimes I'd say 'I can't do that' [but] very often their suggestions were crucial.
>
> I have got to be honest, at the time, there was that much going on that I did not make an issue over it. That was my fault, I should've done and eventually I said 'Okay send him up'. (Hatton interviewed 2012)

One of the controversies surrounding Bond's appointment to Principal Race Relations Adviser derives from the view that this was simply a 'political appointment' because Bond was an active member of Militant who lacked the experience and skills needed for the post. Many arguments have been put forward that both support as well as refute the reasons for Bond's appointment, but both sides agree that having a Militant activist in such a key position would allow the group's political stance on the race-class dynamic to be more forcefully justified and legitimised (at least in theory). At the same time, some Broad Left councillors supported Bond on two counts – firstly, because he was seen as the best candidate and secondly, there was a belief that the appointment of key personnel could be justified on political grounds. In other words, the appointment would support what the council was trying to do. Of course this raises other questions concerning appointing someone who did not ideologically support positive action policies – policies that Broad Left councillors had in fact been advocating and actively supporting. Perhaps this can be explained by the fact that Bond's connection with Militant was not common knowledge.

Paul Lafferty, who was on the appointment panel, was asked

whether he believed Bond was a political appointment and whether it could have been done differently. He explained:

> Well yes, I think so [but] in fairness Derek didn't have to say anything, at all. Most political appointments are done secretly and it's very difficult to prove. You get political people that are unelected and serve the government. I think Derek should have told the truth [about Bond being a Militant member] and we should've had the battle because it just spoilt so many things. If Sam Bond had said 'I'm not a member of the Militants but tell me what they believe in and maybe I believe in that', [or] if Derek Hatton had said 'Yes, he's a member of the Militant' and yes he had spoken to him in London then they would have no case to answer. (Paul Lafferty interview, 2012)

Paul Lafferty believes it was important to appoint those who were sympathetic to what the council was trying to do in terms of policy:

> I was at the interview and I think if someone had come in there and said they thought Maggie Thatcher has the best policies, there's a very good chance that they wouldn't have been appointed [because the candidate] must be able to interpret if not necessarily support the political views [and policies] of the council. They want [that person] to go out there and actually facilitate [council policy]. So I suppose the views that we had as a Broad Left and [Bond's views were] part of it – it was politics. (Paul Lafferty interview, 2012)

This is echoed by Tony Rimmer and Ian Lowes:

> The whole idea was that whoever was chosen [...] could work with the local community. That's why they were chosen because of the qualities that they showed at the interview [...]. The Group went along with that selection [...] and he [Bond] came over as somebody who could get on and do the work. (Tony Rimmer interview, 2012)

> It is the same in any local government, you're talking about a council with a political agenda. The council wants to appoint people to carry out their agenda and their policies. It is not unique because if you look at even national government the Tories in power now, Cameron [et al.]

has appointed all of their mates into positions because they want them to carry out their agenda. (Ian Lowes – workshop interview, 2011)

If you look at when the Liberals were in control who they appointed. I know it was one of the allegations that was always hurled at us about 'jobs for the boys'. I never accepted that we were [out of order] but if we were bad they [Liberals] were infinitely worse – the amount of people that they appointed that were their boys. The first thing that Trevor Jones did – and he got thrown out of office – he appointed his wife as Lord Mayor! That was okay! (Ian Lowes – workshop interview, 2011)

Harry Smith recalls that there was a sense that Bond was the best person for the post:

I was not on the interview panel, but everybody will agree just on interview Sam Bond outshone everyone else on the interview. He would have got it on interview anyway, no matter where when or what. Most of the people who were on the shortlist were put on the shortlist because they had a closed shop thing. A lot of them would not have carried out our policies, so what is the point in employing the chief officer for someone who's going to look after themselves. That is why Sam Bond ended up employed. (Harry Smith – workshop interview, 2011)

Jimmy Rutledge is less certain as to why Bond was offered the job:

I wasn't on the interviewing panel so I honestly couldn't say whether he was the best candidate. He could [have] been a political appointment but he may well have been the best candidate or maybe he wasn't a particularly strong candidate but there was a determination to get him in post anyway. (Jimmy Rutledge interview, 2012)

Bond's appointment was supported by a number of non-Militant Labour councillors, not all of whom shared Militant's views on positive action policies. Tony Rimmer was not part of the interviewing panel but reflects the views of many in the Labour group at the time, including the view that Bond must have been the best candidate for the job and due process had been followed in terms of application form and short-listing:

The people who interviewed him felt, that he was the best man for the job. There was no discrimination against the local group. But how do you appoint somebody for a job? You take their application, you take their CV, you shortlist them in a paper sift if they are suitably qualified and you interview the possible candidates and then make a decision. And on the day, from what I was told, Sam Bond was the best candidate. (Tony Rimmer interview, 2012)

However, the short-listing process has itself been questioned. Critics have argued that Militant duped those both on and off the panel, seen not only in the way it was not openly disclosed that he was a Militant but also in the manner in which Bond was short-listed. As part of the panel Gideon Ben-Tovim explains how Bond was slipped in at the last minute:

Looking back now [...] during the short listing process all the people that had been suggested by the trade union observer and myself were accepted without question by Derek Hatton, the Appointment Panel Chair ... but he insisted on keeping in one candidate who from the summary sheet, seemed ineligible for appointment. He said that the fuller/letter of application demonstrated his expertise – but we were not able to see this. Clearly this was an attempt to pull the wool over our eyes because he and his colleagues agreed all our recommendations from the shortlist. In retrospect, this was the moment when we should have pulled the plug, but we were lulled into a false security because of what otherwise seemed a consensual and constructive approach. (Ben-Tovim interview, 2012)

When it came to the decision as to who would be appointed, the majority (that included six Labour councillors) voted for Sam Bond. For Ben-Tovim, this clearly indicated that Bond's appointment was 'fixed'.

When it came round to the room and all Labour hands were put up for Mr Bond I just couldn't believe it. It just shows how relatively naïve we were at the time. It was unanimous [except the opposition councillor who did not support Mr Bond] and we walked out as did the trade union observer. So obviously it was planned and fixed, because of his politics and background. That was the person they had already decided to appoint but wanted to appear to go through the motions of a legitimate appointment process – a pretty cynical and damaging manoeuvre. I know that following the majority line is of course often part of the political process, but it should not take place in public sector appointments. In crossing that line, and in such an extreme way, the councillors lost all claims to integrity and professionalism, and that was quite an eye opener for me. I just hadn't seen anything like that before. (Gideon Ben-Tovim interview, 2012)

Paul Luckock was also part of the panel and believed Bond was a credible candidate and supported his appointment. However, the response this provoked from what he describes as 'a small group of self-interested professionals' within the black community was not anticipated and he reflects that tactically his appointment was a mistake:

I sat on the interview board so I was culpable I think in tactically making a mistake in appointing Sam Bond. In that it was naïve not to anticipate massive opposition from the self interested professional lobby when one of them was not appointed. He was the best candidate on the day you know, he came across as articulate, respectful and understanding of the issues facing the black and ethnic community. I was aware on the day where he was coming from as I did the other candidates [and] I knew Sam had a Militant background. As I got to know him, I liked him a lot, he was open and not knowing in his style and therefore good at seeking to understand the Liverpool residents' specific need or interest. He conducted himself with great dignity despite the abuse he experienced. (Paul Luckock interview, 2012)

Tony Mulhearn had opposed the creation of a Race Relations Adviser for political reasons and believed this was self-serving:

They had this race relations industry which became a hotbed of careers, as if race was something apart from the general class struggle. Bond was selected strictly in accordance with the council procedures. (Tony Mulhearn – workshop interview, 2011)

So why then did the majority go along with Bond's appointment? Some knew of his connections with Militant, others did not. Ben-Tovim situates the decision to appoint Bond in a wider context:

These were people who could speak, they were good orators who could talk and were quite persuasive, and I think people who dissented from that were dealt with pretty harshly through ideological combat in terms of doing people down personally and playing the 'class card'. (Gideon Ben-Tovim interview, 2012)

Others felt Sam Bond was chosen because there was no credible alternative. Tony Rimmer reflects:

I didn't know the Black Caucus candidate who had applied for the job, but they had obviously not done enough to impress that day at the interview, or maybe they came second that day, I don't know. (Tony Rimmer interview, 2012)

Paul Lafferty was on the interviewing panel and felt there was little competition:

Derek didn't have to push too much because some of the candidates were very poor indeed. I mean, we had one guy who basically said that he'd left his last employer because there was some irregularity with money and there was one guy said that he felt it just seemed like a good idea, something to do after his university placement. But, Sam said all the things you like to hear and he would wouldn't he [laughs]. But it wasn't that he had to do anything overt. It wasn't a hard struggle because he came out as a young black man who's well educated, knew what he had to do, was very keen to do it and he knew what we were trying to do. I mean who wouldn't vote for him? So he didn't have to push. We were happy with him till it all blew up. (Paul Lafferty interview, 2012)

Sam Semoff was not part of the panel but argues that there were other candidates better equipped to serve the local black community. He says that all the candidates bar one (Bond) held progressive anti-racist views and ideas:

One of the two from outside Liverpool was from Sheffield or Birmingham or maybe somewhere else and the sixth one was Sam Bond. Now the interesting thing is of those six, five had what I would call a progressive view on race relations, they knew their ideas – you had to challenge racism as racism. Sam Bond of course who was actually a pretty nice guy personally [...] shared the Militant ideology very much ... but the end of that meeting, Hatton said it had to be Sam Bond, so the panel chose Sam Bond. (Sam Semoff interview, 2012)

Bond had strictly adhered to Militant's anti-positive action stance during the interview:

It was the most extraordinary interview I had ever seen in my life. Even now trying to reflect on the morality, the values, the attitudes of people, I was astonished at the way the Labour councillors, some of who I thought were reasonable people could unanimously put their hands up to appoint somebody with no background, no experience, whose interview was very poor but where he had clearly been primed to say a couple of stock things about race policy 'I don't believe in positive action, I don't believe in record keeping' – and that's about all he had to offer that's compared to three or four other people we interview who all had useful things to say. [They] were perfectly credible and appointable in my view and the view of the trade union observer. (Gideon Ben-Tovim interview, 2012)

Bond's ability to toe the Militant line was one thing, but the question of his suitability has now been questioned 30 years on by Derek Hatton himself:

Once he came up and he was there at the interview, I had to appoint him but he was not the best on the day, [but] there were not many others who were better on the day. (Derek Hatton interview, 2012)

Bond's appointment was a turning point. From that moment on, opposition to the council grew, legitimated by a feeling (even from many who otherwise supported what they were doing) that Militant was illegitimately dominating the council and driving its problematic policies through.

# CHAPTER SEVEN

# CONTROVERSIES

The biggest tactical error that we ever made was appointing Sam Bond. (Derek Hatton interview, 2012)

T he appointment of Sam Bond was one of a number of controversies that backfired and fed into the undermining of Militant's leadership in Liverpool during these years. In addition, allegations of bullying and intimidation formed another strand that would damage Militant's standing in Liverpool in general, and people's perceptions of the legacy of the council in particular.

## Campaign against Bond

Opposition to Bond began during the interview process when adviser Gideon Ben-Tovim and one other walked out in protest following an otherwise unanimous vote in favour of Bond:

I've sat on probably hundreds of interview panels in my life, I have never walked out on one before and never never walked out since, but I just could not stay in the room, nor could the other adviser. (Gideon Ben-Tovim interview, 2012)

This marked the beginning of the campaign against Bond and was followed by opposition from the white collar union NALGO who refused to work with him.

> The unions joined in the opposition to Bond and refused to pass on his post or pass through phone calls. I would not say it was 100 per cent but it certainly limited his capacity to do anything. (Sam Semoff interview, 2012)

Paul Lafferty, a member of the panel, explains, 'There is no question that it had an effect, NALGO decided to not co-operate'. As news spread, 'there was outrage from the black community' (Semoff interview, 2012) and an occupation of Council offices took place with a number of individuals held there, some argue held hostage, for several hours. For Jimmy Rutledge and Derek Hatton, the episode caused a huge split in the Labour group and gave ammunition to opponents such as the Liberals and the national Labour leadership:

> I can remember being at a meeting in relation to it where people from the Black Caucus actually brought padlocks and chains and locked the committee room we were in, we had to sit there for hours. That caused splits within the Labour group because they thought it was a political appointment. I knew something of it because my ward was south city centre it took in all of Chinatown, took in a bit of Dingle and Toxteth which is obviously the traditional black area of Liverpool so you could sense the undercurrents there. Of course there were people quick to exploit [the] inherent right and wrongs. (Jimmy Rutledge interview, 2012)

Derek Hatton adds:

> So we appoint him [Bond] and all hell broke loose, and what that did from that moment on was to split the Liverpool left and aided and abetted brilliantly by the Liberals and *Echo* and everything that goes with it, and certainly aided and abetted by that traitor Kinnock and the national Labour Party. (Derek Hatton interview, 2012)

During the occupation of Council offices, Paul Lafferty was one of those held and though he makes light of the episode, this does not detract from the high emotions and tensions that emanated from all sides:

It all became ridiculous in the end in as much as we got stopped from leaving [the Council offices]. As a councillor I was held prisoner. What happened is that Derek was up on the top floor discussing what was going on when basically the people from the Black Caucus moved into the Council offices and refused to let anyone in or out. I remember getting some lunch from the window, we had to have lunch [winched in] and all the rest of it. [We were there] about nine, eight hours I think, something like that. And they were shouting obscenities and doing all kinds of stuff. And eventually they let us go. (Paul Lafferty interview, 2012)

Sam Semoff recalls meetings, marches and conflicts between individuals in meetings over the Bond affair: 'I remember there were always meetings you know of the opposition, the opposition to Bond' and 'there were rallies and challenges [including] one classic City Council meeting where (anonymous) and (anonymous) got ejected by the police'. Paul Lafferty recalls how the tensions:

went on for months, months and months. It seemed to my mind [that] spoiled a lot of what we were doing because we were in a situation we couldn't get out of really and that it spoiled something that could have been really good. (Paul Lafferty interview, 2012)

Sam Semoff recalls a march against the Thatcher government that was joined by an opposing feeder march from Liverpool 8 – such was the anger and alienation felt by those opposing Bond:

There's a classic example of the strength of the opposition, the anger and the hostility. There were a number of rallies and marches in support of a council controlled by Militant and it supporters and against what Thatcher was doing, against the Thatcher regime. There was one march which was made up of feeder marches – these were small marches that started off in different parts of the city and converged as they reached City Centre and there was a feeder march from Liverpool 8 going into the main march and I remember being on that feeder march. The anger to the Labour controlled council here in Liverpool was greater than it was towards Thatcher. (Sam Semoff interview, 2012)

There were other incidents of anger and hostility towards the council, particularly Derek Hatton who became the focus of much of this:

One of the things that happened was a meeting in Liverpool 8 Law Centre in which Hatton spoke and you can imagine. I mean, you got to give him credit for going into the lion's den [...] and he waffled on the questions [put to him] but there was one question I'll always remember and he was asked basically, 'Why are you supporting Bond?' I always remember he said 'Well the decision to keep Bond in position well it really isn't me, it was the district Labour Party that took the decision' [...] that was a clear manipulation, clear example of how he manipulated when he told the district Labour Party well I had no choice [...] but then when questioned by the black community as to why that decision was taken he said, 'It wasn't me, it was the district Labour Party'. (Sam Semoff interview, 2012)

## Opposition to Bond from the black community

In addition to Bond being a Militant activist, opponents (both black and white) also questioned firstly whether he was qualified to do the job in terms of his experience of race relations work and secondly in terms of his understanding of the specificity of race in the context of Liverpool that was quite different from London. Tunde Zack-Williams had been involved in the Liverpool 8 community and as an academic and left activist, had written and published on race in Liverpool. For him, Bond's appointment was 'an insult to the city'. Firstly, Bond had been given the job of Principal Race Relations Adviser because 'race was not important' and was indicative of Militants perspective that saw the working class in 'monolithic' terms with little understanding of the 'secondary contradictions of capitalism' that came out of class oppression (namely race and gender amongst others). Secondly, Bond had little or no training in social issues since he was a surveyor. As opposition to Bond picked up speed and conflict between the black community and the council intensified, black opposition to Bond came to be viewed and understood by those outside of this group in parochial terms. Demands for the dismissal of Bond in favour of a 'local' appointment came to dominate subsequent perceptions and discourse. Paul Lafferty is perhaps representative of many views within the Labour Council that understood black opposition to Bond in such terms:

> There was a wide expectation that someone from Liverpool would take the post. But that would have been illegal if we'd have said someone from Liverpool [must] take the post. I mean if you'd been from Manchester and you'd heard the job that you've always wanted and you applied for, and had the qualifications to do, but you [are] discriminated [against] because you're not from Liverpool.

> Basically the [Black Caucus] demands were that we sack Sam Bond, re-interview, and take someone on that they knew because of Liverpool's peculiar situation historically and that no one knows Liverpool like they do. Therefore it should be one of them [But] you had to look at the best person for the job. (Paul Lafferty interview, 2012)

Tony Rimmer echoes this view:

> Interviews went on and the person that was selected was a guy from London, who was Sam Bond. Now obviously there was an objection to that from the Black Caucus because he wasn't a local man, he didn't know local issues. (Tony Rimmer interview, 2012)

Tony Mulhearn also supports this view:

> Bond was selected strictly according to council procedures. As Liverpudlians are in Leeds, Liverpudlians are in London, Liverpudlians are in Manchester, this whole business about someone from Liverpool was just a red herring. (Tony Mulhearn – workshop interview, 2011)

However, as Sam Semoff argues, the black community itself was not homogenous in terms of its opposition to Bond's appointment and there existed different perspectives:

> In the black community it varied. For some people in the black community their opposition was because Bond was not local [and he didn't understand local issues] and for some people their opposition was because of the particular politics of Bond. And it's hard to say [but some] opposed Bond for a combination of reasons – the fact that he wasn't from Liverpool and the fact that he also shared the ideology [of Militant]. People opposed Bond for either one of those [reasons] or for a combination of both. (Sam Semoff interview, 2012)

There seems little doubt that there existed a preference for a 'local person' by some but this did not represent *all* black opposition as has been widely disseminated. For others, Bond's appointment was not necessarily about parochialism or localism but was about appointing someone who was *aware* of local issues, and in particular the *specificity of race* in a Liverpool context. So in practice, the person appointed did not necessarily have to come from Liverpool:

> People from the black community who believed in directly challenging racism would not necessarily have objected to a person outside of Liverpool if they shared their views. (Sam Semoff interview, 2012)

Gideon Ben-Tovim again challenges claims of parochialism:

> Those of us who were involved in the interview process walked out because this was clearly a 'put up' appointment. I mean it could have been a Liverpool person that would have been the person appointed, we would still have walked out. It was not because Sam Bond was a Londoner and we 'just wanted one of our own' as we were accused by the Militant leadership at the time. (Gideon Ben-Tovim interview, 2012)

Tunde Zack-Williams' (interview, 2012) opposition to Bond rested on the grounds that he lacked any understanding of local issues pertaining to the specificity of race in a Liverpool context (Gifford, Brown et al. 1989; Small 1991; Zack-Williams 1997). This did not necessarily mean that whoever was appointed had to be born and bred in Liverpool. It did mean however, that whoever was offered the job needed to have a sense of the particularities of Liverpool and the way race was played out here if the post was to carry any leverage and be taken seriously within the black community.

Ray Costello, local black historian, offers another perspective and puts into historical context the 'invisible' status that locally born black people occupied:

On the question of whether or not the local black population were being parochial in not accepting Bond, the history of the Liverpool black community has to be considered. Liverpool's black community, the oldest in Europe, dates back to the eighteenth century, but since then has acquired an unusual cloak of invisibility and to this day very few members of the old black community are to be seen working in Liverpool's central business district, in spite of the area of black settlement being only a short walk away. The City Council (and it should be said that there were individual councillors who struggled to help bring about racial equality), along with the local business community, sometimes offered an illusion of a multi-racial, multi-cultural city by employing black individuals from elsewhere, a precedent easier to break when the need to dispose of these individuals arose, further enraging local black people by presenting a face of respectability seen as a sham; a massaging of figures. (Ray Costello interview, 2012)

There had been other reasons to explain black opposition to Bond that focused around allegations of black separatism. Steve Munby was active in the Communist Party at the time and is dismissive of such claims:

Let me tell you how separatist the black community is, you've got accounts of black seamen from Liverpool and white seamen who worked underground for the ANC from Liverpool. This is a very proud chapter in our history [...] it's not been historically separatist partly because of the nature of the Liverpool black community [...] So the idea that the opposition to Sam Bond and Militant was to do with the kind of separatist not working together is not true. The opposition came from people who were trade unionists who were concerned about independence and respect. (Steve Munby interview, 2012)

Jerry Spencer had little time for either group and saw the subsequent conflict and entrenched positions that arose as attributable to the stubbornness of each, though particular blame is placed at the feet of the Liverpool Black Caucus:

> I think at the time, it's an exaggeration, but they [the two sides] were scorpions in a bottle. Really, there were two groups of people who were pig headed, had countervailing views and were not going to compromise at all over those views. But I think, as well, they couldn't necessarily articulate why, except in terms of the slogans and had no ability whatsoever to compromise or accommodate with each other. I think 90 per cent of that was on the Black Caucus side or more. I mean whatever the balance is, I think it was more on their side than on Militant's side. I think the problem was that they very quickly got themselves locked into positions that they couldn't move out of. (Jerry Spencer interview, 2012)

Peter Kilfoyle on the other hand argues that black opposition was grounded in an understanding that Bond was not all that he appeared:

> As far as Sam Bond's concerned, it strikes me it's very much like the BNP today where they claim that they have black members. Oh, they may have one or two misguided souls who signed up to them, but it doesn't stop them being essentially a racist organisation. That was the same in Militant; Sam Bond may have been a willing dupe but he wasn't going to dupe the people in Liverpool 8, although they were no angels. (Peter Kilfoyle interview, 2012)

Opposition to Bond was not of course confined to the black community or to reasons of parochialism, if that is what it was. A section of the left within the Labour group opposed Bond because of his Militant politics.

> [There were] those who opposed Bond because of his ideology, because he hooked into the ideology [of Militant]. Certainly from the

non-black community the opposition to Bond was purely based on the fact that they were Bennites [and] had a Bennite view of challenging racism, people like myself, we opposed Bond because of his politics. (Sam Semoff interview, 2012)

## An own goal?

Thirty years on, Derek Hatton concedes that offering the job to Sam Bond was a mistake and a heavy price was paid for which he takes responsibility:

> The biggest tactical error that we ever made was appointing Sam Bond. It was one of those things that didn't really matter, that is what infuriated me. We had involved the Black Caucus in many things, they obviously had a voice. [It was] the one thing that lost us the support of a lot in the city, not the majority but a lot in the city and gave us big big problems. I didn't think it through. It destroyed our relationship with the unions, and I take responsibility for that. (Derek Hatton interview, 2012)

For Jimmy Rutledge, the Bond affair was 'with hindsight [and] for various reasons a huge own goal, a huge own goal'. Many of those who were interviewed on the issue of Sam Bond's appointment have argued that the controversy and splits it caused gave those who opposed the council the opportunity they were looking for to stick the boot in. This included the press, the Liberals and the Labour leadership. Paul Lafferty explains how 'The Echo continually dripped that we were corrupt. The Bond issue was investigated probably more than anything I've ever known in my life...' Tony Mulhearn reflects on how opposition to Bond was used by the establishment to criticise the whole Labour group:

> The fact of the matter [is] it was blown out of all proportion and used as a weapon against us. Again that wholly signified the role of the establishment, [the] crazed attitude of the media and the complete distortion of the 47's position. You had this furore egged on by the Liberal party, by the press. The whole of the establishment got hold,

they did not give a damn about the black community, it was to undermine the position of the 47. It was banner headlines, the world's press was in there, and it was on the news every night. (Tony Mulhearn – workshop interview, 2011)

Derek Hatton explains how the Bond issue enabled opponents of the council to split the left in two and cause insurmountable damage within the labour movement:

They called us everything under the sun and we gave them a rod, we gave them a sword to literally split the left in a way that nothing else could have done. All the other [things] the taxis etc. would not have mattered if we had not split the left. What split us was the Sam Bond appointment. I have mentioned it a number of times but perhaps not as clearly as I am saying it now. It was the one thing that caused the biggest split within the Labour and trade union movement in Liverpool, amongst the activists and everybody else. (Derek Hatton interview, 2012)

Those who were part of the left and opposed Bond's appointment have also been accused of jumping on the bandwagon and of using the incident as a rod to beat the council with. Paul Lafferty echoes this:

I think it was probably a mistake in [appointing] Sam Bond, for the simple reason that he gave them an opportunity that they wanted. They wanted that opportunity for all the wrong reasons. (Paul Lafferty interview, 2012)

Jerry Spencer again reiterates how the Bond affair gave those on the left legitimacy to criticise:

Sam Bond gave people a licence to critique without being accused of being right wingers. You could then say, look you don't get new social movements, you don't get gender, you don't get race. That's not being a right winger that enabled people to criticise. I think it legitimised those movements or those people, those voices. (Jerry Spencer interview, 2012)

Steve Munby agrees:

> The most significant point is it gave sanction to other people on the left to oppose Militant. People felt afraid that if they opposed Militant they would be accused of being right wing. This allowed them to attack Militant from the left. Although I thought Militant were completely wrong, I don't have a lot of respect for some of the people who started having a pop at Militant over this. I thought they were gutless, they only felt they could attack Militant from the left. (Steve Munby interview, 2012)

The campaign against Bond and the Labour council was spearheaded by the Liverpool Black Caucus. Their action in turn led to counter-tensions against this group by sections of the council. Moreover, claims that the Black Caucus was used by those who cared little for the black community have also been made. Tony Mulhearn amongst others expresses this tension:

> The so-called Black Caucus inflamed the situation. Derek was called a racist, I was called, the level of vitriol was absolutely appalling. Tell you who supported the Black Caucus Michael Heseltine, Thatcher, the Liberals, the Tories and the Communist Party, the Communist Party leadership because they were incensed that the 47 were doing what they could not do. (Tony Mulhearn – workshop interview, 2011)

Paul Lafferty also believes the Black Caucus was used by others to buttress criticism against the Labour council:

> The irony of course is that all the people who sided with the Black Caucus said we had to do this and we had to do that, [they] all got into power and then quickly forgot them [black community]. A lot of people were looking for something to bash us with and it was very difficult to actually say to the Black Caucus at the time that all these people are your mates. (Paul Lafferty interview, 2012)

James Dillon regrets the split that opened up between the council and the black community and felt the position of Principal Race Relations Adviser was unnecessary:

The press made the most of it, I don't think we needed Sam Bond: in our naïveté if you like, we appointed Sam Bond thinking it would make it better for the black community [...] they fought against us – if they had combined with us and fought the government, it might have been better for all sides concerned. But they decided to fight us and they thought we could give them the world, but we could not give them the world, we did not have the world. I think we handled it pretty well. (James Dillon – workshop interview, 2011)

Nobody could have predicted the strong reaction the Bond appointment would provoke and the damage this would cause the Labour council. While a number of those interviewed concede 30 years on that Bond was a mistake, at the same time, there is a sense within the Labour group that they were trying to do what they thought was right. Paul Lafferty:

We were already under pressure, the press didn't like us, Neil Kinnock didn't like us, the Tories certainly didn't like us, so actually employing him [Bond] was the wrong thing to do, but we did it for the right reasons. (Paul Lafferty interview, 2012)

Sam Semoff reflects that:

While, I disagreed with many of the Militant policies and in particular their position on racism, I never questioned the sincerity of the leaders and their supporters. With exception of one 'leader' nearly all involved in one way or another with Militant believed that their policies were in the best interests of the people they represented and would lead to a fairer and more just society. I can think of individuals, albeit misguided in their politics, were some of the most caring people I have known. (Sam Semoff interview, 2012)

The conflict over Bond eventually resulted in him being removed from post in 1987 but not before the Militant leadership had attempted to create an alternative structure for him to operate through – the Merseyside Action Group. In the end, the Race Relations Liaison Committee was disbanded and the proposed Race Relations Unit never got off the ground. The damage done to community relations fed into further alienation of the black community. For Zack-Williams (interview, 2012), 'the black community was the most oppressed group' in Liverpool and as such the Militant leadership 'should have carried the black population', adding that any left group 'has to know how and when to struggle'. Munby believes the Bond issue exemplified Liverpool Militant's lack of interest in racism and draws a distinction between these and London Militants:

> I think [the Bond issue] exemplified Militant not getting race and never having had a strong base in Liverpool 8. They completely misread the riots, didn't understand about racism or policing.

> Clearly they [Liverpool Militant] weren't cut from the same cloth as the GLC. The GLC left got feminism and anti-racism in a way that Militant never did. Militant wouldn't get involved at all with the Anti-Nazi League. (Steve Munby interview, 2012)

In the context of the Bond affair, Peter Kilfoyle draws parallels between Militant's stance on race and gender issues:

> Now when I think of Sam Bond, they [Militant] didn't seem to have a policy on racism, they didn't seem to have a policy on feminism. In fact they argued theoretically against these things, everything could be reduced to the alienation of the workers ... (Peter Kilfoyle interview, 2012)

Gideon Ben-Tovim echoes this:

> I think the same arguments would be found around the issues of gender, suggesting that the simple class approach isn't good enough to encompass the range of disadvantage and differences involved in inequality. (Gideon Ben-Tovim interview, 2012)

At the same time, sections of the Broad Left did attempt to rectify racial and gender inequalities. Tony Rimmer argues that attempts were made to introduce gender parity in jobs and wages:

> We tried to treat everybody as equal. Where there was discrimination

for instance, such as on parity with wages, we tried to introduce it so that a woman doing the same job as a man got the same pay. (Tony Rimmer interview, 2012)

Sam Semoff explains how positive action policies began to be implemented in Liverpool under a Labour council following Militant's expulsion:

> The interesting thing is of course when Labour came in it was an entirely different Labour council, you had people like Keith Hackett, Liz Drysdale, Sarah Norman, Juliet Herzog who were very much committed to making links with the black community. I mean they supported the Liverpool 8 Law Centre, remember we set up Merseyside Immigration Advice Unit which I was part of, they set up Amadudu, the black women's refuge – the exact opposite of what Militant was all about. I mean can you imagine trying to set up a black women's refuge under the Militant (laughing) administration? (Sam Semoff interview, 2012)

The Sam Bond issue exposed more than anything else the tensions and disagreements over equal opportunities and political appointments and inadvertently mobilised one of Liverpool's most oppressed groups, but not in a way the council could have predicted nor wanted. The Labour Council should in theory have had the support of Liverpool's black groups alongside the wider labour movement in the struggle against the Thatcher government. Labour was the natural constituency of the black community. Bond however became Militant's Achilles heel – a major flaw and weakness in an otherwise powerful phenomenon.

## Allegations of intimidation

The Bond controversy has also raised a number of other issues. This includes allegations of bullying and threats surrounding the Bond issue itself, as well as within the Labour group more generally. With reference to Bond, as well as the occupation of Council offices and the holding of individual councillors here, allegations of threats to Bond himself were made. Such incidents perhaps suggest the actions of a community that was in a position of weakness rather than strength (and were allegedly individual, spontaneous acts rather co-ordinated community responses). Others may claim this was indicative of individuals trying to protect their interests. Without condoning these acts and in an attempt to understand and explain them, it would seem that such actions were indicative of the high levels of anger, frustration and disempowerment that many felt surrounding Bond's appointment. The action surrounding his appointment epitomised and symbolised for many, the tip of a huge iceberg, of a long tradition of marginalisation and invisibility that had dogged this community's history in Liverpool. It was another example of not being listened to, of being side-lined yet again in a decision that would impact this community more than any other. For many, Bond was another example of Militant benignly sticking the boot in while paying homage to a form of 'racial equality' that lacked clout and commitment to the local community. The resistance to Bond can be seen as symptomatic of a wider struggle for greater equality that black groups had been battling over for years.

The Bond issue also brought to the fore for some, what might be seen as a kind of arrogance of the part of the leadership in the sense that they held firm in their belief that the decision made was the right one despite the fallout. There would be no movement, no compromise and no surrender, perhaps for all the wrong reasons? For John Airs, this signalled a sense in which rank and file members were increasingly moving further away from the leadership:

> I think the problem was that they very quickly got themselves locked into positions that they couldn't move out of. I think that was seen, as something else that was wrong with Militant, that it would actually not have the sense to come up with a solution, to come up with some way of actually dealing with this and that it had no power to accommodate. There was a power structure there that if you didn't fit yourself into it then you were going to get crushed.

> I think this was the first sense, that perhaps we'd let the genie out of the bottle as it were, that something had got loose; we'd created a monster, if you like. Those are exaggerations, but the idea that in actual fact we're not in charge anymore. You know the movement from below, the rank and file, the foot soldiers, the ordinary people, we're not part of this, we can't trust the leadership on this issue. I think

that, as much as anything, it hardened the attitudes, it convinced the leadership that they were right or that in order to hold the coalition together they had to take a strict line, a hard line, all the time. And if you're not with us then you're against us. (Jerry Spencer interview, 2012)

And just as allegations of intimidation and threats made against those who opposed Bond have come to light, so too claims of creeping bullying by Militant members have also been made.

Alleged bullying and intimidatory tactics against those who even remotely dissented or challenged what Militant and others were trying to do have been made by some. Such allegations focus on intimidation from rank and file members as well as increasing centralised control exercised through strong individual leaders. Particular reference has been made in this context to the nature of the District Labour Party, chaired by Militant Tony Mulhearn. In some cases it was the style or manner in which things were said rather than the content. In such cases, it is important to distinguish intimidation from the 'rough and ready' nature of working class politics that was moored in Liverpool's casualised port economy where the day to day struggle to survive bred a straight-talking culture. Peter Kilfoyle gives some context to this and acknowledges that there were distinctions to be made between passion for a cause and intimidation.

It depended on the personality. I'm one of 14 children and when we used to get together [people who didn't know us] thought we were going to come to blows because of the arguments that would take place between us would be so passionate. It wasn't, it was just a very, very passionate way of expressing yourself and there was an awfully great deal of that. For people like me, and there were lots like me who had similar kinds of backgrounds, this was all part and parcel of debate. But not everybody's from the background and some people felt extremely intimidated; many women or older people, a lot of people who'd come into Liverpool from outside. That was difficult and I've been at meetings where people have tried to physically threaten and intimidate and I'm not an easy person to intimidate, but they'd still give it a go. So that was not unknown. (Peter Kilfoyle interview, 2012)

Jerry Spencer reflects on the robustness of debate within the DLP that was dominated by white, male trade unionists and how this might have been intimidating for some groups:

> At the DLP there was a lot more debate about things like housing, about industrial relations, about social policy and issues; I found it a lot more interesting. You know there were still the battles between left and right and that sort of thing, but I thought they were more muted, interestingly, and far more productive therefore, the discussions and debates there.

> I think that's why there was far more organising outside or alongside the DLP [...], but I didn't think there was anything necessarily wrong with that, but that was just how Labour politics was [in the '80s]. (Jerry Spencer interview, 2012)

Kilfoyle reflects on the way a no-nonsense 'workerist'-infused language was common within the wider labour movement and not just Militant, and again how this could be alienating to those outside Liverpool and who did not understand the sturdy local culture:

> Lord King flies in and he wants to decide where they're going to have the maintenance for British Airways; Cardiff or Liverpool. Ironically, this guy described himself as an anti-Militant, he was a man called John Farrell who ran for deputy General Secretary of the then T & G union and he was based over in Birkenhead. But it's the mentality, it's the workerist approach. It's the 'us against the world' kind of approach. King arrives, and there was a strike going on which involved the cleaners and he's there and he was the most foulmouthed man I'd ever met. He was effing and blinding at Lord King, in the most foul language, as he came through. King made up his mind there and then, there was no way in which investment was coming into Liverpool. Now you may say, oh well that's an individual, but that individual reflected a stand of thinking that was common in the broader Labour movement at the time which was aggressive, it could express itself in a way which might've been appropriate, arguably, in some workplaces but wasn't appropriate in a public place like that. It was just alienating; it was just horrible, hostile. (Peter Kilfoyle interview, 2012)

Derek Hatton again puts into context a working class culture of 'rough and readiness' that made its way into local political debates:

> You're talking about lads who had been dockers, who had been fireman who had been building workers who had been print workers. You're talking about lads who had been as kids, scrapped every day, you're talking about lads that had been involved in boxing, in football, lads who had been with lads in every single way in Liverpool. You are talking about ordinary Scousers. There is no way in this world that that gang of people were going to sit down there and argue and discuss [in the same way] that they would in the GLC or Islington. That was not going to happen, that was not the type of people we were and there was no way that we could have changed that.

> The people who were actually really opposed to that was in the Labour Party [and] who made the comments [of intimidation] in the main were people who were not from Liverpool. You never heard, even the likes of Eddie Rodrick or Bill Snell who were opposed to us, comment about the way we argued. They were just the same. Eddie Rodrick was very fierce or Paul Ore [...] we used to argue like mad but you know exactly the way to argue. (Derek Hatton interview, 2012)

Louise Ellman recalls how increasingly she began to hear stories of bullying tactics by Militant members:

> Over time, stories emerged from Labour members about physical and political bullying by Militant. I heard this as a member of North West Labour Party Executive [people who were very supportive of the Labour Party and very hostile to the Tory Government]. (Louise Ellman interview, 2012)

Alex Scott Samuel (interview, 2012) was a socialist and member of the DLP. He explains his relationship with Militant as one in which whilst not disagreeing with their policies, particularly the way Militant were fellow 'socialists opposing the horrendous stance and strategy of Thatcherism', he did however detest what he terms Militant's *style*. He argues: 'the way they worked was totally unacceptable' citing intimidation and aggressiveness as a tactic that was used, particularly in the

DLP, against those who disagreed or challenged their views. This was not aimed at the right wing elements, but against fellow socialists. Samuels argues that much of this became personalised. According to him, there were around 10 members in the DLP out of approximately 120 who were collectively labelled by non-Militant but 'fellow traveller' Tony Byrne as the 'bourgeois elements'. Samuels accuses others of taking the political moral high ground through the use of dismissive and belittling labels. Terms like 'class enemy' were used to put people down who were accused of betraying the people of Liverpool. Peter Kilfoyle echoes this again with reference to the District Labour Party meetings:

> Mulhearn was the chair in the crucial period, if you got the chair there was a line and a tremendous bias and prejudice and it was allied with vitriolic attacks upon leading lights in the Labour Party. You don't want to expose yourself, willingly, to being abused, pressurised, called a traitor, all sorts of things you were accused of in this tremendously wound up atmosphere that was part and parcel of the DLP. (Peter Kilfoyle interview, 2012)

Paul Luckock offers an alternative perspective of DLP meetings:

> Tony Mulhearn I would say was a sort of a giant in a sense of political leadership in terms of not just the Militant's position but the way in which he chaired the district Labour Party. The way he smoothed out things, in what I would say historically, you would have wanted your most honourable shop steward to be [...]. So I hold Tony Mulhearn in great status. (Paul Luckock interview, 2012)

John Airs remembers the efficiency with which business was dealt within the DLP, but also of the manipulation:

> My experience of [Militant] were [they were] actually very efficient. I mean Tony Mulhearn was one of the best chairs I've ever seen, he just got through masses of stuff. I also knew that they could be quite manipulative and calculating. I remember they got one guy, he'd objected to something that they wanted to do, so they made him talk for it, they set him up to actually propose it at the GMC. (John Airs interview, 2012)

Others like Michael Parkinson, whilst not personally witnessing intimidation, doubts whether systematic and organised intimidation went on. He contextualises the manner in which 'aggressive politics' came to the fore, arguing that this was a left-over from the Liberal administration and the insular character of Liverpool at the time:

> I knew Peter [Kilfoyle] and I always thought he overegged his pudding really. I was around when the *Echo* and Peter Phelps made all the allegations of intimidation and I don't think they invented it but I never really saw it [perhaps] I'm being naïve? But I think that's a bit exaggerated you know. I may be wrong on this but I think it was more cock up than conspiracy. Liverpool's a very interesting, fascinating, peculiar place. The voice [accent] is fairly harsh but they're not that harsh. There's different Liverpools and my Liverpool is not actually the only Liverpool but I thought that organised intimidation was way overstating it. [Liverpool had become inward looking and insular] [...] I think that's the difference now: you will hear foreign voices on the street whether they're German tourists or whether Spanish because of the footie and I think at that time it sort of reached its apogée. [...]
>
> The Liberals will always hate me for saying this but I thought in a certain way their decade of pavement politics, fairly aggressive politics didn't help raise the tone. Frankly I would say we all shared a bit of responsibility for what happened, rather than saying there was an organised criminal conspiracy and we didn't know what was going on. I think it was just people not facing up to their own responsibilities, myself included. (Michael Parkinson interview, 2012)

Gideon Ben-Tovim offers another perspective in which he recalls the way in which increasingly, those who dissented from Militant's line would be accused of betraying the working class. For him and others, Labour during the Militant years in Liverpool became a form of 'municipal Stalinism':

> As far as the Labour Party was concerned you had a period of fear of dissent and an atmosphere that we refer to in our book [Liverpool Black Caucus 1986] as 'municipal Stalinism' – a very powerful well run machine in the Labour Party where if you didn't go along with the line

you were treated pretty heavily. So for me as a Labour Party member who was not happy about what he was seeing, mainly because what I was experiencing on the race relations front, there was I thought a particularly negative atmosphere within the Labour Party. This was detrimental to opening up the debate, discussion and reflection, which in my view should be the hall mark of democratic politics. (Gideon Ben-Tovim interview, 2012)

Others like Jerry Spencer describe how the democratic centralist tendencies of Militant left little room for dissent or reflection, even when mistakes were made. This militated against him joining:

What made me never join was the democratic centralism, that line, you know, there was no scope for dissent, there was no scope for exploring new ideas, different ideas and I think this was the worst of it really, there was no scope for exploring why things had gone wrong, why things weren't working and a denial that things weren't working. There's no reflection within the organisation. There might have been higher up, but that wasn't transmitted downwards. There wasn't any dialogue between the foot soldiers and the leadership around what works and what doesn't work. (Jerry Spencer interview, 2012)

Indeed, for some of those who gave interviews, there is a suggestion that as Militant came under attack or made mistakes, the tendency to keep a tighter rein of control increased:

Once you were in Militant that was it, the Party line ... so that's why I never joined. I think the tragedy was that the more and more it became ... the more the possibility of power became real and the converse side, the more and more the possibility of ultimate defeat became more and more real, they became more and more centralist. (Jerry Spencer interview, 2012)

The District Labour Party has been singled out by several interviewees as the place where Militant's influence and alleged bullying could be most clearly seen:

The District Labour Party was a crucial power base for the leading

Militant faction within the Labour Group. In a situation where Labour Party branches were somewhat moribund it was possible to work to organise and control the delegates who were then able to deliver what the core group wanted. Thus the District Labour Party over-turned the initial appointment of a so called 'right winger' to the Leader of the Labour Group on the council in 1983 and installed John Hamilton instead .The DLP was used to overturn the 'agreement' Derek Hatton made [doubtless cynically, knowing this was would be revoked] to rescind the appointments to the Principal Race Adviser Post. [In later reforms of the Labour Party in Liverpool, the DLP lost this kind of direct power over council decision-making.] (Gideon Ben-Tovim interview, 2012)

Alex Scott Samuels recalls another more benign tactic used by Militant in the DLP that involved waiting until the end of a meeting when the majority of members had left, to push through motions that might otherwise be defeated. He also recalls more threatening behaviour and alleges that some trade union activity (including a branch of the GMB union) was 'particularly unpleasant for Militant intimidation'. As well as being unacceptable, this formed part of a wider strategy that undermined the democratic process. The vandalism of greenhouses in Calderstones Park containing rare orchids was said to have been a revenge attack against gardeners there who refused to support wider strike action.

John Airs offers an alternative perspective, arguing that intimidation and underhand tactics became very apparent when the Labour Party expelled Militant:

I really did not see any intimidation at all, it might have been going on? When I thought the nastiness came in was when the Militant were purged. It was the other way round. It came very suddenly. It was Kilfoyle who had been sent back to Liverpool clearly to cleanse the city, Kinnock's 'Labour Party' [mocking Welsh accent] having a go about the redundancy notices. I mean, we knew what was going on then.

Then the clearout started and that's when I got really angry. This was before Blair. This was Kinnock. And I remember going to one constituency meeting, and about 5 or 6 people who were always there, weren't there, and we asked, 'Where are they?' and they had been barred, you know, thrown out. They were Militants.

It came out of the blue. At a usual monthly meeting of the constituency, [people] in the room started to talk about some issue, and someone said something about a missing member, and we looked round, and I think there were five who were barred from attending. And I thought that's disgraceful, there was no discussion, we knew nothing about it, suddenly they were gone. And I thought I'm not going to stick with this, and it did seem to me that the party started to move rightward again after that [...]. It could be that they were pushed that way by their experiences of fighting the revolutionaries, but there were a lot of people that I respected and had worked alongside but who now seemed to be going rightwards very quickly. (John Airs interview, 2012)

Clearly then, what was seen and described as intimidatory by some, was perceived and understood by others as a form of 'no-nonsense straight talking' working class style of doing business. This was simultaneously acceptable to some, and out of order and alienating to others. Moreover, as the above transcript points out, the expulsion of Militant from the Labour Party was seen by many, including non-Militant Labour Party members, as alienating and unacceptable. This, alongside the disbarring of the 47 Labour councillors, came on the back of a number of developments that ran parallel to and beyond the Bond issue and allegations of bullying. Whilst these and other events collectively amounted to an eventual undermining of the council's standing in Liverpool, the question we must ask is what is the legacy of those years? Was Liverpool set back, as critics have argued, or did the council steer Liverpool back on track?

## CHAPTER EIGHT

# THE LEGACY

'We've a Lib Dem run council in Liverpool and they have worked like Trojans to undo the damage caused by the militant Labour council of the '80s.'[9]

C ritics of the Labour Council of the early 1980s called Liverpool the 'city of missed opportunities' (Parkinson and Bianchini 1993). They argue that the council put off the revitalisation of the city by not doing what Manchester did, opting instead to fight the government for more resources. Geographer David Harvey has argued that:

If, for example, urban entrepreneurialism is embedded in a framework of zero-sum inter-urban competition for jobs, resources and capital, then even the most resolute and avant-garde municipal socialist will find themselves, in the end, playing the capitalist game and performing as agents of discipline for the very processes that they are trying to resist. (Harvey 2001: 349)

To what extent then did these developments put Liverpool's revitalisation back a decade? Or was this the time the city began to stand up and fight back?

## Disbarred, purged – and re-elected

In January 1986 the disbarred councillors of 48 went to court to challenge the District Auditor's decision. In their affidavit, they argued that that District Auditor (DA) had been wrong to fine and disbar them as there was no set date to set a rate, and that it was honest and reasonable for councillors, bearing in mind the needs of the inhabitants of the city of Liverpool, to use their discretion to try to get the best deal possible from the Secretary of State. In acting as they did they argued, they had behaved honestly and with advice, not recklessly. The only financial loss Liverpool had suffered was through the actions of the Government in withholding central funding that the city needed to address its problems. It was not a case of delay itself being used 'as a weapon or lever to prise money from the Government'. From the councillors' point of view they believed they were acting in the best interests of the ratepayers and inhabitants of the city by trying to negotiate an improvement in the city's position before they set a rate, not unlawfully or wrongly and with reckless indifference to the results. Thus they argued the DA was wrong to substitute his political judgement about what the likely result of the councillors' actions would be in the future, before the negotiations were over.

More prosaically, John Hamilton wrote his own justification, 'Why we're in court':

> Since the Tory government took office in 1979 Liverpool City Council has lost £350 million in rate support grant, unemployment has increased, and the social needs of the area have risen. To carry out its programme of housebuilding, increasing the number of nursery places and helping to provide more work for people the city council has pleaded with the Government for more money, or, at least, not to continue to cut back on our existing grants. The District Auditor says it is wilful misconduct for councillors to try and negotiate money from the Government and not set a rate until you know the result of your appeals.

> Where is the liberty and freedom in the country when a District Auditor removes councillors from office, takes away their citizenship makes them bankrupt and confiscates their homes and possessions, because they had the effrontery to ask the Government for more

resources for the city and its people? Is it right to punish people who stand up and ask for help to relieve poverty and suffering?

Contemporary speech notes by a Militant supporter provided a more forcefully political and confrontational approach to the relationship between the DA and the councillors. The removal of the councillors, Militant argued:

> ... will, if it is highlighted and used properly, enormously raise the consciousness of the proletariat. It will represent a direct attack on local government democracy and will without doubt further under-mine support for the Tories and increase the sympathy for and support for Labour. Our role in this will be vital: by propaganda, speeches, written material and meetings we can explain the class motives of this action ... our programme must include the need for the Trade Union movement to take over running of the council to prevent a Liberal take over – a policy of non-co-operation.

Between February and March 1986 the Labour National Executive Committee voted to suspend the Liverpool Party, and Peter Kilfoyle began to organise against Militant in Liverpool Labour Party. In the run up to the May 1986 local elections the Alliance (formerly the Liberals, now allied with the Social Democratic Party who had split from Labour over the role of the left in Labour) printed 100,000 leaf-lets stating: 'Gangsters run our town hall'. At the same time, Labour used Michael Heseltine's views against their critics: in 1981, in the aftermath of the riots, Heseltine argued 'The private sector cannot play the prime role. Only public funds can buy out the accumulated legacy and despair and decay.' (Taaffe and Mulhearn 1988: 441) Labour argued this was still the case, and campaigned strongly in support of the council's legacy. The *Liverpool Echo* commented on the eve of poll:

> *Militant*, masquerading under the banner of Labour, have taken the city to the brink of bankruptcy, saddled it with an impossible debt burden, damaged its education service, left its streets dirty, its dust-bins un-emptied and given it an international image of industrial anarchy. And that takes no account of the 'jobs for the boys' scandals, or the intimidation of council officers, of the revenge on those who

dared to step out of line and of the anxiety inflicted on thousands of families who for months never knew for certain whether they would be paid. (Taaffe and Mulhearn 1988: 443)

In the local election of 1986, Labour's share of the vote was 39 per cent, while Liverpool's Tories were wiped out by the Alliance (now the Liberal Democrats) who won 41.76 per cent (2.76 per cent more than Labour's share of the vote). Labour gained one more seat and retained power. The new council consisted of Labour 55 seats, Alliance 37, and Tories 7 (Taaffe and Mulhearn 1988: 446–7). The election day's *Liverpool Echo* front page showed a jubilant Derek Hatton, with headline 'Militant's vote of confidence', with further comment (9 May 1986: 6) acknowledging what it called 'a confounding Militant Victory'. It continued:

> No scouser could have been under any illusion that a vote for Labour in this city was a vote for Militant … no one who went to the polls yesterday did so in ignorance of the price Liverpool would pay for endorsing Militant misrule … The biggest losers remain the city and people of Liverpool, who more and more will find themselves written off by the rest of the country which looks simply at seats won rather than votes cast and will decide that they have the leadership – and the votes – they deserve.

Less than two weeks later, on 21 May 1986, the first Liverpool councillor Tony Mulhearn was expelled, while 11 others were threatened with expulsion. On 26 May, after a three month investigation, Labour's NEC charged 16 Labour Party members with Militant membership, including Derek Hatton, and raised the possibility of charges against another 16. Dennis Skinner proclaimed this was a case of 'kicking people when they are down' as the 47 were due before the court of appeal the following Wednesday (*The Times* 27 May 1986). In contrast, the Eldonian's Tony McGann, vice chair of Vauxhall Labour Party, argued that this is not personal, but that Militant was a 'cancerous growth' within the Labour Party (*The Times* 27 May 1986). In June, Derek Hatton and the 11 others were expelled from Labour and in July the Appeal Court upheld the DA's decision. In September eight of the eleven expelled members appealed to the Labour conference, but in a closed session the Labour Party conference voted 20:1 to uphold the expulsions.

In January 1987, the 47 councillors began appeals to the Law Lords, only to have them dismissed in March. Following the failed appeals, the councillors had £242k costs imposed on them on top of the £106k surcharge. They were finally dismissed from office and a Tory-Alliance coalition briefly took control of the council for seven weeks. The Alliance leader Sir Trevor Jones argued: 'Everyone accepts that we have been left a city in a filthy mess. We have taken steps to clean up the city centre as part of the need to improve the image of the city to the outside worlds to begin to attract more inward investment and jobs.' (Dunn 1987: 3) Militant, they argued, had borrowed almost £229 million, mainly from foreign banks, for 'a monolithic and unresponsive municipal approach to housing and the environment, which no longer met people's aspirations'. However, the *Liverpool Echo* also criticised the coalition for failing to show a strategy for the city. It argued that a 'responsible' Labour administration would be better placed to undertake the intensive measures and care the city needed.

In May 1987 (a general election year), Labour fought the local election based on the council's record since 1983 and under the slogan 'We Support the 47', without a clear leader. In the meantime, Keva Coombes convened a rump of the remaining 11 Labour councillors. Politically on the left but not a Militant, Coombes expressed a desire to continue with the Urban Regeneration Strategy. He argued that a neglected Liverpool had been in decline for 10 years before Labour came into office, and stated that he was proud of the council's record and the houses it built: but he also commented 'We have learned from our mistakes'. Coombes recognised that fundamental problems remained on Merseyside. In an article in the *Liverpool Echo* (1 May 1987: 7) entitled 'Keva Coombes: Presenting a brighter and better face to the world' that appeared just before the election, Coombes argued that Labour was happy to work with the private sector to promote the image of the city, but also pointed out that 'Image, however, is less important than reality and only if the people of Liverpool have a city with decent homes, do they have the right to try and sell our city to the world'. He argued that the house building programme must be defended.

The 1987 local election saw a victory for Labour with many of the new Labour councillors now taking a more centrist position. The Tories were reduced to four councillors. A new anti-Militant leader, Harry Rimmer, took over the council and met the new Tory Environment

Secretary, Nicolas Ridley, in what was described as a 'cordial, friendly and constructive meeting'. Rimmer said that after the general election:

> In Labour controlled authorities there is an acceptance of the reality in the situation. Mrs Thatcher has won a fresh mandate. Past experience is that trying to defend ourselves by confrontational tactics has been counterproductive to say the least ... we intend to be constructive, seeking common ground, and working with the Government to achieve a solution to our problems. (Hamilton Fazey 1987)

Ridley responded by saying this was not a case of burying the hatchet 'as the analogy is inappropriate because the hatchets had been wielded by Labour councillors no longer in office'. Nonetheless Ridley was not prepared to cut the city any slack: he proceeded to rate cap Liverpool, which left a huge gap between income and projected expenditure – again. Rimmer tried to bridge the gap by seeking Labour support for a redetermination of the rates, standing down as leader in September having failed to do so. Militant's commentary argued this demonstrated that co-operation had not been more successful than conflict: 'There are only two roads: whether to 'co-operate' with the Tories and make cuts or fight for more resources.' (Taaffe and Mulhearn 1988: 493)

In early October 1987 Keva Coombes took over as leader and again met with Ridley to seek a new start. He asked to be allowed to make a small rates increase to cope with the £43–£51 million budget deficit he had inherited, but Ridley held firm in his hard-line attitude towards Liverpool and turned him down. Ridley argued it would be wrong to put up rates 'just as businesses are returning to the city' (*Liverpool Echo* 4 February 1987: 6). In the comment 'Tories torpedo Liverpool' (4 February 1987: 6) the *Liverpool Echo* argued that the Tories had undermined Coombes and missed the opportunity for better relations with the city: again co-operation was being rebuffed, and the blame lay squarely with the Tory government. Uncertainty remained the last thing Liverpool needed as it tried to rebuild its economy.

Despite Margaret Thatcher famously stating in the 1987 election that 'we must do something about those inner cities', seemingly the Government did not think that Liverpool Council was fit to run the city. Perhaps Liverpool's inner city was still enemy territory.

## Merseyside's revival begins

In May 1988, Labour under Coombes again fought the election under the slogan 'fighting the cuts, rebuilding the economy, creating local jobs and good homes for all'. Confrontational rhetoric aside, there was a new attitude in the Town Hall. The council under Coombes put its differences with Merseyside Development Corporation to one side now that waterfront regeneration was bearing fruit. New policies emerged encouraging local enterprise, developing training and infrastructure development, as well as a number of anti-poverty measures. In a promotional newspaper produced at the time to encourage businesses to invest in the city entitled '*Making it on Merseyside: a celebration of Liverpool's amazing economic revival*', Merseyside Chamber called the plans 'imaginative, realistic and on the whole sensible', and said 'we wish to co-operate'. By 1988 Heseltine was saying:

> When I came to Liverpool the impression outsiders had of the city was a total lack of partnership. I think the attitude is much better now ... the 'psychology of failure' had received a dent in its assumptions.

On 3 June 1988, the *Liverpool Echo*'s Stephen Suckley wrote of the 'Merseyside revival!' in which 'Businessmen enjoy wealth of culture in BOOMing city' (*Liverpool Echo* 3 June 1988: 7).

The 47, now half way through their 5 year ban, had by 1988 nearly raised enough to pay off their surcharge. An agreement was made to pay off the debt at £4,000 a month, but a staggering £10,000 a month came in from supporters. In 1989, the District Labour Party was said to be still asking candidates not to pay their poll tax and those who did were refused places on the council's candidates list. The *Liverpool Echo* (9 May 1989) reported 'candidates prepare for war' as 'Militant still have a hold in this city'. By 31 January 1991, sufficient funds (£500k) had been raised to pay off the debts hanging over the councillors. This included the £106k surcharge, the £232k legal costs imposed by the DA, and £162k legal costs for the House of Lords appeal.

Time was now limited for the Left in Liverpool. In May 1990 Keva Coombes was again replaced with anti-Militant Harry Rimmer. In July 1990, 14 Liverpool councillors were suspended for voting against rent rises and in the 1992 Liverpool Walton by-election, Militant Lesley Mahmood stood against Labour's Peter Kilfoyle and lost heavily. The council moved towards no overall control. Commentators reflect negatively on this period:

> By the end of this period the city had become a byword for political turmoil and militancy: not an attractive destination for inward investment. Whatever gains the 'militants' thought they might have made were almost certainly dwarfed by the lost investment and poverty of council services over the subsequent decade. (Couch 2003 cited in Murden 2006: 463)

Michael Parkinson argued:

> Liverpool's leaders ... failed to demonstrate the necessary political skills to construct a stable coalition to promote regeneration. But they also lack many of the resources that underpin regeneration capacity. The public and private sectors are both weak, and relations between them are strained. Liverpool's relationship with central government has been controversial, and the city has attracted little goodwill or money ... the most obvious aspect of the city over the last two decades [to 1990[ has been regime instability ... the city has been characterised by highly volatile and partisan party politics, limited administrative and governmental capacity, a lack of powerful business leadership, and an inability to construct coalitions between the public and privates sectors. (Parkinson 1990: 241–2)

By 1990, two decades of economic failure, compounded by political failure, had led to a degree of cynicism in public life that was corrosive. Parkinson (1990: 255) argues that a major legacy was a city council seen as inward looking, fragmented and negative, not recruiting good people: 'There is clearly a cultural dimension to the city's failure that goes beyond the statistics of economic decline.'

Others blamed bad press for the city's continuing woes. In an article in 'Merseyside Today', a supplement of *North West Business Leader* entitled 'From Militancy to Moderation', Trevor Furlong, Chief Executive of Mersey Docks and Harbour Company asked the press:

Why do you have to report it? Other places, such as several London boroughs, and Sheffield, have their political problems, but those of Merseyside ... always seemed to be reported more often and more sensationally, undermining the area's considerable progress.

Malcolm Kennedy further argued:

We've spent the last 20-odd years trying to live down what happened in the eighties. This was no heroic [battle] ... [it] destroyed attempts to rebuild Liverpool post-Thatcher for years ... the recovery would've been much easier if it hadn't have been for what happened in the eighties.

Confrontation, Kennedy argued, did not help:

I can remember one of the Conservative ministers coming out, who was actually sympathetic to the city ... and there were people like Michael Heseltine who was sympathetic to what was happening in the city ... we were all opposed to what Mrs Thatcher was doing but you didn't make the situation worse than it had to be. (Malcolm Kennedy interview, 2012)

In 1998 the Liberal Democrats took control of the council and kept hold of it until 2010 when Liverpool, again against the national trend, voted in a Labour administration. Labour's Joe Anderson was elected Mayor in 2011. He would take a noticeably co-operative stance with the Government.

Mike Henesey worked at Merseyside Task Force at the time. He argues:

the presentational damage that was done to Liverpool was huge. Why would the private sector come and invest in Liverpool in those days when you had a council that wasn't looking to work with the private sector? They were looking to take on the government. Why would you invest in Liverpool given those circumstances? And I think that was for me the biggest thing that we lived with. I think we finally nailed it only when we had Capital of Culture and where people came and saw what has happened to the city in recent years. (Mike Henesey interview, 2012)

In contrast, Michael Parkinson argues that blaming Liverpool's misfortunes on the council is misplaced:

> It was being said at the time, [Militant's actions] will deter investors, the private sector. I thought that was exaggerated, I may be wrong but at the time I thought that was exaggerated ... The Merseyside Development Corporation was set up in '81, it was struggling to get investment in the mid '80s. The larger structural things and the economic things [really mattered, and], to some extent people were blaming the Militant for deterring investors who didn't actually exist to be honest ... The idea that there was billions of investment waiting to happen and Derek Hatton stuck his head above the parapet I just don't think that happened. (Michael Parkinson interview, 2012)

The 47 responded with a defence of their achievements including the houses, leisure centres and parks that were built (Mersey Militant pamphlet 1991 'Liverpool 47: success against the odds'). They argued that while nationally, Labour did lose the general election, its programme in Liverpool was popular:

> Their election [Labour] in May 1983 was part of the social whirlwind following on from the recession of 1981–82 and the riots in Toxteth. The Liverpool Labour Party stormed to power on a radical socialist programme with the intention of defending jobs and services. If the national Labour party leadership had emulated Liverpool, we wouldn't have gone through the nightmare of a further eight years of Tory Government [...] In the field of housing, jobs, services, rents, sports facilities and education, the 47 translated socialism into a language which people could instantly recognise and identify with.

Peter Kilfoyle adds:

> Their claim to fame was housing and the sports centres. Now I go to the gym in one of the sports centres a couple of times a week, I don't reject the fact that they built those sports centres, fine. They built houses, but what I do say is that you've got to make balanced judgements.

For Kilfoyle, the real problem was what he regards as the damage Liverpool Council did to the Labour Party nationally:

> Their real legacy, wasn't in bricks and mortar, it was in the image that they created and that was extremely damaging certainly within the British Isles towards Liverpool and towards potential investors. It was seen as a bunch of loony tunes running the city and I think that alienated a lot of people, certainly potential investors. That was one part of the damage. The other damage that they did was to the Labour party because the Labour party was associated with madcap ideas. I've found those two things together unforgivable. (Peter Kilfoyle interview, 2012)

Those interviewed for this work deny that the council wanted conflict to serve Militant's deeper revolutionary agenda and as such did not care about the city. Moreover, as previously stated, Militant members constituted a small minority on the council; the majority were Broad Left non-Militants. What does come across most strongly from these reflective accounts is that such councillors *cared* about their city, and wanted to banish the poverty they saw around them. John Flamson worked at the Merseyside Development Corporation at the time. He argues,

> There is no doubt that they had an impact through the media on the image of the city. Some would think that it was a deliberate attempt to rubbish the city, I think that's totally wrong in that if you talk to the individual councillors they love the city, still do, so I don't think they hated the city and wanted to see the city tarnished but they probably didn't realise the extent of the politicking. (John Flamson interview, 2012)

Critics of the council understand that the city was objectively having a hard time, however it was the response to that hardship that they challenge. Malcolm Kennedy argues:

> Well yes [the private sector] was disinvesting, it was disinvesting all across the country. It's not as if even the figures in Liverpool were worse than where I'd come from. ... It was as if Liverpool always had

it worse than everybody else and nobody else was suffering anything like the same problems. It just wasn't true. (Malcolm Kennedy interview, 2012)

Peter Kilfoyle puts it this way:

I'm not for one minute suggesting the Militants on the council at that time were responsible for the flight of capital from the city, initially. That was one of the things which gave them traction, the fact that that had happened in the first instance. What was actually happening was a shift in trade patterns of course in that Liverpool, instead of being a gateway to the world, was being bypassed and you've got to think this through again. They were going to the Rotterdams, the Bremerhavens, the Cherbourgs.

As the trade patterns changed and containerisation came in, ports like Rotterdam were equipped for the modern era. The employers [in Liverpool] were happy with outdated [technology and working practices] … You needed a longer term vision of what was required. That's where the disinvestment came, because of the failure of British capital to understand. (Peter Kilfoyle interview, 2012)

John Flamson argues that more could have been achieved through co-operation with central government agencies:

if they had a policy of co-operation with MDC then they could have said 'OK, not quite a coalition, but these are some of the things that we're looking for, can you help through these developments? a) in terms of jobs for local people, b) in terms of helping our housing, putting some social housing in amongst the private housing or whatever' and actually MDC might have been open for that discussion, as such we never really got to that strategic level of agreement and so the council tended to see the docks as just, that's over there we need to get on with stuff in the city. (John Flamson interview, 2012)

Mike Henesey worked for the Merseyside Task Force at the time. He argues that the council did not recognise what support *was* available:

If you looked at the amount of monies that were made available through the Merseyside Task Force from '81, we had the Merseyside special allocation, you had massive amounts of urban programme monies, huge amounts in terms of housing. I would've thought it more than made up for the £23 million ['stolen' by central government] ... I always got the feeling that it was more about 'we're going to take on Thatcher and how can we do that?' And the way they did it was say, 'No, we're not going to set a budget. We're going to spend all our money on housing'. If you look at what Liverpool was like in those days when you have a vacuum and we seem to keep just being battered, somebody comes along. The Militant came in and a lot of people got behind them. You paid your money you take your choice of where you see that. (Mike Henesey interview, 2012)

John Flamson also argues that the problems the city was facing were so deep that any council at the time would have struggled:

If there had been any other council at the time, would the economic fortunes of Liverpool have changed radically? No I don't believe so. I think the structural economic problems were so deep [...] did they put people off coming to Liverpool? Well maybe, certainly had an effect on the popular perception of Liverpool fuelled by some of the national media. Did they have a serious impact on serious investors? Well maybe marginally, because serious investors look at the figures. I suppose where an investor is more worried, it's more about the political stability in an area and you couldn't describe Liverpool as politically stable at that time, almost irrespective of which party was in control. So it was a bit of instability there. I think sometimes people conflate the Militant policies with political instability. You can have political instability without Militant. (John Flamson interview, 2012)

## Moving on

Mike Henesey recalls how a perception of Liverpool as a problematic place on the part of ministers took some time to dislodge:

we used to have ministers coming on a regular basis in the '80s and we used to have senior civil servants come in and even into the '90s and you only had to listen to them and it was clear that they had an image of Liverpool. What we always used to say to them was if you can get them up here and actually see the place, take them round, attitudes changed literally overnight. There is reality and perception, and the perception was 'You don't want to go to Liverpool. You get mugged on the corner, your car stolen', all the stereotypical images of Liverpool ... once you got people here there was a real transformation and a new understanding when they saw what was going on, when they saw the people and the passion the people had, and the real desire to want to change things. (Mike Henesey interview, 2012)

Michael Parkinson argues that Liverpool turned in on itself in the 1980s.

I think the wider story is that Liverpool really had become a closed society. It wasn't listening or hearing other voices from other places in retrospect [...]. I think in a way we had become too insular, the level of public debate was narrow and the political debate I think had been debased for a long period of time. (Michael Parkinson interview, 2012)

Maurice Gubbins worked for the Government Office on Merseyside from the 1990s through the city's revitalisation. He recalls the long process of building up trust between the council and central government when, with the replacement of Margaret Thatcher with John Major, Michael Heseltine took control of government policy towards the cities. Councils, ignored by Mrs Thatcher, got a new, more central role as partners, not pariahs (Stewart 1995). Gubbins reports that trust was built up slowly:

a fair degree of people skills came into play. Working in a scenario where a close relationship with John Flamson and his team became more proactive. He would say 'I wouldn't do that if I were you', or 'Why don't you try and present that a little more like this, or that?' so we became, rather than critical head bangers, on opposite sides of the table, we gradually evolved it into a more constructive, ongoing critical but constructive relationship. And we found surprisingly that Ministers, Tory Ministers, moved on too, and were proactive, visited regularly. We had good working relations, even handedness.

This openness from government, post Thatcher, contrasted with that of the 1980s, but even then, problems remained: Gubbins recalls continuing bad press knocking Liverpool long after the departure of the militant (with a small 'm') Labour Council

> The more balanced people were in that mindset of moving on, and proving to people that they were moving on. And one of the biggest issues that they struggled with was how do we get over this continual bad press? How do we persuade the London media and people in the South that things are changing, and demonstrate that things had changed, as the media mindset was still stuck in the '80s. How do we get the good news stories out, and we accepted that that would be a long term process, a drip drip drip, so communications and ways of working with friendly media?

Some in the media wanted to reproduce stereotypes about Liverpudlians, but others recognised the very deep structural problems that remained. Such issues were only addressed when large amounts of European Union funding came online. Again, this contrasts with the Labour Council of the 1980s where no such funds were available and instead it was forced to struggle against major government cuts in its budget. Gubbins recalls:

> There was a mixture of all that going on. 'Oh, they feel so sorry for themselves all the time, why don't they move on,' or 'there's so much unemployment, how [do] you work with them?' and there was the more thoughtful, Liverpool is where it is, physically, its out on a limb, there is so much work to do, this feels like a mountain to climb. And even the beginning of Objective One, EU funding, if felt like throwing a pebble into a large lake in terms of the impact that was going to have, how long it's going to take to make a difference.

Unhelpful distinctions were made with Manchester:

What you found was a lot of people from all sectors that were deeply committed to making a difference and turning it around, and I think that they were all conscious that they had been talking to senior officials in Whitehall that it was a long term job as there was the mixed-up attitude, 'that's been a problem place, that's been a difficult place, where is the evidence that is changing or has changed?' So while there was a lot of earnestness from a wide range of people, the back-cloth of the decline that had taken place, the physical location of it out on a limb, and the comparisons that began to emerge at that time, the constant comparisons with Manchester, and at least Manchester's ability to present itself so much more positively, more eloquently, without so much of the baggage of poverty, still applies today. The political baggage seems to have got Manchester in a different place. So it was all mixed up. They were all aware of the economic problems, the location problems, the history problems, the unemployment issues, the chippy scouser, it was all there.

Gubbins argues that things only began to change when central government began to see a council as a partner, someone to be worked with, not fought against:

In all fairness to Tory governments, it was only in the 1980s that we started to see cities as generators of jobs and opportunities and leisure in a way that we didn't in the 1950s, '60s and '70s … The job was enormous. The lack of investment, the lack of proactive work by the previous councils, lack of private sector engagement and confidence, there must be government culpability for allowing a city to fall into such a decline and not addressing it earlier. Perhaps politicians weren't as focused as they could have been on what they should have been doing. The private sector was not as involved as it could have been. But the job was enormous: we are very aware of how many billions have been poured into it and look at the job that there is still to do. The size of the job is important, to keep in balance.

It took the Capital of Culture year to show that things have changed:

One of the things I didn't expect was the massive turn around in perception about the city that happened around the time of Capital of

Culture. It seems obvious now, but that was more of a turning point than many of the other really, really good things that have been done. It grabbed the media attention in a really good way.

People who are scousers, have always lived here, used to say to me: 'We've lost our confidence'. And that's where this chippy exterior comes from. When you have inflexible, bureaucratic civil servants saying things should be better than this and people scrabbling around not getting the support they need, you'd get problems. Fault lies on both sides,

Mike Henesey argues that the revitalisation of Liverpool has largely been achieved by public, not private money:

When you get people up here, particularly people who remember that period, they come up and they go 'Wow, look at it now, look at the changes' and I just think it's slightly ironic that the bulk of the changes have been on the back of European and public sector money. Yes, you can't dispute Liverpool One and the impact that's had, massive but I question whether Liverpool One would have happened if there wasn't all the other stuff going on and the investment of European money. That's been the big show, and the impact that that's had has been significant. (Mike Henesey interview, 2012)

In contrast to the 1980s when central government adopted a more punitive approach to local councils through rate capping, budget cuts and through the imposition of unelected quangos, today things are very different. The greater willingness of local authority, central government, and the wider public, private and voluntary sectors to work together in collaboration is a radical departure from the 1980s. Mike Henesey argues,

when I think about my early time in the benefit office where there was a thing about closing the door, turning off the light, throwing away the key and I look at where we are and think 'God help us' if we were still in that position with what's going on now. We would've just been a basket case. We have lifted ourselves up, and Capital of Culture was a key in the sense that it just changed perceptions and people are prepared to be interested in investing, you look at tourism and you look at the universities. What was the universities' involvement in this city back in the early '80s? They weren't involved. Now they are, now they're a key partner in everything that goes on. And I think that's been a big change in terms of what's gone on. (Mike Henesey interview, 2012)

## Beyond confrontation – housing

For its supporters, the council became known for its successes in building houses, leisure centres and Everton Park. The focus was, some would say, 'monomaniacal' regarding housing. Former councillor Paul Lafferty recalls:

> Tony Byrne wasn't a Militant but he was brutal in getting money and saying this is going to the housing budget. I suppose the answer was always you know if you haven't got a decent house to live in, you might have a sports centre up the road but if you're living in damp conditions, the greatest need would be housing. After that [it may be] somewhere to take the kids to swim and exercise. So housing and exercise/leisure facilities were the priorities and everything went to that. (Paul Lafferty interview, 2012)

The focus on housing was concrete, bricks and mortar:

> The Broad Left agreed that whilst we had the majority [in the council], we'd go for housing and building. They couldn't knock them down after we'd gone. They were there and whether they sold them or whatever they did, it didn't make any difference because people were in them. I think you've got to [remember] the terrible and absolutely disgraceful conditions people were living in. (Paul Lafferty interview, 2012)

The house building programme was for some, symbolic of Militant's and the Broad Left's ability to listen to what people needed but also to fulfil their promises. Jerry Spencer explains:

If there was any reason why I liked Militant, or respected them; it was because I actually thought they would do what they said they'd do. Was there a plan to build 5,000 houses, for instance? No. But are we going to build houses? Yes, we are. Are we going to reorganise the schools? Yes, we are [...] they'd listen to working people, ordinary people. Look to the state of the cities and say that we've got to do something about this ... I think it was a very genuine understanding of what ordinary people wanted and needed and a determination to give it to them. (Jerry Spencer interview, 2012)

This does not mean that there were no other priorities. Derek Hatton argues:

We would not have been able to do what we did unless we understood how the local government worked and how the local committees worked. We had to empty the bins. We had to create jobs. We had to build houses. We had to do all that. We all had to be the best councillors. (Derek Hatton interview, 2012)

Councillors were seen as good managers, giving clear instructions. Officers knew what was expected of them. Former councillor Harry Smith argues:

We were the only authority in the country to build any nursery schools. When you see athletes on the TV they are at the Centre for Excellence in the Dingle, we rebuilt that. They never say the 47 did that.

John Airs recalls how initiatives like the Parent School Partnership, which was under constant threat, offered a 'life-line' to some:

My wife worked for Parent School Partnership, working with parents in schools, I got to know some brilliant working class parents through her. The PSP was under threat every year, we had to go and lobby and demonstrate so they did not withdraw it. There were people who said 'this saved my life'. (John Airs interview, 2012)

Paul Lafferty echoes the sense of commitment and accountability councillors felt towards their communities:

[as a council] we were saying this is a way forward we felt then and I'm sure we still feel now that if you say you're going to do something then you do it you have to represent people and if you say this is what you are going to do then you do it [...]. It sounds simplistic doesn't it? (Paul Lafferty – workshop interview, 2011)

Heather Adams is still proud today of the contribution the Labour council made to greater levels of social justice in spite of obstacles:

When I think of social justice I think of raising people out of poverty, helping people reach their full potential. Whether it is children doing well in the education system, helping elderly people stay independent as long as possible, helping disabled people achieve their full potential I think we made a contribution to that in Liverpool in the '80s. I do not think that these things can be tackled on a large scale unless we have a government that is committed to doing it. (Heather Adams – workshop interview, 2011)

But things were not always so rosy. Ian Lowes reflects on the tensions encountered by a socialist council working within the restrictions of the system:

Tony is right, you can't have socialism in one country, certainly can't have [it] in one city, but it was a question of raising people's conscious-ness. We have a Labour socialist council [we] should try to do things within the confines of the system in which we are working and we would like to do more but we can't. We would like to build 20,000 houses, we would like to create 10,000 jobs and so on and so forth. Working within the capitalist system it is limited what you can do. They [the council] demonstrated in a practical way what could be achieved so it was a question of politicising people who think there was a fair amount of success. (Ian Lowes – workshop interview, 2011)

Jerry Spencer reflects that perhaps the council's determination to fulfil its pledges ultimately became its weakness:

I think potentially you might say that that was their undoing in the end. I think you can call it integrity, but that sticking to what we said we would do became, in a sense, the last line of defence. We wrapped ourselves in the red flag as it were, and went down blazing, as it were. But, I can't attack that. You can say that that was not necessarily the sensible thing to do and perhaps we should've modified and bent a little bit, but you can't criticise people for doing what they said they were going to do. (Jerry Spencer interview, 2012)

Nevertheless, this does not detract from the fact for some, winning control in 1983 and beyond and the subsequent achievements were

a vindication of working class politics. It shows that a radical agenda can succeed. It was a sort of vindication of Militant politics as well when it said we were going to take power in '84 and then suddenly we're in power. It shows what we can do. When the working class sets its mind to something, it shows what can be achieved. (Jerry Spencer interview, 2012)

Many simple but practical initiatives were introduced to improve communities:

One of the things that we actually did was really funny [laughs[. Pavements for instance, all the lighting on pavements point out onto the road, [and we thought] why don't we turn them round and point them on the people? And I think that says everything about us really. (Paul Lafferty – workshop interview, 2011)

In a recent letter in the *Liverpool Echo* (13 April 2012) supporting Tony Mulhearn's candidacy for Mayor in 2012, significantly reference is made to the housing, school and nursery legacy of those years:

[Mulhearn] and his colleagues from the so-called 'militant era' fought the Tories when Thatcher was in power, so they could build houses for people in Liverpool and I mean built council houses not private houses that people can't afford. Also they built schools and nurseries. You only have to look around Liverpool to see the proof. If that's being militant, bring it back. People only believe what the press feed them.

Opponents of the council have made charges that it was not interested in working with the private sector. Former councillors recall many examples of perhaps unsung, public-private initiatives:

> There were certain projects for the elderly that I wanted to do and I was looking at ways in which we could actually tie in with the government – have a sort of joint funding between the council and private [funds]. We actually identified a few places, had the borough solicitor start looking at whether we could buy them to actually mingle community with some private money. If I'd have still been on the council that would have been a major thing we'd have done because we'd identified the property, identified where we could get the money ... did a feasibility study on them.

> At the time they were selling off lock, stock and barrel the older people's homes. My idea was to have some community involvement by paying for some of it through community and not just leave it to private enterprise which was a disaster and still is. Some businesses were expanding private homes and they would happily have gone in with us because they would have had our expertise, the size of the council, and we'd been happy to have their money. It would've been an equal partnership [...] On principle the Broad Left [agreed] and [appreciated] what [I was] trying to do, but Byrne said that's what we should be doing next year. Course we never had a next year. (Paul Lafferty interviewed 2012)

Councillor John Nelson recalls working with city centre business:

> In 1985 the City Council spent £6000 on the Christmas lights and it was a disaster and we said 'Look, it is the big thing for the businesses within the city'. In 1986 I was chair of the licence committee. Everything was going for house building, and I said [to a group of local businesses including Chairman of Marks and Spencer's] that we will give you up to £25,000 for the lights if you go pound for pound. And we had £50,000 for the lights. We had the most fantastic Christmas lights. We certainly did things like that. (John Nelson – workshop interview, 2011)

Late night shopping was brought into the city centre in the face of trade union opposition. John Nelson recalls:

> USDAW wanted to stop at eight o'clock on Thursday night. I thought it was a nonsense and I persuaded the group, Thursday night people in Liverpool wanted to go to the shops. To be honest with you I did it under the delegated powers as soon as they made me the chairman I just went and did it ... There was pandemonium over at first but then everyone said great. We did things like that sometimes it was unpopular I never always kowtowed to the trade unions because they were not always right and quite often I was unpopular, but we did do things like that it certainly wasn't a one-way street. (John Nelson – workshop interview, 2011)

Dave Lloyd recalls working closely with business:

> With the crisis and other things going on we always used to talk to business, Clayton Square development, the Cavern Quarter, Liverpool City Council money went into that. They were all under our administration. I remember going to a Chamber of Commerce meeting. And the Chamber of Commerce has actually given credit for the employment that we created because of the positive attitudes we had to industry.

He argues:

> I guarantee that that housing building programme created at least five times the jobs, proper jobs, trained jobs, apprenticeships, than jobs in Liverpool One and if Liverpool One is looking for business what does someone do when they go into a home? They buy curtains, they buy flooring, and they buy TVs. So we create an economy. (Dave Lloyd – workshop interview, 2011)

Tony Mulhearn remembers working with the Task Force and Merseyside Development Corporation:

> As a general principle we did work with all agencies from the point of view of getting as much as we could out of them. Often Derek

and Tony arranged meetings with the Task Force over something or other just to try and extract what they could out of the situation. [As an example], the Garden Festival was trumpeted by Heseltine and we were cast as the villains who opposed. Our position was very clear. We said, you want to develop the Garden Festival, fine. What Heseltine did was the money was extracted from our budget to pay for the Garden Festival. I mean it was just a blatant discrimination and of course Heseltine took all the credit, blamed the council for being obstructive, when it was a gigantic lie. We were prepared to work with any agency providing we could maintain our socialist programme and extract what we could from what was available, government funding. (Tony Mulhearn – workshop interview, 2011)

Paul Lafferty argues that the council was not opposed to what government agencies were doing, but it did not think that they had the right priorities: 'it was fireworks and the big profile things but we had a programme to actually improve the lives of people. It is first things first and that is 'what we believed in.' (Workshop interview, 2011) John Nelson argues 'at no stage did we have an obstructive attitude we never said we would get in their way or that we would be awkward, it was just that if they wanted to talk to us we would talk to them. If we thought we would get something out of them we would go and meet them.' (Workshop interview, 2011) The 47 argued that accusations claiming they did not work with other agencies were overblown.

## What does it all mean?

The choices taken by the Labour Council in the 1980s are routinely contrasted with the pragmatism of the following Labour administrations of Harry Rimmer and then Joe Anderson, and that of the Liberal Democrats under Mike Storey and then Warren Bradley. Under a more pragmatic administration, it is argued, the city turned the corner. In the current environment of cuts and austerity, Joe Anderson continues to speak out. In January 2013 he organised a summit in Liverpool of the leaders of northern cities similarly affected by the cuts. He organised an online petition arguing for fairness. Again, the current Bishop of Liverpool argued in defence of the city. But no one in power argued that today's councils should follow the example of the Liverpool Council of the 1980s.

That's not to say that the new pragmatism is unchallenged. Tony Mulhearn stood against Joe Anderson in the Mayoral contest on an anti-cuts platform. In his election manifesto, Mulhearn argued:

> All the parties in the council chamber have shamefully voted to carry out eye-watering cuts decided in Whitehall and Westminster by the bankers' best friends. My colleagues and I in the Trade Unionist and Socialist Coalition say: 'The bankers brought on this crisis, let them pay for it'.

Current MP Louise Ellman argues that Tony Mulhearn's approach was rejected at the ballot box, fairly decisively:

> The political situation is now completely different as shown by the 2012 mayoral election result where Joe Anderson received 58,448 votes [59.3 per cent] for the Labour party and Tony Mulhearn came 5th with 4,792 [4.86 per cent] votes for the Trade Unionist and Socialist Coalition. I support Joe's approach. He led the march through the streets of Liverpool against government cuts but also faced up to the consequences of government attacks on funding for Liverpool. At the same time, he tried to secure the best deal for the city in, for example, securing the cruise ships terminal, enabling cruise ships to stop and start in Liverpool, and City Deal. Both of these policies required negotiating with a Tory Minister.

> We must make our strong opposition to Tory/Lib Dem cuts clear, but at the same time, negotiate with Ministers and encourage positive investment. I don't think the approach taken in the '80s would resonate now. (Louise Ellman interviewed 2012)

Militant opponent Gideon Ben-Tovim agrees:

> If there is a benign side to their making a contribution to Liverpool, then to go to that edge of expelling themselves from office clearly was a mistake. To suggest now in the current context in 2012, as I think some former Militant people are still saying, 'oh you

shouldn't be doing this you should be standing up to the government, you should refuse to pass on Government cuts, you should set an illegal budget' then I think that is just irresponsible [...] I think a Labour council has no choice but to try to get the best deal possible for its citizens, to try to make the least harmful cuts, to try to take people with you, to fight the good fight with the government as hard as you can, but stay within the bounds of legality – this is the strategy being adopted by the Labour Council in Liverpool and I fully support that approach. To just say 'Well we don't want to do this. We are fighting the Government. We are all resigning by acting illegally, that would be the principled thing to do,' that would be making a gesture but doing no favours to the people of Liverpool and to the transformed reputation of the City. Local politics is about continuing to try to get the best deal you can, trying to keep your values and principles, and trying to work them through in the real world, as, inclusively as you can with local citizens. (Gideon Ben-Tovim interview, 2012)

Derek Hatton defends his legacy but argues that it needs to be seen as of its time. 'If we could not do it in the '80s there is not a chance in this world that even thinking about it now. Not even a chance', he now argues. In the *Liverpool Echo* (14 May 2011), Hatton argued that today's Labour Council would have committed 'political suicide' if it had set an 'illegal' budget, as it has come to be known. While Hatton argued that if he had his time again he would not do anything differently, he felt that the city was unlikely to see the kind of resistance that saw thousands of people take to the streets of Liverpool to oppose the Tories in the 1980s. He argues:

People accept the status quo now, but history has shown time and time again that without challenge there's no change [...] There are people out there who still take the line that we should do what we did in the 1980s, but the danger with that is assuming the conditions are the same as they were in the 1980s. The fact is, they're not. I remember the editor of the *Echo* at the time saying he could 'taste the pre-revolutionary sentiment walking down Dale Street'. When you look at the situation now [...] the comparison is virtually non-existent.

While it's OK to say they should put up a fight, in all fairness to Joe [Anderson] I think it's probably unrealistic. [...] I would not be one of those to argue he should do what we did in the 1980s. It would be political suicide.

In the '80s, we thought it was worth a go [...] Everyone gets some of the tactical things wrong, but overall I don't regret one bit of it. (Waddington 2011)

Proponents of a new struggle today against the coalition led by local authorities argue that the lessons of the 1980s Liverpool Council are many. Its stand was part of a much longer process throughout the 1970s of slowly building up the movement that took power in 1983, developing policies through the District Labour Party, and building support in the wider community and in the trade unions. Many speak of the way Liverpool was politicised during those years, elements of which remain today:

I think that the legacy that it has left in those years [is that the] municipal elections had over 50 per cent voting. It has never happened again we actually politicised the people and some of those policies and some of those ideals that we left are still there now in the community, for future generations.

However, Mark Campbell reflects that the world is very different now:

I was involved in preparing food parcels for miners and standing on picket lines at Sutton Manor colliery and the rest of it and it was right at that time. But, there's no doubt that after the miners' strike everything changed. I'd go with Joe Anderson, because he's an honest man of the day. I think the political landscape has changed so much, It was right at the time. (Mark Campbell interview, 2012)

Current councillor and Militant opponent Steve Munby feels that one of the lessons from the Militant period is the need to look after ordinary working class Liverpudlians: those who lost out when the manufacturing and port jobs left the city, and who have been marooned ever since. He argues,

There was a wave of working class people in their 30s, 40s and 50s who lost their jobs from the decimation of unskilled manual occupations. They'd be in their 50s, 60s or 70s now. Militant particularly appealed to that layer of people. They'd been left high and dry and we haven't really known what to do to help them – I mean they're stuffed. Capital of Culture didn't help them, or they've just ended up on the long term sick.

We haven't come up with good political solutions for them. Militant had something that spoke to their beliefs and values and needed them. But it ended up leaving a lot of them betrayed, stranded. I think that challenge is still there … particularly in north Liverpool, and as an administration now we are trying to address that in different ways. We shouldn't walk away from that responsibility politically to unskilled working class people. They are not unskilled – there is a generation of really funny, literate, interesting people in Liverpool who were left high and dry by Thatcherism, and they matter. (Steve Munby interview, 2012)

This is a group that the Labour Council of the 1980s stood up for, though not always as effectively as it could have done. Attitudes to Liverpool's black community and towards identity politics were deeply problematic. Opportunities to make deals with Government were missed through a misplaced triumphalism. The political culture was, at best, robust. Of course, every political party has its wilder side, and makes mistakes: but to characterise the whole of what is lazily called the 'Militant' period as a missed opportunity is too simplistic. The Liverpool Labour Council of the early 1980s was composed of ordinary Liverpool folk, with all their passions and faults. It spoke for many of those who have been left behind by Liverpool's revitalisation – that is worth acknowledging. Perhaps only when *all* Liverpudlians feel part of a prosperous, inclusive, equal and sustainable city will we be able to call Liverpool's revitalisation a success and a cause for celebration.

# BIBLIOGRAPHY

Alcock, P., 'Welfare rights and wrongs: the limits of local anti-poverty strategies', *Local Economy*, vol. 9, no. 2 (1994), pp 134–152.

author unknown, 'Economic Change in Liverpool and the role of the Local
Authority', (1985).

Beckett, A., *When the Lights Went Out: Britain in the Seventies* (Faber and
Faber: London, 2010).

Ben-Tovim, G. (ed.), *Equal Opportunities and the Employment of Black People
and Ethnic Minorities on Merseyside* (MAREE: Liverpool, 1983).

Bennett, A., *Untold Stories* (Faber and Faber: London, 2005).

Beynon, H., *Working for Ford* (Penguin Educational: Harmondsworth, 1973).

Boddy, M. and Fudge, C. (eds), *Local Socialism* (Macmillan: London 1984).

CDP, *Gilding the Ghetto: The State and the Poverty Experiments* (CDP Inter-
Project Editorial Team: London, 1977).

Couch, C., *City of change and challenge: urban planning and regeneration in
Liverpool* (Ashgate: Aldershot, 2003).

Crick, M., *Militant* (Faber and Faber: London, 1984).

Darlington, R. and Lyddon, D., *Glorious Summer: Class Struggle in Britain, 1972*
(Bookmarks: London, 2001).

David, R., 'Why the Mersey Sound is off Key', *Financial Times,* 2 February
1979, p. 6.

Du Noyer, P., *Liverpool – Wondrous Place: Music from the Cavern to the Capital of
Culture* (Virgin Books: London, 2002).

Dunn, A., 'Liberals look for Liverpool victory in the wake of Labour troubles',
*The Guardian*, 21 March 1987, p. 3.

Frost, D. and Phillips, R. *Liverpool '81: Remembering the Riots* (Liverpool University Press: Liverpool, 2011).

Gifford, A. M., Brown, W., et al., *Loosen the Shackles: First Report of the Liverpool 8 Inquiry into Race Relations in Liverpool* (Karia Press: London, 1989).

Hain, P., *Radical Regeneration: Protest, Direct Action and Community Politics* (Quartet Books: London, 1975).

Hamilton Fazey, I., 'Liverpool in dialogue with Ridley', *Financial Times*, 5 August 1987.

Harvey, D., 'From Managerialism to Entrepreneurialism: the transformation in urban governance in late capitalism', *Geografiska Annaler*, Series B, Human Geography, vol. 71, no. 1 (1989), pp 3–17.

Harvey, D., 'From Managerialism to Entrepreneurialism: the transformation in urban governance in late capitalism', *Spaces of Capital* (Edinburgh University Press: Edinburgh, 2001), pp 345–368.

Hatton, D., *Inside Left: the story so far* (Bloomsbury: London, 1988).

Hernon, I., 'Echo correspondent Ian Hernon interviews Lord Heseltine on the Toxteth riots', 6 July 2011: http://www.liverpoolecho.co.uk/liverpool-news/toxteth-riots/toxteth-riots-stories/2011/07/06/echo-correspondent-ian-hernon-interviews-lord-heseltine-on-the-toxteth-riots-100252-29001276/#ixzz2BdewCKtd. Last accessed 14 February 2013.

Heseltine, M., *Life in the Jungle: My Autobiography* (Hodder & Stoughton: London, 2000).

Hickling, P., 'It's like San Francisco – with greyer weather', 21 February 2007: http://www.guardian.co.uk/culture/2007/feb/21/europeancapitalofculture2008.liverpool. Last accessed 14 February 2013.

Humphrey, D. and John, G., *Police Power and Black People* (Panther: London, 1972).

Hunt, T., *Building Jerusalem: The Rise and Fall of the Victorian City* (Phoenix: London, 2005).

Kilfoyle, P., *Left Behind: Lessons from Labour's Heartland* (Politicos: London, 2000).

Kilroy-Silk, R., *Hard Labour* (Chatto and Windus: London, 1986).

Lane, T., *Liverpool: Gateway of Empire* (Lawrence & Wishart: London, 1987).

Liverpool Black Caucus, *The Racial Politics of Militant in Liverpool: The black community's struggle for participation in local politics 1980–1986* (Merseyside Area Profile Group and Runnymede Trust: Liverpool and London, 1986).

Mackintosh, M. and Wainwright, H. (eds), *A Taste of Power: the Politics of Local Economics* (Verso: London, 1987).

McNabb, P., 'Integration in Liverpool: a Definition of the Problem', Parliamentary Select Committee on Race Relations and Immigration, 'The Problems of Coloured School Leavers'. Evidence taken at Liverpool in March (HMSO: London, 1969).

McSmith, A., *No Such Thing as Society: a History of Britain in the 1980s* (Constable: London, 2011).

Melish, I., Ben-Tovim, G. S., et al., 'Patterns of Discriminatory Behaviour by Police and in the Courts Facing the Locally Born Black Population in Liverpool', Parliamentary Select Committee on Race Relations and Immigration, Police/Immigrant Relations, vol. 2 (HMSO: London, 1972).

Melish, I., McNabb, P., et al., 'The Relevance of "Race" to Education Opportunity in Inner City Liverpool', Parliamentary Select Committee on Race Relations and Immigration, 'Education', vol. 3 (HMSO: London, 1973).

Merseyside County Council, *Agenda for Merseyside* (Merseyside County Council: Liverpool, 1985).

Merseyside Socialist Research Group, *Merseyside in Crisis* (Merseyside Socialist Research Group: Birkenhead, 1980).

Militant, *Liverpool Fights the Tories* (Militant Publications: London, 1984).

Munby, S., 'Municipal Militancy', *Marxism Today* (September 1985), pp 45–46.

Murden, J., 'City of Change and Challenge: Liverpool since 1945' in J. Belchem (ed.), *Liverpool 800: Culture, Character and History* (Liverpool University Press: Liverpool, 2006).

O'Brien, M., 'Liverpool 1911 and its era: Foundational Myth or Authentic Tradition?' in J. Belchem and B. Biggs (eds), *Liverpool: City of Radicals* (Liverpool University Press: Liverpool, 2011).

Parkinson, M., *Liverpool on the brink: one city's struggle against Government cuts* (Policy Journals: Hermitage, Berks, 1985).

Parkinson, M., 'Liverpool's fiscal crisis: an anatomy of failure', in M. Parkinson, B. Foley and D. Judd, *Regenerating the cities: The UK crisis and the US experience* (University of Manchester Press: Manchester, 1988).

Parkinson, M., 'Leadership and Regeneration in Liverpool: Confusion, Confrontation, or Coalition?' in D. Judd and M. Parkinson, *Leadership and Urban Regeneration: Cities in North America and Europe* (Sage Publications: London, 1990), pp 241–257.

Parkinson, M. and Bianchini, F., 'Liverpool: a tale of missed opportunities' in F. Bianchini and M. Parkinson, *Cultural Policy and Urban Regeneration: the West European Experience* (Manchester University Press: Manchester, 1993) pp 155–177.

Parkinson, M. and Duffy, J., 'Government's Response to Inner City Riots: Minister for Merseyside and Task Force', *Parliamentary Affairs* 37, vol. 1 (1984), pp 76–96.

Peck, J. and Tickell, A., 'Business goes local: dissecting the "business agenda" in Manchester', *International Journal of Urban and Regional Research*, vol. 19 (1995), pp 55–78.

Phelps, P., 'Hard Left is a Hard Fact', *Liverpool Echo*, 10 December 1981, p. 6.

Quilley, S., 'Manchester's "Village in the City": The Gay Vernacular in a post-industrial landscape of power', paper presented to Conference 'The Politics of Cultural Change', University of Lancaster, July 1994.

Shennan, P., 'Derek Hatton: I'll never retire … but I'd have a facelift', *Liverpool Echo*, 16 January 2008: http://www.liverpoolecho.co.uk/liverpool-life/ liverpool-lifestyle/2008/01/16/derek-hatton-i-ll-never-retire-but-i-d-have-a-facelift-100252-20355998/. Last accessed 14 February 2013.

Singleton, K., 'Revolting Tenants: The Great Abercromby Rent Strike of '69' *NERVE* 15 winter (2009).

Small, S., 'Racialised relations in Liverpool: A contemporary anomaly', *New Community*, vol. 18, no. 1 (1991), pp 511–537.

Stack, P. and Watson, M., 'City in Crisis: the Liverpool Experience', *Socialist Worker Review*, vol. 76 (1985), pp 10–11.

Stewart, M., 'Between Whitehall and Town Hall: the realignment of urban regeneration policy in England', *Policy and Politics*, vol. 22, no. 2 (1995), pp 133–146.

Taaffe, P. and Mulhearn, T., *Liverpool, a city that dared to fight* (Fortress Books: London, 1988).

Waddington, M., 'Derek Hatton: Repeating what militant did would be "political suicide" for Labour in Liverpool today', *Liverpool Echo*, 14 May 2011: http://www.liverpooldailypost.co.uk/liverpool-news /regional-news/2011/05/14/derek-hatton-repeating-what-militant-did-would-be-political-suicide-for-labour-in-liverpool-today-100252-28692408/#ixzz1VI8OSwg8. Last accessed 14 February 2013.

Wainwright, H., *Labour: a tale of two parties* (Chatto and Windus: London, 1987).

Watson, M., 'The Bleeding of Liverpool', *Socialist Worker Review*, vol. 80 (1985), pp 16–17.

Zack-Williams, A. B., 'African Diaspora Conditioning: The case of Liverpool', *Journal of Black Studies*, vol. 27, no. 4 (1997), pp 528–542.

# ENDNOTES

1 Dunlop, English Electric (planes), Albright and Wilson (chemicals), Kodak, BICC (cables), John Dickinson (stationery), Hartley's Jam, Crawford's Biscuits, Bird's Eye, AC Spark Plug, Fisher-Bendix, Kraft Foods, Otis Elevator, Yorkshire Imperial Metals, Distillers, Glaxo.

2 See Singleton, K. (2009) 'Revolting Tenants: The Great Abercromby Rent Strike of '69' *NERVE* 15 Winter for a discussion of this in the Abercromby area.

3 www.merseybasin.org.uk

4 BBC News: 'History repeats itself for Heseltine', 6 March 2006. Available at http://news.bbc.co.uk/1/hi/uk_politics/4778766.stm

5 Ibid.

6 'Capitalisation' means moving spending (in this case on housing repairs) from day to day spending – revenue – which needs to be raised from the rates to long term spending on infrastructure that did not count against day to day spending – capital.)

7 Ben-Tovim, G. (1980) (ed.) *Racial Disadvantage in Liverpool: An Area Profile*. Liverpool; Ben-Tovim, G. (1983) *Equal Opportunities and the Employment of Black People and Ethnic Minorities on Merseyside*. 'Liverpool; Race and Housing in Liverpool – a research report' (1984), Commission for Racial Equality

8 'Race and Housing in Liverpool – a research report' (1984), Commission for Racial Equality

9 Liberal Democrat Party election leaflet, Liverpool, mid-1990s.

# INDEX

Adams, Heather 106, 142–3, 198
Airs, John
    intimidation allegations 173–4
    Labour supporter 39, 43–4, 125
    Militant arrogance 169
    Militant expulsions 176–7
    public support for policies 73
    social conditions 9, 10
Alliance Party (Liverpool) 181, 183
Anderson, Joe 3, 187, 202, 203
Association of Metropolitan Authorities
    116

Benn, Tony 72
Bennett, Alan 67
Ben-Tovim, Gideon
    council co-operation (2012) 203–4
    equality initiatives 141–2, 144, 167
    Militant strategy criticized 113
    'municipal Stalinism' 129, 174–5
    political responsibility 92–3
    Sampson Bond affair 151–2, 153,
        154, 155–6, 160
Benyon, Huw 40
Birchall, Tommy 33
black community (Liverpool)
    council initiatives, post-Militant 168
    Council's discrimination 144–5, 147

marginalization, history of 130–3
marginalization, reaction to 138–9,
    169
Militant's disinterest 39, 128, 134–5,
    141–2
race equality, call for 133–4
Sampson Bond, Black opposition
    147–8, 156, 158–63
Bleasdale, Alan 2
Blunkett, David 2, 69, 72, 102, 108–9
Bohanna, John 65
Bond, Sampson
    appointment, opposition to 123–4,
        129–30, 141, 155–63, 166–7, 169
    appointment process 128, 147–54
Booth, Anthony 39
Byrne, Tony
    budget crisis 1985 105, 107
    equality measures sidelined 142
    housing programme 98, 99–100,
        196–7
    Jenkin's settlement 83–4, 97
    left wing councillor 29
    Stonefrost Report, response to
        117–18
    Swiss bank loans 119–20

Campbell, Mark 11, 77, 90–1, 114, 205

city councils
    funding cuts, response to  2, 67–70
    'no rate cut' budgets  102–4
    'nuclear-free' status  70, 123
    post-Thatcher partnerships  192
    protest and compromise  113
Community Development Programme
    (CDP)  11–12
Coombes, Keva  183, 184, 185
Costello, Ray  161
Crick, Michael  71
Crossland, Anthony  68
Croxteth Comprehensive dispute  53–4
Cunningham, Jack  72, 80, 81

Daily Post  15, 46, 133
Deane, Brian  33
Deane, Jimmy  33
Dillon, James  50–1, 60, 166
District Auditor
    budget illegality  103–4
    councillor dismissals  106, 107, 108–9
    dismissal challenged  180–1
Dunlop, Pauline  79

Ellman, Louise  63, 112, 124, 172, 203

Farrell, John  171–2
Fields, Terry  48
Financial Times  15
Flamson, John  19, 28, 63–4, 189, 190,
    191
Ford, Gerald, President  67
Furlong, Trevor  186–7

Garden Festival  25
Gilding The Ghetto (Alcock)  12
Ginsburg, Allen  8–9
GMWU  14
Grant, Ted  33
Gubbins, Maurice  192–4

Hain, Peter  43
Hamilton, John  29, 45, 75, 84, 96,
    180–1
Harrison, Terry  33, 41, 48
Harvey, David  68, 179
Hatton, Derek
    anti-cuts campaigns  102

budget cuts, national issue  72–3
    character analysis  122
    council choices (2011)  204–5
    councillor priorities  62–3, 197
    docks, decline of  10
    election '83 success  56–7, 58
    election '86 success  182
    funding victory  84–7
    funds shortage  118
    Labour Party expulsion  182
    'middle class' leftists  97
    Militant, belief in  35, 36
    ministerial rebuke  73–4
    ministerial visit  82
    MP candidate  48
    municipal enterprise  46–7
    policy implementation  61–2
    public spending cuts  14–15
    redundancy backlash  108
    residents' opinion  101
    Sampson Bond appointment  128,
        129–30, 148–9, 151, 154, 156–8,
        163, 164
    Thatcher rebuke  97
    'workerist' mentality  172
Heath, Ted  41–2
Henesey, Mike  18–19, 21–2, 24, 187,
    190–2, 195–6
Heseltine, Michael  4, 20–1, 25, 26, 54,
    71, 181, 185, 192
Heysel Stadium tragedy  104
Hodge, Margaret  2, 102
Hogan, Mike
    anti-cuts campaigns  102
    campaign unit activities  95–6
    funding victory  88
    Militant sell-out?  121
    Militant supporter  34, 76–7
    redundancy notices  114–15
    social conditions  18
    union relations  110–11, 120

Jenkin, Patrick
    budget mishandling  73–4, 79–80, 96,
        98–9
    financial legislation  100
    funding settlement  83–4, 85
    Liverpool's poverty realised  81–2
Jones, Trevor  80, 134, 183

Joseph, Keith 54

Kemp, Richard 16
Kennedy, Jane 115–16
Kennedy, Malcolm
    confrontation, wrong strategy 90,
        187
    government confrontation 64
    Labour supporter 32–3
    Militant opponent 37–8, 189–90
    redundancy notices 115–16
    Swiss bank loans 120
Kilfoyle, Peter
    anti-Militant campaign 181
    city's political history 125, 126
    council leadership failures 27–8
    docks, decline of 20, 190
    election '92 win 186
    Heseltine's efforts praised 26
    intimidation allegations 170–2, 173
    job security 40–1
    left wing councillor 29
    Militant's legacy 188–9
    Sampson Bond affair 162, 167
    Swiss bank loans 119–20
    unequal opportunities 131–2
Kilroy-Silk, Robert 16–17
King, Thomas, Lord 171
Kinnock, Neil
    budget cuts 72, 75
    budget talks 81
    Conference speech (1985) 1–2, 116
    Liverpool addressed 118–19
    Liverpool militancy, attitude to 2–3,
        96–7, 122

Labour Party (Liverpool)
    1950s–70s 32–3
    bullying and intimidation allegations
        170–1
    changing membership 43–8, 49–51
    election '83 campaign 54–6, 58–9
    election '83 success 48, 53, 56–8
    election '86 181–2
    election '87 success 183
    intimidation allegations 172–5
    Labour Party expulsions 182
    local election success (1984) 80
    Militant arrogance 176

Militant policy, distrust of 37–9
Sampson Bond protest 156–8, 162–3
'sensible six' split 75, 90–1
suspension 122, 181
suspension and expulsion 122
'workerist' mentality 171–2
Labour Party (National)
    council budgets 72
    Liverpool Militants' expulsion 122,
        176–7, 181, 182
    settlement advice sort 92
Lafferty, Paul
    campaign against Militants 165
    city's militant reputation 109
    councillor responsibility 51, 197–8,
        202
    equality initiatives 137–8, 141,
        143–4, 145
    housing programme 196–7
    public private initiatives 200
    Sampson Bond affair 148–9, 153,
        157, 159, 163, 164, 166
    social conditions 50
Lane, Tony 40, 41
Liberal Party (Liverpool) 42–3, 46, 79
    see also Alliance Party
Liverpool
    '80s riots 4
    Capital of Culture boost 194–6
    challenging perceptions of 191–4
    Chinese community 143–4
    docks, rise and decline 8, 10–11, 20,
        41
    economic problems 190–1
    European Union funding 193, 195
    football hooligans 104
    job loss and economic decline 16–20,
        99
    leadership failure, legacy of 183–7
    Liverpool 8 unrest 138–9
    militant reputation 39–40, 109
    Militant Tendency, founding of 33
    motor industry 8, 40
    politics, sectarian divides 31–2, 125,
        126
    poor social conditions 7, 9–10, 13–14
    private sector policy 14–16
    race inequality 130–1
    regeneration schemes (1970s) 11–14

regeneration schemes (1980s) 21–7
reinvention, post 2000 3–4
Liverpool Against Militant 116, 118
Liverpool Black Caucus 141, 145, 156–7,
  162, 165
Liverpool City Council (1970s–80s)
  Broad Left initiatives 137–8
  equality measures sidelined 141–2
  gender inequality 135–6
  leadership failures 27–8, 42–3
  left wing not Militant 28–9
  Liberal proposals 16
  Liberal/Tory coalition 17
  Race Relations Liaison Committee,
    role thwarted 133–5, 139
  racial inequality 130–1
  rent strikes 41–2
  social services, ineffective 139
Liverpool City Council (1983–1985)
  arrogance and lost trust 169–70
  Budget Day, March 1984 76–80
  budget hopes dismissed 96, 97–9
  bullying and intimidation allegations
    172–3
  campaign against Militants 163–5
  campaign unit activities 95–6
  councillor dismissals 106, 180–1,
    182–3, 185
  councillor priorities 62–3, 201–2
  cuts, campaign against 2, 69, 70–5
  deficit budget and illegality 102–6
  deficit budget debate 107
  dissenters removed 146–7
  Equal Opportunities Committee, lack
    of 131, 141, 143, 145–6
  equality initiatives, mixed response
    141–5, 167–8
  finances examined 81
  funding victory, reactions to 83–9
  government confrontation, support
    for 63–5
  government funding demands 62
  introductory review 4–6
  Kinnock's response to militancy 2–3
  Militant sell-out? 121–2
  Militant strategy criticised 89–91,
    92–3, 112–13
  Militant's influence 123–5, 128–30
  Militant's legacy 189–91, 205–6

private money for housing 99–100
public private initiatives 200–1
public service achievements 196–9
public services debate 100–1
public support for policies 80
redundancy backlash 107–8, 110–11,
  114–16
Sampson Bond, Black opposition
  158–63, 166
Sampson Bond, protest against
  156–8
Sampson Bond, selection process
  147–54
'sensible six' councillors 75, 90–1
Stonefrost Report, response to
  117–18
Swiss banks to rescue 119–20
Thatcher snub 97
Liverpool City Council (1987–2010)
  183–7
Liverpool City Council (2010–) 203–4
*Liverpool Echo*
  budget talks 81
  city revival 185
  Kinnock's message 119
  Militant supporters 36–7
  Militant Tendency, legacy of 181–2
  Mulhearn supporter 199
  municipal enterprise (Hatton) 46–7
  Sampson Bond affair 163
  'Save our City campaign' 80
  Tory relations with city 184
  unemployment 104
Liverpool Inner City Partnership 12
Liverpool Labour Left 116, 117, 121
Livingstone, Ken 2, 69
Lloyd, David 49–50, 201
Lowes, Ian 44, 133, 136–7, 139–41,
  149–50, 198
Luckock, Paul
  budget crisis 1985 105
  dissenters removed 146–7
  election '83 campaign 54
  funding victory 87–8
  Mulhearn and intimidation 173–4
  Sampson Bond affair 152
  social conditions 13–14
  social services, ineffective 139

McCartney, Paul  122
McGann, Tony  182
Merseyside Community Relations
  Council  134, 141
Merseyside County Council  23–4, 26–7
Merseyside Plan (1944)  8, 9
Merseyside Structure Plan (1972)  9–10
Merseyside Task Force  21–4, 71, 83,
  190–1
Merseyside Urban Development
  Corporation  24–6, 28, 185, 190
Militant Tendency
  arrogance and lost trust  169–70,
    175–6
  bullying and intimidation allegations
    170–1, 172–3
  campaign against  163–5
  councillor dismissals  181
  founding of  33
  influence within council  29, 44–6,
    123–5
  Labour members' disquiet  37–9
  Labour Party expulsions  122, 176–7,
    182–3
  Labour Party liability  96–7, 189
  Liverpool Council leadership  2
  oppression only by class  135, 137,
    159, 167
  policies, attraction of  33–6, 44–5
  positive action sidelined  128–30
  proposed achievements  188
  rallying support  76–80, 89
  strikes and occupations  41–2, 76
  supporters sold out?  121–2
  'workerist' stance, appeal of  125–7
Mooney, Ted  33
Mulhearn, Tony
  campaign against Militants  165
  capitalism at fault  99, 202
  city politics  17
  councillor dismissals  109
  dispute activist  41
  election '83 campaign  59
  equality initiatives  144
  funding victory  89
  intimidation allegations  173
  Labour Party expulsion  182
  Labour Party fears  45
  Mayoral candidacy  199, 203

Militant supporter  33–4
Militant's influence  129
Militant's local support  71–2
MP candidate  48
redundancy backlash  108
Sampson Bond affair  152, 159–60,
  163
Munby, Steve
  confrontation, wrong strategy  78–9
  councillor responsibility  206
  Militant criticised  111, 113
  Sampson Bond affair  161–2, 165, 167
  Stonefrost Report  118

Nelson, John  50, 200–1, 202
Northern cities, attitude to  4

Parkinson, Michael
  funding settlement  84
  government confrontation  64–5,
    97–8
  intimidation allegations  174
  leadership failures  28, 42–3
  Liverpool, Tory dismissal  71
  Liverpool's misfortunes  188, 192
Patten, Brian  9

Race Relations Act (1976)  130, 134
rate support grant
  Liverpool's shortfall  62, 63, 72–3
  national recalculation  58
  rate capping  98
Redgrave, Vanessa  54
Revolutionary Socialist League  see
  Militant Tendency
Ridley, Nicholas  184
Right to Work campaign  17, 18
Rimmer, Harry  183–4, 185–6
Rimmer, Tony
  election '83 campaign  55–6, 60
  funding victory  86, 92
  Labour supporter  32
  making a stand  48
  ministerial visit  82–3
  Sampson Bond affair  149, 150–1,
    153, 159
Rutledge, Jimmy
  Budget Day rally 1984  78
  council policy  47–8

councillor dismissals 106
election '83 success 57–8
poor social conditions 15, 27
Sampson Bond affair 150, 156, 163
Rutledge, Paul 70, 88, 91

Samuels, Alex Scott 172–3, 176
Sefton, Bill 42
Semoff, Sam 135–6, 153–4, 157–8, 160, 163, 166, 168
Sheppard, David, Bishop 74–5, 116
Skinner, Dennis 182
Smith, Harry 49, 59, 130–1, 145–6, 150, 197
Social Democratic Party (SDP) 48
Socialist Review 111–12
Sorenson, Eric 83, 85
Speke Enterprise Zone 25
Spencer, Jerry
  initiatives reduced 146
  intimidation allegations 171
  Kinnock's speech 122
  Militant, contribution of 35–6, 124–5, 196–7
  Militant arrogance 175–6, 198–9
  Militant strategy criticised 112
  poor social conditions 19
  redundancy notices 114
  Sampson Bond affair 162, 164–5
Stonefrost Report 116–17, 122
Straw, Jack 73
strikes and occupations
  apprentice strike 1960 33
  Liverpool, reputation for 40–1
  rent strikes 1972 11, 41–2

Taaffe, Peter 17, 71–2, 108
Thatcher, Margaret
  dispute management 85, 91, 184
  Hatton rebuked 97
  Heseltine's efforts praised 26
  private sector policy 1, 16–17
  public spending cuts 14
Tinnion, Jeff 118
Tory Government (1979-1990)
  commissioner plan 81
  dispute management 85–6, 91, 184
  Liverpool, dismissal of 12, 71
  Liverpool demands unrealistic 97–9
  public spending cuts 14–15
Toxteth 4, 14
trade unions
  Council support withdrawn 118
  nomination rights and equality 136–7, 139–41
  power of 41–2, 126–7
  redundancy backlash 108, 110–11, 115–16
  Sampson Bond, opposition to 156
  selective membership 133

Urban Programme 11, 83

Wall, Pat 33
Warlock, Derek, Archbishop 75, 80, 116
Westbury, Bill 105
Wilson, Harold 31, 39–40
'winter of discontent' (1979) 14

Zack-Williams, Tunde 158–9, 161, 167